EDWARD KESSLER

# Jews, Christians and Muslims in Encounter

scm press

© Edward Kessler 2013

Published in 2013 by SCM Press
Editorial office
3rd Floor
Invicta House
108-114 Golden Lane,
London
EC1Y 0TG

SCM Press is an imprint of Hymns Ancient & Modern Ltd
(a registered charity)
13A Hellesdon Park Road
Norwich NR6 5DR, UK

www.scmpress.co.uk

All rights reserved. No part of this publication may be reproduced, stored in a retrieval system, or transmitted, in any form or by any means, electronic, mechanical, photocopying or otherwise, without the prior permission of the publisher, SCM Press.

The Author has asserted his right under the Copyright, Designs and Patents Act, 1988, to be identified as the Author of this Work

British Library Cataloguing in Publication data

A catalogue record for this book is available from the British Library

978-0-334-04715-5

Typeset by Manila Typesetting Company
Printed and bound by
Ashford Colour Press

# Contents

| | | |
|---|---|---|
| *Preface* | | *v* |
| *Introduction* | | *xi* |

## Part 1 Jewish–Christian Relations: *status quaestionis*    1

| 1 | Jewish–Christian Relations: The Next Generation | 3 |
|---|---|---|
| 2 | Jewish–Christian Relations in the Global Society: What the Institutional Documents Have and Have Not Been Telling Us | 18 |
| 3 | Land and Memory | 42 |
| 4 | Contemporary Questions about Covenant(s) and Conversion: A Public Dialogue | 59 |

## Part 2 Jews, Christians and the Bible    77

| 5 | 'Whom do men say that I am?' (Matthew 16.13) | 79 |
|---|---|---|
| 6 | Mary – The Jewish Mother | 93 |
| 7 | Bound by the Bible: Jews, Christians and the Binding of Isaac | 110 |
| 8 | The Sacrifice of Isaac (the Akedah) in Christian and Jewish Tradition: Artistic Representations | 131 |
| 9 | The Jewish People and Their Sacred Scriptures in the Christian Bible | 152 |
| 10 | Reasoning with Violent Scripture: With a Little Help from Job | 171 |

**Part 3 Jews, Christians and Muslims**     189

   11   A Jewish Approach to Dialogue with
Christians and Muslims     191
   12   The Sacrifice of Abraham's Son in Judaism
and Islam     201
   13   Changing Landscapes: Jewish–Christian–Muslim
Relations Today     213
       Postlude     Martin Forward     235

*Further Reading*     245

*Acknowledgements*     252

*Index of Biblical References*     255

*Index of Names and Subjects*     258

# Preface

The chapters in this volume consist of articles and lectures delivered over 15 years, beginning in 1998, the year the Centre for the Study of Jewish–Christian Relations (later to become the Woolf Institute) was founded.

During this period, interfaith relations has changed dramatically, both in the UK and overseas. For example, in 1998, Pope John Paul II was in the process of taking major steps in fostering reconciliation between the Roman Catholic Church and the Jewish people, the first Jewish statement on Christians and Christianity in modern times (*Dabru Emet*) was in preparation, and the Israeli–Palestinian Peace Process appeared to be making tangible progress in resolving the long-running conflict.

How things appear to have changed for the worse during the following 15 years! The rise of religious radicalism and extremism, notably the 9/11 and 7/7 attacks, the failure of the Israeli–Palestinian Peace Process and regular outbreaks of violence in the Middle East, as well as the apparent decline of religious institutions in the West, have led to a perception that interfaith dialogue has failed.

Individually and in combination, these factors make many people today ask whether relations between faiths is part of the problem, not the solution, of many challenges facing society. For my part, I remain convinced of the positive value of the interfaith encounter and continue to pursue the vision outlined by the pioneers of interfaith dialogue, such as Martin Buber and Wilfred Cantwell Smith, with vigour and also optimism.

Buber set the bar high when he wrote as early as in 1929, 'a time of genuine religious conversations is beginning – not those so-called but fictitious conversations in which none regarded and addressed his partner in reality, but genuine dialogues, speech from certainty to certainty, but also from one open-hearted person to another open-hearted person'.[1] Buber emphasized the importance of experiencing 'the other side' of a relationship that transforms itself from the 'I–It' involved in everyday encounters to the 'I–Thou' of a genuinely human encounter.

Similarly, Wilfred Cantwell Smith insisted that 'religions' were not to be reified as 'impersonal theoretical systems' that could be juxtaposed and compared. 'Ask not what religion a person belongs to but ask rather what religion belongs to that person' is the rationale behind the first principle.[2] Smith affirmed that the distinctive quality of the human being was faith rather than his or her holding a set of beliefs ('the alleged ideal content of faith'), and therefore dialogue was always from faith to faith, in Buber's words, from 'one open-hearted person to another open-hearted person'.[3]

As a scholar of interfaith relations and an active participant in the practice of interfaith dialogue, I have learnt that there is a danger in seeing everything in terms of two dimensions: of being either true or false; that there can only be one perspective. There is always more than one perspective. This is essential for a genuine understanding of the nature of interfaith reality. Each of us sees the world from different perspectives and, in the words of Jonathan Sacks, we must seek to confer the dignity of difference on how the world looks from one perspective as well as how the world looks from another.

---

[1] Martin Buber, 1947, *Between Man and Man*, London: Routledge & Kegan Paul, p. 9.

[2] Wilfred Cantwell Smith, 1963, *The Meaning and End of Religion: A New Approach to the Religious Traditions of Mankind*, New York: Macmillan, p. 332.

[3] Kenneth Cracknell, 'Dialogue', 2005, in Edward Kessler and Neil Wenborn (eds), *A Dictionary of Jewish–Christian Relations*, Cambridge: Cambridge University Press, p. 125.

# PREFACE

Another way of saying this is that the interfaith world is an irreducible multiplicity of perspectives.

There is, in other words, the view of Isaac. But there is also the view of Ishmael. There is the view of Jacob. But there is also the point of view of Esau. There is the view of Adam, but also Eve. Interfaith dialogue is an attempt to do justice to the fact that there is more than one point of view.

Since we see things differently and have different perspectives on reality, how should we proceed under those circumstances? Well, we can talk. We can converse. You can tell me how the world looks to you. I can tell you how the world looks to me. We can have a dialogue. We can, through interfaith dialogue, learn what it feels like to be different, and bridge the distance between perspectives.

Interfaith dialogue is based on the principle of an 'irreducible multiplicity of perspectives'. Personally, I do not believe that out of the many comes one. I believe that out of the one come many; there is an emphasis on the unity of God alongside the diversity of human existence. That, it seems to me, is the goal of a genuine religious dialogue, as outlined by Buber and Cantwell Smith, and the reason why I have immersed myself in the study of interfaith relations and the practice of interfaith dialogue for 25 years.

It has been no easy task selecting writings that shed light on the encounter between Jews, Christians and Muslims. That it has turned out to be so rewarding is due to a significant number of people. I would first of all like to thank my editor, Natalie Watson at SCM Press, who initially encouraged me to put this book together. I would also like to thank Martin Forward for offering his thoughts in a postlude, Shoshana Kessler, who devoted much of the summer of 2012 to editing the book and unifying a disparate array of writings, and Martin Borysek, a graduate of the Centre for the Study of Jewish–Christian Relations, who has kindly provided the indices.

There are a number of colleagues without whose help this book would not have been completed. I would first like to express thanks to all the staff at the Woolf Institute: Mohammed Aziz, Dr Shana Cohen, Claire Curran, Dr Emma Harris, Esther

Haworth, Trisha Oakley Kessler, Dr Lars Fischer, Dr Josef Meri, Tina Steiner, Matt Teather and Alice Thompson.

The students at the Woolf Institute, Cambridge University, and the Cambridge Theological Federation have been, for the most part, a privilege to teach. In fact, teaching is the greatest source of learning, and much of the material in this book originated in classes and conversations with my students. I am fortunate to work in a rich learning environment, which provides an engaging forum for the study and teaching of interfaith relations. Needless to say, any mistakes in the following pages are entirely my own.

My fellow Trustees have encouraged me to write as well as to direct the Woolf Institute and I thank them all – Professor Waqar Ahmed, Lord Ian Blair, the Revd Professor Martin Forward, Bob Glatter, Peter Halban, Lord Khalid Hameed, Lord Richard Harries, David Leibowitz, Professor Julius Lipner, Martin Paisner, Lady Marguerite Woolf, as well as the previous Chairs, the Revd Dominic Fenton, Clemens Nathan and John Pickering.

I would also like to acknowledge the support of colleagues and friends in the study of interfaith relations and the practice of interfaith dialogue, who have been kind enough to offer support and encouragement in the divinely inspired task of fostering reconciliation and furthering understanding. They include Professor Akbar Ahmed, Professor Phil Cunningham, the Revd Dr Susan Durber (and numerous colleagues at Westminster College), Sir Brian Heap, Dr Amineh Hoti, the Revd Dr Toby Howarth, Professor Geoffrey Khan, Professor Paul Luzio, Professor Ibrahim Al-Naimi, Adrian Nicholas, Dr James Carleton Paget, the Revd Dr Peter Pettit, the Revd Professor John Pawlikowski, Professor Philip Renzces, SJ, Dr Robert Sansom, the Revd Martin Seeley, Martyn Sakol, Paul Silver-Myer, Professor Yasir Suleiman and the Revd Guy Wilkinson.

I am particularly grateful to two mentors, who for many years have been extremely generous in offering me their time and wisdom during the more challenging moments of leading the Woolf Institute: HRH Prince Hassan of Jordan and Lord Harry Woolf, both of whom I deeply respect and admire.

## PREFACE

Finally, none of these chapters would have been written without the support of my family, which (in the words of George Santayana) is one of nature's masterpieces: my parents, Willie and Jo Kessler; my wife Trisha; and our children Shoshana, Asher and Eliana. Together they remind me daily of the priorities in my life, and I am deeply grateful for their love and affection. This book is dedicated to them.

I commend to all readers of this book the following words of Mother Teresa:

> 'What can you do to promote world peace? Go home and love your family.'

# Introduction

**Part 1 Jewish–Christian Relations:** *status quaestionis*

This book begins with an analysis of the state of play in Jewish–Christian relations. Chapter 1, which originated from the first memorial lecture in memory of Holocaust survivor Rabbi Hugo Gryn, describes how the Shoah and the State of Israel have dominated relations for 50 years, since the end of the Second World War. Yet there are dangers if these two immense events of the twentieth century provide the only topics for discussion between Jews and Christians. Although the Shoah and the creation of the State of Israel spurred an intense desire among many Christians and Jews to learn about the history, theology and other aspects of Jewish–Christian relations, there are dangers when the agenda becomes dominated by either or both of them.

For example, the need to tackle the Holocaust is self-evident, but it needs to be conducted in perspective. Emil Fackenheim's proclamation that the Shoah resulted in a new commandment, the 614th, which stressed that it was incumbent upon Jews to survive as Jews, is a case in point. According to Fackenheim, one remained a Jew so as not to provide Hitler with a posthumous victory. However, as a result, Jewish identity can easily become Shoah-centred – as can Jewish–Christian relations. While reaction to the Shoah is an important driving force, positive relations cannot be built solely on responses to antisemitism and Christian feelings of guilt.

A similar picture can be drawn about the State of Israel. After more than 60 years of sometimes perilous existence, Israel is no longer a recent creation and, after the large *aliyah* from the former Soviet Union in the 1980s and 1990s, no longer attracts significant numbers of Jewish immigrants. While Israel will retain a significant place in the Jewish–Christian relationship of the future, especially as the resolution of the Israeli–Palestinian conflict remains some way off and the gap between Israel and the Jewish diaspora widens, other matters of mutual interest to Jews and Christians will take their place.

Other topics that deserve attention include the consequences of the social and economic transformation of Europe, the importance of the Orthodox Christian–Jewish relationship, the growing desire for greater theological reflection and the implications of the scholarly re-evaluation of the encounter between Christians and Jews in the early centuries of the Common Era.

Chapter 2 considers the major institutional statements and charts their development. I point out that although open and direct consultations have taken place and formal declarations and guidelines have been issued, something is missing – the implementation of these statements into Jewish and Christian communal life.

Three themes can be identified in Christian documents published in recent decades, each of which has resulted in a Jewish response. First, a realization that Christians and Christianity have made a significant contribution to Jewish suffering; second, a reawakening to the Jewishness of Christianity; third, a recognition among some Christian leaders that the formation of Christian identity today is dependent upon a right relationship with Judaism.

Jewish responses to these themes have been as follows: first – distrust of Christian overtures; second – defensive involvement in dialogue (in other words, involvement for the sake of combating antisemitism); third – developing awareness of commonality as well as an appreciation of a common purpose. It is the third theme that provides the best opportunity for developing positive relations between Jews and Christians.

As the subject of Israel–Palestinian conflict is rarely far below the surface, and regular outbreaks of violence in the region result in significant pressures far away from the Middle East, Chapter 3 deals with peace and understanding (or perhaps more realistically, conflict and misunderstanding), whether they take place in meetings between Christians and Jews in churches and synagogues,

## INTRODUCTION

in Lambeth Palace and in the Chief Rabbi's Office or in the coffee parlours of Jerusalem and Bethlehem.

Discussions are often divisive and controversial, as participants tend to be advocates of one side or another. Chapter 3 considers why it is so rare to find Christians or Jews who are both pro-Palestinian and pro-Israeli. Blinkered views prevail and conversations brim with emotion and passion.

While for Jews the reasons are more obvious: the centrality of the land of the Bible, as well as the survival of over a third of world Jewry, is at stake. Christians not only disagree as to the place of Israel in Christian theology, they also feel particular concern for Christians who live in the Holy Land as well as for Palestinians in general. There are of course also many Christians and Jews who are deeply concerned about the 'Other', making this a complicated picture to understand.

The chapter outlines the history of Jews and Christians in the Holy Land during the last millennium, explores the significance of Jerusalem and reflects on the challenges faced by Christians today, whether they live in the Jewish State of Israel or in Arab countries – in both, they face increasingly militant religious voices. Those who are committed to genuine reconciliation between Israelis and Palestinians may realize that good neighbours are better than good guns, but they face increasing problems, created by those who are moving away from genuine dialogue towards a megaphone monologue, who generate noise but not hope.

Chapter 4 explores some of the theological questions that Jewish and Christian theologians are now beginning to tackle. In recent years, several theological controversies have beset official relations between Jews and Christians. These include whether Christians should pray for the conversion of Jews, whether the purpose of interreligious dialogue is to lead others to Christian faith, and whether Christians should undertake non-coercive 'missions' to Jews. An underlying theological topic in all these disputes is how the biblical concept of 'covenant' is understood in Judaism and Christianity and in their interrelationship.

Originating from a public dialogue with leading American Catholic scholar Professor Philip Cunningham in 2008, Chapter 4 reflects on a modern re-reading of Paul, especially Romans 9—11, which concerns the role of the Jewish people after the appearance of Christianity. The traditional Christian teaching of 'replacement' or 'substitution' – that with the coming of Jesus Christ the Church has taken the place of the Jewish people as God's elect community – has been repudiated by Christian theologians, but there is less agreement about what replaces replacement theology.

Clearly, the rejection of replacement theology entails some affirmation of the continuing validity of God's covenant with the Jewish people and the continuation of their covenantal relationship with God, as expressed by Pope John Paul II's comment 'the people of God of the Old Covenant, which has never been revoked'. However, constructing a new theology of the Church and the Jewish people remains an unresolved and formidable undertaking, because, as German theologian Johann-Baptist Metz has argued, the restatement of the Church's relationship with the Jewish people is a fundamental revision of Christian theology.

## Part 2   Jews, Christians and the Bible

The Bible provides a fundamental connection between Jews and Christians, and Part 2 explores the similarities and differences in respective approaches to Scripture and what they tell us about Jewish–Christian relations. During the last two decades, there has been increasing Christian interest in both the Jewish context of the New Testament as well as in the influence of Jewish biblical interpretation on the formation and development of Christianity.

For understandable reasons, it has generally been assumed that Judaism influenced Christianity, but relatively little attention has been given to the other side of the same coin – the question of the influence of Christianity upon Judaism. I suggest that neither Jewish nor Christian interpretations of Scripture can be understood properly without reference to the other. This is because both Jews and Christians lived – and continue to live – in a biblically orientated culture.

## INTRODUCTION

Part 2 begins with Chapter 5, with reflections on changing Jewish attitudes towards Jesus and their implications for Christian self-understanding. Over the centuries, primarily because of Christian persecution, Jews have been indifferent or hostile to Jesus and his teachings. Yet attitudes on both sides have changed in recent years and this chapter explains why.

One of the certain facts about Jesus is that he was a Jew. He was a child of Jewish parents, brought up in a Jewish home and raised in accordance with Jewish tradition. Throughout his life, Jesus lived among Jews and his followers were Jews. Indeed, no other Jew in history has rivalled Jesus in the magnitude of his influence, but when the Church persecuted Jews in an effort to convert them, Jewish indifference to Jesus turned to hostility. Up until recently, most Jews have chosen not to think of him at all.

Chapter 5 charts the dramatic change in the writings of Jewish scholars who have come to study the teaching of Jesus and their influence on Christians who, for their part, have come to admire Judaism and to appreciate the immense debt of Christianity to it. Although the hostility of centuries cannot be eliminated in the blink of an eye, the signs are encouraging. Similarly, the traditional Jewish attitude of indifference (and at times hostility) to Jesus is also being overcome. Of course, the death of Jesus cannot have for Jews the same significance as for Christians, and his significance lies in his life. For the majority of Jews, Jesus can never be what he is to Christian hearts, yet an increasing number are proud that Jesus was Jewish – that he was born, lived and died a Jew.

Chapter 6 considers the significance of Mary as a Jewish mother. Although, as Chapter 5 shows, the Jewishness of Jesus is increasingly recognized, and that in its origins Christianity was a first-century Jewish group, rarely is the mother of Jesus portrayed as a Jew. This is partly because Christianity forgot its Jewish roots, but as Christians recovered a respect for their Jewish siblings and asserted the Church's debt to its Jewish heritage, it is well overdue that we reconsider Mary in Jewish terms. As a teacher of Christian–Jewish relations, I occasionally have to remind my students that Mary was a first-century Palestinian Jewish woman, not a Roman Catholic.

Chapter 6 examines New Testament descriptions of Mary, as well as early post-biblical Christian ones, which either ignore Mary's Jewishness or adopt an anti-Jewish position. In the centuries that followed, Christian anti-Judaism grew, and Jews were accused of desecrating Marian images as well as deriding her cult.

The chapter concludes with suggestions as to how Christians can celebrate that Mary was Jewish like her son, Jesus of Nazareth, and followed a Jewish way of life. It is argued that as a 'daughter of Israel',[4] she should be remembered as a Jewish mother.

Chapters 7 and 8 explore Genesis 22, the Sacrifice of Isaac, which is one of the most famous stories in the Bible. As a piece of writing, the biblical account has tension and drama and enough action for a five-act play or a Hollywood blockbuster. Yet it is compressed into only 18 verses. It is packed with energy and dynamism, a paradigm of Aristotle's catharsis, arousing both terror and pity. It deals with the biggest themes and touches the deepest emotions.

The story focuses on Abraham's relationship with God and how his faith in God, and his commitment to him, was demonstrated by his willingness to sacrifice his long-awaited son at God's command. Abraham's attempted sacrifice of Isaac has been an important passage for Judaism and Christianity from an early period. For Jews, from at least as early as the third century CE, the Binding of Isaac (as it is called) is read in synagogue on Rosh ha-Shana, the Jewish New Year. For Christians, from around the same period, the Sacrifice of Isaac is mentioned in the Eucharist prayers and the story is recounted in the period leading up to Easter.

A study of traditional Jewish and Christian biblical interpretations of Genesis 22 shows that both the church fathers and rabbis asked the same question of the biblical text; both were very close readers and interested in the detail of Scripture. Rabbi Ben Bag Bag, who lived in the first century CE, could have been writing on

---

4 *Mary: Grace and Hope in Christ*, 2004, Anglican–Roman Catholic International Commission, at www.anglicancommunion.org/ministry/ecumenical/dialogues/catholic/arcic/index.cfm

behalf of the church fathers when he stated, 'turn, turn and turn it again, and you will find something new in it'.

This highlights a more constructive and mutually beneficial encounter between Christians and Jews during the formative centuries than had previously been realized. Indeed, it is possible to uncover a fruitful two-way encounter between Jewish and Christian biblical commentators, when each side was aware of the other's interpretations, for good, not just for ill. When Jews and Christians read traditional post-biblical interpretations, they will often discover a willingness among the rabbis and church fathers to be open to, and to engage with, each other's teachings.

I call this an 'exegetical encounter' and suggest it is found not only in Jewish and Christian writing, but also in art. Artistic interpretations of Genesis 22 show similarities between the representations of Jewish and Christian artists. They also indicate a positive interaction as well as a rich diversity, and some of the artistic representations mirror literary interpretations; on other occasions, they are unique and not found elsewhere.

Chapter 9 examines the 2001 Vatican document on Jewish–Christian relations entitled *The Significance of the Jewish People and their Sacred Scriptures in the Christian Bible* (*JPSSCB*). The document is important for three reasons: 1) it explores the positive significance for Christians of the fact that the history of Judaism did not end with the destruction of the Second Temple in 70 CE, but developed an ongoing innovative and living religious tradition; 2) it attempts to understand Judaism as a living faith and strives to learn by what essential traits Jews define themselves in the light of their own religious experience; 3) it is the first statement on Jewish–Christian relations issued by the Pontifical Biblical Commission, illustrating that Roman Catholic consideration of the Christian–Jewish relationship extends beyond the Pontifical Commission for Religious Relations with the Jews. It is the concern of the Roman Catholic Church as a whole.

Most noteworthy is *JPSSCB*'s call for the use of Jewish commentaries by Christians since, it explains, Jewish interpretation of Scripture can be viewed as legitimate. The document's affirmation that the 'Jewish messianic expectation is not in vain' is also significant, preparing the ground for future Catholic encounters with the Jewish people that may consider theological issues such as messianism, because, as the document concludes, 'this people has been called and led by God, creator of heaven and earth. Their existence is not a mere natural or cultural happening . . . It is a supernatural one. This people continues in spite of everything to be the people of the covenant, and, despite human infidelity, the Lord is faithful to his covenant.'

The handling of violent Scripture is the subject of Chapter 10, the final chapter in Part 2. Religion is often portrayed, with justification, as being a cause of destruction and there is little doubt that it has, at times, been a force for evil in the world and violent actions have been justified with reference to Scripture. This chapter considers how to interpret violent biblical texts and proposes a hermeneutic that can be embraced by both Jews and Christians. If religion per se is part of the problem, then religious thinkers and leaders need to put their minds to it becoming part of the solution.

This chapter takes as a starting point Deuteronomy 20, especially verses 16–18, in which God commands the Israelites to destroy the cities of the Hittites, Amorites, Canaanites, Peruzites, Hivites and Jebusites and kill every breathing thing – men, women, children and even animals. Rabbinic tradition made an ethical decision not to understand the command literally and annulled the genocidal meaning of the text, by declaring that military power could no longer be used. The reality was that, living as a minority in Christian and Muslim societies, Jews were instructed to follow a model of passive acceptance.

The Shoah, and the creation of the State of Israel, changed all that. The quietist approach gave way to one in which a more aggressive response to violence seemed appropriate. But as Israel has moved over the years from using military force sparingly and defensively to employing it liberally and belligerently, the danger of such violent texts re-emerged. In response, I propose a new hermeneutical principle, 'exegetical relativity', and suggest that it is no longer appropriate to search for the one and only correct meaning of a text. Rather, it is essential to examine, as the rabbis

INTRODUCTION

have traditionally done, a number of different interpretations, each with its own context. With reference also to the Christian Syriac hermeneutical tradition, I suggest it takes a high degree of maturity to let opposites coexist without pretending that they can be made compatible and that the 'plain and obvious interpretation' of the text does not hold its final meaning.

## Part 3  Jews, Christians and Muslims

The final part of this book extends the study of the Jewish–Christian encounter to include Islam. It begins with Chapter 11, with a revised 2008 lecture, which took place at London's Hellenic Centre, home of the Greek Orthodox Church in Great Britain, and explores a 'Jewish Theology of Dialogue', the basis for which, I suggest, is Leviticus 19.33–4 ('You shall love the stranger as yourself . . . because you were strangers in the land of Egypt'). This is followed by a reflection on the state of play in Jewish–Christian–Muslim relations today.

From the Jewish perspective, Jews need to ponder the purpose behind the creation of Christianity and Islam, such as the significance for Jews of the Jewishness of Jesus and the existence of two billion Christian followers who read the Jewish Bible. As for Islam, Jews need to reflect on the fact that over 1.6 billion Muslims share many of the same rituals and customs as Jews and, like Jews, adhere to a strict monotheism.

One of the few pieces of good news in today's encounter between religions is that Christian–Jewish dialogue arose despite profound theological differences and many centuries of alienation and distrust. The fact that Jews and Christians have built mutual respect and understanding does not, of course, mean that this model can be wholly applied to relations with Islam. Jews and Muslims today carry far different memories and issues than the historical baggage brought to encounters with Christians. Building positive relations with Muslims is in its early stages and represents a new challenge.

Chapter 12 explores the story of the near sacrifice of Abraham's son in Islam (the festival of *Eid al-Adha* commemorates Ibrahim's willingness to sacrifice his son at Allah's command) in comparison with Judaism and Christianity. The willingness of someone giving up his own life for a greater cause is not unknown to the three Abrahamic faiths, the virtue of which stands at the heart of each.

In particular, I explore similarities between the Jewish and Muslim approaches to Scripture. For Muslims, the most reliable Qur'anic commentary is contained in the Qur'an itself, and commentary (*tafsir*) begins on this principle. Like the rabbinic hermeneutical principle, 'Scripture explains Scripture', Muslim commentators clarify one verse with reference to another and this approach is regarded as the most significant form of commentary. Thus *tafsir* is similar to midrash, a Hebrew term for asking, searching, inquiring and interpreting.

Chapter 12 briefly identifies interpretations of the attempted sacrifice of Abraham's son. They demonstrate parallel thinking as well as shared interpretations and indicate a common approach to the sacred text. Such was the closeness of the interpreters that these interpretations moved between and among Jews and Muslims.

The final chapter of Part 3, Chapter 13, considers some of the similarities and differences in contemporary encounters between Jews, Christians and Muslims. Despite the potential symbiosis, there are barriers to dialogue and the chapter reflects on the impact of the Israeli–Palestinian conflict and the sometimes harmful influence of collective memories: for example, Jews think of Christianity in terms of suffering and persecution; while Muslims have not forgotten the Crusades, and see in Western aspirations an old Crusader mentality in a new guise.

Although I acknowledge that commemorations of past events help preserve a sense of historical continuity and identity, a preoccupation (some might call it an obsession) with the past may be damaging if it results in a negative identity and self-understanding, especially if it becomes the only or primary lens through which reality and the changing world is viewed. One way to disarm an obsession with the past is to adopt a critical approach to it in order not to become victims of an ideological 'vindication' of the past that is nostalgic, dogmatic and sometimes irrational. If the past is approached critically, it can reveal new interpretations and understandings of the world that can be liberating and constructive.

The book ends with a call for a *memoria futuri* – memory for the future – and for Jews, Christians and Muslims to reflect on the more positive aspects of memory. For example, Christianity has recognized that traditional views of Jews are unacceptable and has worked to create a new relationship, shifting from what was, for the most part, an inherent need to condemn Judaism to one of a condemnation of Christian anti-Judaism. It has also led to a closer relationship with 'the elder brother' and not, as some feared, to the undermining of Christian teaching. The rediscovery of a positive relationship with Judaism will facilitate a positive formation of Christian identity and memory. For Jews, *memoria futuri* may help view diaspora life not primarily in negative terms (exemplifying a history of oppression), but in positive terms (as a fruitful environment facilitating dynamic development). For Muslims too, developing a vibrant diaspora existence will help the communities adapt from living in a majority Muslim culture to a minority culture, among other minorities. In my view, a 'memory for the future' provides the basis for fostering understanding and constructive relations between adherents of the three Abrahamic faiths.

PART I

# Jewish–Christian Relations:
## *status quaestionis*

# I

# Jewish–Christian Relations: The Next Generation

### The Foundations of Jewish–Christian Dialogue Today

If we take the twentieth century as our starting point, it is quite clear that two immense events have combined to provide a dual focus to Jewish–Christian Relations today:

- the Shoah
- the creation of the State of Israel.

Both spurred an intense desire among many Christians and Jews to learn about the history, theology and other aspects of Jewish–Christian relations.

For Christians, the Shoah resulted in an awareness of the immensity of the burden of guilt carried by the Church not only for its general silence (with some noble exceptions) during 1933–45, but also because of the 'teaching of contempt' towards Jews and Judaism that it carried on for so many centuries. As Jules Isaac showed immediately after the Second World War, it was this that sowed the seeds of hatred and made it so easy for Hitler to use antisemitism as a political weapon.

As a result of the soul-searching that took place after 1945, many Christians began the painful process of re-examining the sources of the teaching of contempt and repudiating them. Christian institutions, most notably the Vatican, the World Council of Churches (WCC) and certain Protestant denominations have since then issued declarations against the perpetuation of this teaching.¹

It is, therefore, not surprising that many of the studies on Jewish–Christian relations examined, in particular, Christian antisemitism. This tendency was reinforced by the publication of a number of key works, including institutional publications such as *Nostra Aetate* and individual studies such as Rosemary Radford Ruether's *Faith and Fratricide*. The agenda of Jewish–Christian dialogue was heavily influenced by such works.

The Shoah not only caused Christianity to reassess its relationship with Judaism, but also stirred greater Jewish interest in Christianity. Jonathan Sacks spoke for many when he stated that, 'today we meet and talk together because we must; because we have considered the alternative and seen where it ends and we are shocked to the core by what we have seen'.²

The need to discuss and to tackle the Shoah in Jewish–Christian dialogue is self-evident, but it must be conducted in perspective. Fackenheim famously stated that the Shoah resulted in a new commandment, the 614th, which stressed that it was incumbent upon Jews to survive as Jews after the Shoah.³ One remained a Jew so as not to provide Hitler with a posthumous victory. As a result, Jewish identity became Shoah-centred and, at the same time, Jewish–Christian dialogue became Shoah-centred.

---

1 For a summary of Vatican statements, see E. Fisher and L. Klenicki (eds), 1990, *In Our Time: The Flowering of Catholic–Jewish Dialogue*, New York: Paulist Press; for a summary of Protestant statements, see A. Brockway (ed.), 1988, *The Theology of the Churches and the Jewish People*, Geneva: World Council of Churches.

2 Helen Fry, 1996, *Christian–Jewish Dialogue*, Exeter: Exeter University Press, p. xi.

3 'We Jews are, first, commanded to survive as Jews, lest the Jewish people perish. We are commanded, second, to remember in our very guts and bones the martyrs of the holocaust, lest their memory perish. We are forbidden, thirdly, to deny or despair of God, however much we may have to contend with Him or with belief in Him, lest Judaism perish. We are forbidden, finally to despair of the world as the place which is to become the kingdom of God lest we help make it a meaningless place in which God is dead or irrelevant and everything is permitted. To abandon any of these imperatives, in response to Hitler's victory at Auschwitz, would be to hand him yet other posthumous victories.' E. Fackenheim, 1969, 'Transcendence in Contemporary Culture: Philosophical Reflections and a Jewish Theology', in H. W. Richardson and D. R. Cutler (eds), *Transcendence*, Boston: Beacon Press, p. 150.

There is a danger that by focusing solely on the Holocaust, Jews and Christians will gain a distorted view of Judaism and the Jewish people.

The second event that underpins Jewish–Christian relations today is the creation of the State of Israel, which has brought renewed confidence to Jews in their dealings with Christians. As Norman Solomon has pointed out, the ongoing existence of the State of Israel has resulted, on the one hand, in Jews feeling less threatened by dialogue and more willing to participate and, on the other, in abandoning an apologetic stance that defines dialogue simply as the education of Christians about Judaism.[4]

Jewish–Christian dialogue became Israel-focused as Israel displayed many of the tensions of Jewish–Christian relations – the significance of a holy land, the problems of religious and secular divisions, and the consequences associated with power and weakness. Then there is the subject of Christian attitudes towards Israel, and Jewish responses. For example, the Christian Zionists, who strongly support Netanyahu and the Israeli 'right', have – understandably – only received a partial welcome by Jews.

Great emotion surrounded, and continues to surround, Israel in Jewish–Christian dialogue. Discussions often result in controversy as, for example, by the immediate and volatile reaction of Jewish communities throughout the world in response to the Vatican's document published in 1985. This document affirmed the Jewish people's attachment to the land of Israel and the existence of the State of Israel under international law, but cautioned against religious interpretations of the State of Israel. At that time, the fact that the Vatican did not recognize the State of Israel only served to increase the furore still further.[5]

The significance of the State of Israel to the Jewish world explains both the enormous satisfaction, as well as the sense of

---

4 Norman Solomon, 1991, 'Themes in Christian–Jewish Relations', in L. Klenicki (ed.), *Toward a Theological Encounter*, New York: Paulist Press, p. 31.

5 *Notes on the Correct Way to Present Jews and Judaism in Preaching and Catechesis in the Roman Catholic Church* VI.25, at www.vatican.va/roman_curia/pontifical_councils/chrstuni/relations-jews-docs/rc_pc_chrstuni_doc_19820306_jews-judaism_en.html

relief, felt by most Jews when the Vatican did belatedly recognize the State in 1994. The recognition of Israel marked an important stage in Jewish–Christian dialogue as David Rosen, who was intimately involved in the negotiations with the Vatican, explained:

> This is the end of the beginning. The implications of *Nostra Aetate* and the subsequent documents called out for full relations between the Holy See and the State of Israel. Their absence had suggested that the reconciliation between the church and the Jewish People was not a complete one. Accordingly, for the last three decades, Jewish representatives have called on the Vatican to take this step. The agreement that was signed last week, therefore, has historical and philosophical importance as well as diplomatic significance. Now we can address the meaning of our relationship and get on to many other matters of common interest.[6]

The question is: what are the 'other matters of common interest'? To be sure, both the Shoah and the State of Israel will continue to be pillars of Jewish–Christian dialogue, but they can no longer bear the load on their own. They can no longer be the only items on the agenda. Is it not possible that the Shoah will suffer the same fate as the First World War – that is, remain a pivotal event to those who suffered during those years, as well as their children, but for some of the grandchildren and following generations become one more terrible incident of history that can be studied in books and viewed in newsreels?

A similar picture can be drawn about the State of Israel. After 50 years of perilous existence, Israel is no longer a recent creation[7] and, after the large *aliyah* from the former Soviet Union, no longer attracts significant numbers of Jewish immigrants. Its own

---

6 Quoted from D. O'Brien, 1998, *The Hidden Pope*, New York: Daybreak Publishing, p. 383.

7 For instance, 91 countries were admitted to membership of the United Nations between 1949, when the State of Israel joined the United Nations, and 1979. Cf. E. Osmanczyk (ed.), 1990, *Encyclopedia of the United Nations and International Agreements*, London: Taylor & Francis, pp. 960–1.

interfaith efforts are directed more towards the Arab Islamic communities than the Christian. While Israel will remain a significant factor in the Jewish–Christian dialogue of the future, the increasing tension between it and the Jewish diaspora will serve to allow other 'matters of common interest' to take their place.

On their own, neither Israel nor the Shoah will provide the cornerstone for Jewish–Christian relations in the future. Other issues will come to the fore, and I would like to turn to two of them.

## Jewish–Christian relations in a New Europe

The first issue concerns the consequences for Jewish–Christian relations of a New Europe. Even though it was a few years ago, it is clear that 1989 has marked a significant turning point in European history. At that time, and shortly afterwards, there was widespread euphoria at the collapse of communist governments in Central and Eastern Europe. Democracy and prosperity were promised. But the euphoria has now vanished; the promises have yet to be redeemed. Unemployment and social unrest have increased, and the people go hungry. Strife prevails. At the same time, the affluent West is fearful of succumbing to a bout of recession.

Superficially, the problems are economic. How does one move from a socialist to a free market economy? What sort of skills, training and infrastructure are needed? What help is required from the outside? If these problems could be isolated, perhaps they could be solved.

However, economic problems cannot be isolated from social, political and moral ones. Economics cannot of itself tell us how to create a happy and prosperous society. The free market system needs a favourable environment in which to operate and, as Adam Smith himself noted,[8] its operation must be subjected to moral and political constraints.

The turmoil in Central and Eastern Europe clearly prevents the possibility of building a 'favourable environment'. This turmoil is

---

8 *An Enquiry into the Nature and Causes of the Wealth of Nations*, 1776, IV.9.

at its most extreme in the Balkans, where there exists a denial of citizenship – that is, equal rights – to persons of the 'wrong' ethnic or religious group. The naked meaning of 'ethnic cleansing' is 'Get out! Leave the home where your mother and father lived before you were born! Because of your race or religion you are not fit for me to grant you equal rights on my territory!' Those with ideologies do not pause to enquire by just what perverse logic Bosnian A can tell Bosnian B, whose ancestors may well have lived in the country longer than his own, 'This is my country, not yours'.

What an appalling tragedy this is. The economic cost is staggering: a country poised to be among those who could lead the economic revival of ex-communist Europe has reduced itself to poverty and deprivation and wantonly destroyed the infrastructure needed for future growth. The social cost is even greater: hundreds of thousands of families have been ripped apart, friends turned into enemies, the flames of hatred fanned to a fury whose bitterness may persist for generations.

Another example of turmoil is Poland, a country that presents contradictory pictures. Some senior clerics have been playing on the antisemitic prejudices inherent in Polish society. Semi-ignorant clergy continue to teach Catholicism with attitudes towards Jews and Judaism that differ little, if at all, from the traditional teaching of contempt.

On the other hand, promising work is being done by Catholic intellectuals in Cracow. The Catholic Academy of Theology in Warsaw, in partnership with a college in Chicago, is educating its young ordinands in Jewish–Christian relations. In line with the Church's new teachings on Jews and Judaism, the Polish bishops have produced excellent guidelines on Christian–Jewish relations. But the bishops and the new clergy still have an uphill task fighting antisemitism, as the controversy over the crosses at Auschwitz makes clear.

Although I do not think that the establishment of a Carmelite convent at Auschwitz some years ago was a deliberate provocation, it was naïve of the Church not to see that Jews would read it as an attempt to take over a sacred Jewish memorial. Now the convent has been moved out, the crosses have been moved in, and old sores are reopened.

Although no one can doubt that the Catholic Church today has a far more constructive and benevolent attitude to Jews and Judaism than ever before, how long will it take for the new teachings to percolate down from the Vatican to the pew? How will new teachings reach the newly free churches of ex-communist Europe?

A third example of the significance of the New Europe for Jewish–Christian relations can be seen in Russia and, in particular, in the Orthodox Christian–Jewish relationship.

Let me set the scene: over a century ago – that is, before the formation of the NCCJ (1927) in the United States and CCJ (1942) in the United Kingdom – a number of important Orthodox Christian theologians attempted to defend Jews during a period of state-supported persecutions. In particular, the most important Orthodox theologian in the nineteenth century, Soloviev, argued that a healthy understanding of the profound relationship between Judaism and Christianity was needed for the sake of both.[9] Like James Parkes and Claude Montefiore, Soloviev was a forerunner of the current dialogue between Christians and Jews.

We also need to take into account that, unlike the West, where the Shoah forced a reassessment of Christian attitudes towards Jews and Judaism, the Shoah has not played a significant role in Jewish–Orthodox Christian relations. The Russians view their suffering under the occupation of the Nazis as a pivotal event in their history, just as Jews view the Shoah in Jewish history. In addition, the Orthodox Church has not gone through a reformation nor a Vatican II council. The Orthodox liturgy, in particular, is problematic, particularly at Easter time, and the changes that have taken place in the Protestant and Catholic liturgies have not happened in the Orthodox Church.

---

9 In one eschatological vision, he portrayed a new unity between the best elements of Orthodoxy, Catholicism and Protestantism, assisted by the return of millions of Jews to their biblical homeland. 'Christianity and the Jewish Question', in S. M. Soloviev and E. L. Radlov (eds), *Sobranie sochinenii Vladimira Sergeevicha Solovieva*, 2nd edn, St Petersburg: Prosveshchenie, 1911–13, vol. IV, pp. 138–9.

Rather, the reassessment of Orthodox Christian–Jewish relations must be found elsewhere. It may well be based on the fact that the Orthodox sense of the unity of the Old Testament and the New Testament makes it impossible to see any difference in the One God who is manifested in both. There is no such thing as Law versus Gospel; the God of Justice versus the God of Love. The attempt to make such contrasts have caused enormous difficulties in relations between Jews and Christians in the West, and is seen by Orthodox Christians involved in dialogue as a Western pseudo-problem. Western Christian theologians should take note.

These three developments in the New Europe – in the former Yugoslavia, Poland and Russia – provide the context for a new challenge in Jewish–Christian relations, and we must respond to that challenge.

We have to take up the challenge of the New Europe because we live in Europe. In the words of Martin Luther King, 'we are caught in an inescapable network of mutuality. Whatever affects one directly affects all indirectly.' Greville Janner, a UK Jewish community leader, tells the story of a private dinner with some leaders of the black community in aid of establishing a Race and Community Group in Parliament. One asked him, 'Why are you Jewish people so interested in this work?' He replied, 'Because it is right. Because it is needed. Because we want to be useful, in passing on just a little of the experience which we have gained, as earlier immigrants than you.' 'Wrong,' Rabbi Hugo Gryn intervened, 'we are interested because this work is in our own interests. Our community can only flourish in a decent society which respects the rights of all minorities. So attacks on the black community are a direct threat to us. And any flexibility or strength which we can provide for the black community is a direct asset to us Jews.'

He is right! And it also applies to the New Europe. Christian–Jewish relations lies at the heart of the transformation of Europe. Get it right, and we can entertain a rosy vision of the New Europe, one in which ethnic and religious diversity are the foundation for a cohesive social life within which an economy can flourish. Get it wrong, and that very same ethnic and religious diversity will destroy society and frustrate economic progress. Jewish–Christian relations is a central issue in the construction of a New Europe. We must get it right.

## Dialogue in the Mainstream of Judaism

The second issue deals with the place of dialogue in Judaism. From a Christian perspective, the justification for Jewish–Christian dialogue is quite clear: there exists an urgent need to understand Judaism and Jewish–Christian relations because Christianity was born of Judaism. The recent Christian reassessment of Judaism *qua* Judaism has resulted in a Christian 'return to its Jewish roots'.

From a Christian perspective, an understanding of Christianity is, to some extent, dependent upon a proper understanding of Judaism. From a Christian theological perspective, this view would be understood as follows: that God's revelation through Christ was for all humanity. Since God's revelation came first to Jews (and since God does not break his promises), it is essential to explore the meaning of God's mission to Israel. Christians need to enter into dialogue with Jews in order to preserve and understand God's faithfulness with Israel.

In the earlier stages of dialogue in the twentieth century, Christian reacquaintance with Judaism resulted primarily in an increased awareness of the Jewish origins of Christianity – that Jesus was born, lived and died a Jew; that the first Christians were Jews; that the New Testament is, for the most part, a Jewish work. However, more recently, there is a growing realization that for nearly 2,000 years – not only the first 100 years – living Judaism has interested Christians and has influenced Christianity. Paul explored 'the mystery of Israel' (especially in Romans 11), and it is the significance of this mystery that has continued to challenge and engross Christians.

Thus the justification for Jewish–Christian dialogue is unambiguous from a Christian perspective. However, the issue from a Jewish perspective is more complicated. At first glance, there is no theological or other imperative to view the relationship with

Christianity as more special than the Jewish relationship with any other faith group. This view is reinforced by the popular assumption that the influence was wholly one-way: Christianity did not influence Judaism; rather, Judaism influenced the development of Christianity.

However, the influence was not one-way, for Christianity has influenced Judaism in a number of ways. Most significantly, there is a growing awareness in academic circles of the influence of Christianity on rabbinic Judaism. This is particularly important because rabbinic Judaism is viewed by both Orthodox and Progressive Jews[10] as the cornerstone of Judaism today. Research is showing that not only was there influence, but that an exegetical encounter between Judaism and Christianity took place. This means that on the basis of a shared textual tradition – the Bible – Jews and Christians maintained a meaningful relationship. And remember, as far as Jews were concerned, those were perilous times.

Why was the Bible the meeting ground? Because Jews and Christians shared – and continue to share – the same textual tradition. The rediscovery of this interaction, which today we call dialogue, can provide an impetus to Jewish–Christian dialogue in the future.

This exegetical interaction indicates that a 'special relationship' existed between Judaism and Christianity from a very early period. Although it is well known that after Christianity became the official religion of the Roman Empire the position of the Jewish communities became more and more precarious, it is not so well known that the rabbis allowed, consciously or not, Christian ideas and interpretations to enter into Jewish thought and life. This happened because dialogue stood in the mainstream of Jewish life.

The rabbinic writings offer an insight into the relationship. They illustrate not only awareness of Christian teaching, but also a rabbinic ability to listen, learn and incorporate those teachings and traditions that were deemed relevant to Jewish life. Jewish–Christian dialogue is, therefore, not a modern phenomenon. If

---

10 I use this term to include all non-Orthodox religious groupings.

Jews and Christians examine post-biblical interpretations, they will discover a shared emphasis on the importance of certain biblical texts as well as a willingness to be open to, and influenced by, each other's teachings. The exegetical encounters that took place so long ago point the way forward.

Let me give you one example of the exegetical interaction between the rabbis and the church fathers from my own research. My PhD examines the interpretations of the rabbis and the church fathers on the Akedah, the Binding of Isaac.

The focus of the biblical story concerns Abraham's relationship with God and how his faith in, and commitment to, God was demonstrated by his willingness to sacrifice his long-awaited son at God's command. Little attention was given to Isaac.

Both the rabbis and the church fathers reflected a great deal on the story. In the rabbinic writings, Isaac is no longer portrayed as a peripheral figure but becomes equal, if not superior, to Abraham. The rabbis portray Isaac as the willing martyr, who volunteers to give up his life for his people. Indeed, such is the merit of Isaac's action (the *zecut avot,* 'merit of the fathers') that Israel benefits from his actions in the future.

The rabbinic portrayal of Isaac parallels a number of aspects of the Christian understanding of Jesus. Among the interpretations there is one comment that is particularly striking. The rabbis explained Isaac carrying the wood for the sacrifice on his shoulders as follows: '"And Abraham placed the wood of the burnt-offering on Isaac his son". Like a man who carries his cross on his shoulder.'[11]

The reference to a cross (*tzaluv*) is clearly influenced by the New Testament description that Jesus carried his cross to the

---

11 Genesis Rabbah (GenRab) 56.3. Some modern Jewish commentators have suggested that this interpretation merely explained why Abraham did not place the wood on the donkey. Cf. M. Mirkin, 1980, *Midrash Rabbah (Heb),* vol. 2, Tel-Aviv: Yavneh, p. 286. Mirkin offers two suggestions – first, that it enabled Abraham to fulfil God's command in every way, and second, that condemned men carry their stake to their own execution. However, such explanations fail to explain why such a clear reference to Christianity was retained by the midrash.

crucifixion.[12] The rabbi who offered this interpretation, whose name is not mentioned, decided that the comparison between Isaac carrying the wood and a man (Jesus) carrying a cross to his execution was valuable. The editors/redactors of the midrash, *Bereshit rabbah*, concurred since they did not censor the comparison in the final redaction.[13]

There are a number of factors, other than a reference to the cross and execution, that provide further evidence that the rabbinic interpretations of the Akedah were influenced by Christian teaching. Like Jesus, Isaac was willing to give up his life; like Jesus, Isaac was not forced by human hand to carry the cross but carried it freely; like Jesus, Isaac was not forced to offer himself as a sacrifice but willingly gave himself up to his father. Like Jesus, Isaac was described as weeping bitterly when told by Abraham that he was to be sacrificed;[14] like Jesus, Isaac shed blood; like Jesus, Isaac is depicted at the gates of hell (gehinna);[15] finally, the Akedah was described as atoning for all, Jew and non-Jew, in a similar way to Paul's assertion concerning baptism.[16] All of these examples can be found in the rabbinic writings.

Thus Jewish interpretations of Isaac at the Akedah cannot be understood properly without reference to the Christian context and should be viewed as an example of an exegetical encounter, for the rabbis were not only aware of Christian exegesis but were influenced by it.

These exegetical encounters between Jews and Christians in bygone times should inspire Jewish–Christian dialogue in the

---

12 John 19.17.

13 The reason why such a controversial statement was retained can be partly explained by the use of Aramaic, which implies that the interpretation was popular. Cf. Irving Jacobs, 1995, *The Midrashic Process*, Cambridge: Cambridge University Press, p. 17.

14 Midrash composed under the Holy Spirit, J. Mann, 1940, *The Bible as Read and Preached in the Old Synagogue*, Ohio: Union of American Hebrew Congregations, p. 65.

15 Song of Songs Rabbah (SoSRab) 8.9.

16 Leviticus Rabbah (LevRab) 2.11: 'whosoever, Jew or Gentile, man or woman, slave or maidservant, reads this scriptural text . . . the Lord remembers Isaac's Akedah'; Galatians 3.28: 'There is neither Jew nor Greek, there is neither bond nor free, there is neither male or female; for you are all one in Christ.'

future. Since the writings of the rabbis and the church fathers provide the cornerstone for Christianity and Judaism today, a study of Jewish and Christian biblical interpretation should become a pillar of Jewish–Christian dialogue in the future. I suggest the growing realization that rabbinic Jews were concerned with and influenced by Christian interpretations (and vice versa) should result in Jews and Christians becoming reacquainted with each other's interpretations.

## The Way Forward

What is the way forward? I have argued that the future dialogue will take place not only in Western Europe but also in Central and Eastern Europe; it will not only include Catholics and Protestants, but also the Orthodox; the dialogue will not only deal with the Shoah and Israel, but also with our shared textual tradition.

Most importantly of all, the future of dialogue – the future of Jewish–Christian relations – depends upon *education*; not only an education of the elite but an education for all.

This means that Jews should examine the writings of the Church and be willing to examine these in a new light. We Jews cannot escape our obligations in the new framework and this includes an examination of our education concerning Christians and Christianity. In Jewish classrooms, little has been done to change negative or infantile perceptions of Christianity. The school doors need to be opened to the winds of change blowing through. To achieve this we need Jewish scholars who can offer a Jewish theology of Christianity; who are willing to put dialogue back into the mainstream.

I call upon Jewish thinkers to face the world of contemporary Christian ideas, to respond to the imperative of dialogue. Although it is understandable that some Jews look upon dialogue with an element of mistrust, perhaps viewing it as a veiled attempt at Christian conversion, our Christian partners are beginning to say, 'We have made many changes and offered new thinking, isn't it your turn now to respond?'

On the Christian side, it means that Christian seminaries should not only offer courses in Judaism, but should consider rabbinic interpretations of Scripture. The results of these studies must find their way not only into the classrooms of seminaries, universities and teacher training colleges; they must also be discussed in the churches as well as the synagogues. Only then shall we truly begin to discover the significance of a shared textual tradition.

New attitudes are of little use if they are confined to an elite, and the true test is the extent to which they have affected teaching at all levels. This means we have to tackle the 'nitty gritty' issues. We need to teach not only about the Jewish understanding of the Sabbath, Passover, life cycle and so on, but we have to tackle the subject of the Pharisees, the relationship between Jesus and Jews, the two covenants – and how to deal with polemical texts. We have to tackle the fact that the plain text of the New Testament and the teachings of churches leaves Jews in a position of inferiority and will induce feelings, if not of genocide, then at least of scorn.

The serious study of Judaism as a living faith and its relationship with Christianity is an essential non-marginal part of Christian formation today. A Vatican directive states, 'Christians must strive to acquire a better knowledge of the basic components of the religious tradition of Judaism; they must strive to learn by what essential traits the Jews define themselves in the light of their own religious experience.'[17] Similar pronouncements have been made by the Anglican and Free Churches.

Some seminaries and theology departments are addressing these needs. But, let's be honest, most ignore it, lack competence, or treat it as an 'optional extra, time permitting'. Hardly anywhere is the new theology on Jews and Judaism effectively integrated into the curriculum.

---

17 *Guidelines and Suggestions for Implementing the Conciliar Declaration 'Nostra Aetate' (n.4)*, 1974, Commission for Religious Relations with the Jews, at www.vatican.va/roman_curia/pontifical_councils/chrstuni/relations-jews-docs/rc_pc_chrstuni_doc_19741201_nostra-aetate_en.html. See also *Notes*, op. cit., 1985, 'The Jews and Judaism should not occupy an occasional and marginal place in catechesis; their presence there is essential and should be organically integrated.'

It is time to bring dialogue back into the mainstream. Both Jews and Christians have compelling reasons to continue the dialogue and to develop it further. Together, we must not run away from it. And if there is one thing that I have learnt about Hugo Gryn from my conversations it is this: Hugo was not a man to run away from things but was willing to speak out. We must also not run away from the issues in Jewish–Christian relations. We must also speak out. Why? For all our sakes and for the sake of the next generation.

As the rabbis tell us, 'You are not free to complete the work, but neither are you free to cease from it.'[18]

---

18 Ethics of the Fathers 2.21.

# 2

# Jewish–Christian Relations in the Global Society: What the Institutional Documents Have and Have Not Been Telling Us

### Introduction

In the last 50 years or so, we have witnessed a massive change in Jewish–Christian relations. This has, for the most part, been so far-reaching that the time has now come to consider new directions in the Jewish–Christian relationship. If we Jews and Christians really are standing at the threshold of a new age, how do we proceed?

The purpose of this chapter is to outline the development of institutional statements in recent years and to point out the gaps and to suggest that (to adapt imagery from Isaiah 29.17) while the land may have been ploughed and seeds may have been planted, a fruitful field has yet to develop.

To offer an overall perspective on Jewish–Christian relations – past, present and future – is practically impossible. The task is made even more complicated by the sharp divisions within our faiths – if there is one thing I have learnt from my Christian brothers and sisters in dialogue it is this: the analogy of 'two Jews three views' is as true of Christians as Jews!

Yet this is the task that has been set, and with some trepidation I shall begin.

I will suggest that three themes can be noted from Christian documents published in recent times, each of which has resulted in a Jewish response. From the Christian perspective, the documents illustrate what might be called 'the Principle of the 3 Rs':

1 **Realization** that Christians and Christianity have made a significant contribution to Jewish suffering;
2 **Reawakening** to the Jewishness of Christianity;
And most recently . . .
3 **Recognition** that the formation of Christian identity today is dependent upon a right relationship with Judaism.

The Jewish responses, which might be described as 'the Response of the 3 Ds', have been as follows:

1 **Distrust** of Christian overtures;
2 **Defensive** involvement in dialogue (in other words, involvement for the sake of combating Christian antisemitism);
3 **Developing** awareness of a commonality with Christianity as well as an appreciation of a common purpose.

In this chapter, I will outline each of these stages, as expressed by the documents, and while we need to be vigilant about points 1 and 2, I will suggest that point 3 provides the basis for relations today.

One final point in this introduction – why the reference to the global society in the chapter title? The adjective 'global' is put in front of many a noun today, and as any glance at the burgeoning literature on globalization indicates, little consensus exists on the precise character of globalization. A new vocabulary has developed, but there is disagreement on the nature, extent and direction of the change caused by globalization.

Globalization is probably as big a historical shift as was industrialization. I shall suggest that we need to contemplate the scale of the challenge of globalization and apply our conclusions to Jewish–Christian relations. It is wrong to see globalization as either wholly positive or wholly negative. However, humankind can use it for good but also for evil. It therefore represents an opportunity as well as a threat.

## The Christian Contribution to Jewish Suffering

*The legacy of the* Adversus-Iudaeos *tradition and Christian antisemitism*

The first theme deals with the awareness among Christians of the Christian contribution to Jewish suffering. We begin in 1948, when the World Council of Churches (WCC) held its first meeting in the city of Anne Frank – Amsterdam. In the introduction to its *Report on the Christian Approach to the Jews*, it made reference to the fact that the conference was taking place 'within five years of the extermination of six million Jews'.

The report marked a new stage in the attitude of the Protestant churches towards antisemitism, for it disassociated itself from previously held views. These either denied the existence of religious antisemitism or, alternatively, blamed it on Jews. Typical of these views was this statement by Dr Frank Gavin in 1931:

> Judaism, when practised by observant Jews, certainly appears to the non-Jew a religion apart from the ordinary world. Within the quite limited meaning of the word 'religious intolerance', there is some basis for its existence, but the creating word, *the determining factor, is not to be cast up to the gentile but to the Jewish side of the ledger* [my italics].

In other words, antisemitism is the fault of Jews![1]

The WCC not only acknowledged the existence of religious antisemitism but also accepted Christian involvement in it. This was a very important step. The report openly accepted that 'the churches in the past have helped to foster an image of the Jews as the sole enemies of Christ, which has contributed to antisemitism

---

1 F. Gavin, 1931, 'The Christian Approach to the Jews', in *Christians and Jews*, New York: International Missionary Council, p. 49.

## JEWISH–CHRISTIAN RELATIONS

in the secular world.'[2] It called upon 'all churches we represent to denounce antisemitism'. Thus Christian awareness of the Christian contribution to antisemitism was placed firmly on the agenda of Christian–Jewish relations. The WCC report marked an admission that not only was Christian history linked to the history of antisemitism, but that it was one of the causes.

The magnitude of the step taken by the WCC can be seen more clearly when compared with the failure of the Anglican Lambeth Conference of 1948 even to mention antisemitism. The nearest the Lambeth Conference came to confronting prejudice in terms of relations between Christians and Jews can be found in a section entitled 'Palestine', which stated that the conference 'greatly appreciates the efforts made to restore peace, and expresses its sympathy with all of every race, and particularly Christians of every Church, who are suffering'.[3]

During the 40 years before the subject of Christian–Jewish relations appeared on the Lambeth Conference agenda, a large number of Protestant churches tackled the problems arising out of the legacy of the *Adversus-Iudaeos* tradition – not however the WCC General Assembly, which has failed to produce a document on the Christian–Jewish relationship. The WCC encompasses over 300 non-Catholic churches, and any statement has to undergo a complicated process of decision-making due to the many different attitudes prevailing among the WCC Member Churches.

The WCC encounter with Judaism has only ever been an issue within the broader discussions by the delegates on interreligious affairs. At this (lower) level, a number of documents have been issued, such as the 1988 Sigtuna statement, which affirmed that the Jewish people have not been rejected by God but remain the continuation of the biblical Israel. On antisemitism it stated:

> We deeply regret that, contrary to the spirit of Christ, many Christians have used the claims of faith as weapons against the

---

[2] *The Message and Reports of the First Assembly of the World Council of Churches*, 1948, London: SPCK, p. 77.

[3] *Lambeth Conference*, 1948, vol. 1, London: Lambeth Palace, p. 31.

Jewish people, culminating in the Shoah, and we confess sins of words and deeds against Jews in all centuries. Although not all Christians in all times and all lands have been guilty of persecution of Jews, we recognize that in the Christian tradition and its use of Scripture and liturgy there are still ideas towards Jews and Judaism that consciously or unconsciously, translate into prejudice and discrimination against Jews.[4]

Yet neither this nor other documents were promulgated at the top level of the WCC, because they would not be passed by the Central Committee. And here lies the key to the problem. The WCC is not only divided, but is deeply involved in the struggle of the Liberation Groups in the Third World. This involved them in support for the PLO in its early years. The strongly pro-Palestinian Middle East Council of Churches is a constituent body of the WCC and has influenced its attitudes beyond the political issues of the Middle East. And the WCC Assembly, held every seven years, has regularly endorsed anti-Israel statements. The hostile attitude to Israel underwent a certain thaw during the Peace Process, but more recently has reverted to the critical.

Fortunately this is not typical of Jewish–Protestant relations elsewhere. For example, the *Adversus-Iudaeos* teachings of Martin Luther were repudiated by the Lutheran World Federation, who rejected 'Luther's violent invective against the Jews and express deep and abiding sorrow over its tragic effects on subsequent generations'.[5] In particular, it deplored the appropriation of Luther's words by modern antisemites and called for increasing Lutheran–Jewish co-operation.

---

4 *The Churches and the Jewish People: Toward a New Understanding*, Consultation on the Church and the Jewish People, 1988, Geneva: World Council of Churches, 1988, at www.jcrelations.net/The_Churches_and_the_Jewish_People_Toward_a_New_Understanding.1512.0.html

5 *Declaration of ELCA to Jewish Community*, 1994, The Church Council of the Evangelical Lutheran Church in America, at www.elca.org/Who-We-Are/Our-Three-Expressions/Churchwide-Organization/Office-of-the-Presiding-Bishop/Ecumenical-and-Inter-Religious-Relations/Inter-Religious-Relations/Christian-Jewish-Relations/Declaration-of-ELCA-to-Jewish-Community.aspx

We now turn to the Roman Catholic Church and the Second Vatican Council. It is worth noting that during the preparatory work, which lasted three and a half years, the 1961 WCC Assembly took place in Delhi. Although the Catholic Church took no part in the WCC, the pre-conciliar climate and the Assembly undoubtedly influenced each other. For example, the Holy See sent observers to the Delhi Assembly.

The significance of the Second Vatican Council for Jewish–Christian relations began to be recognized when shortly before Easter in the same year, John XXIII changed the Good Friday liturgy during which Catholics said, 'Let us pray also for the perfidious Jews'. A year later, the Pope received wide attention for publicly greeting Jewish visitors with the words, 'I am Joseph your brother.'

*Nostra Aetate* marked the beginnings of a fresh approach to Judaism when the Roman Catholic Church 'came in from out of the cold'. According to Edward Flannery, it 'terminated in a stroke a millennial teaching of contempt of Jews and Judaism and unequivocally asserted the Church's debt to its Jewish heritage'.[6]

Some 30 years on, the short passage does not betray signs of the tensions in which it was born. Although *Nostra Aetate* provided no new general Christian thinking – omitting, for example, any mention of the Shoah or the State of Israel – it was forceful in its condemnation of antisemitism. Most importantly of all, it ushered in a new era, fresh attitudes, a new language of discourse never previously heard in the Catholic Church concerning Jews. The concept of a dialogue now entered the relationship.

There were a number of questions raised that the Secretariat decided not resolve formally in a conciliar document and to leave until a future time. One of these concerned the issue of Christian antisemitism. The document stated that nothing was to be taught or preached that was 'out of harmony with the truth of

---

6 Edward Flannery, 1988, 'Seminaries, Classrooms, Pulpits, Streets: Where We Have to Go', in R. Brooks (ed.), *Unanswered Questions: Theological Views of Jewish–Catholic Relations*, Notre Dame, IN: University of Notre Dame Press, pp. 128–9.

the Gospel'.[7] Yet it was still too soon to consider why the texts of Matthew and John tended to excuse the disciples, but accuse more and more Jews by excluding more and more Romans.

How did Jews respond? For the most part, Jews responded to Christian recognition of the legacy of the *Adversus-Iudaeos* writings with distrust – a legacy of the consequences of the 'teaching of contempt'. There was, among the Jewish community, no general desire to engage in dialogue with Christians and Christianity.

It is true that the leaders of the World Jewish Congress (WJC), Nahum Goldmann and Gerhart Riegner, established an international Jewish dialogue body – the International Jewish Committee for Interreligious Consultations (IJCIC), with the participation of the WJC, the Synagogue Council of America, the American Jewish Committee, the B'nai B'rith and Anti-Defamation League and the Israel Interfaith Committee – but the desire among the majority of Jews was lacking.

This was the result not only of suspicion of Christian motives but also because of the mark that the *Adversus-Iudaeos* tradition had left on the Jewish psyche. Most Jews did not trust Christian motives. But there was also another reason for Jewish distrust. Jews responded to the Christian *Adversus-Iudaeos* tradition, and although there is little evidence of an *Adversus-Christianos* tradition, Christianity was dismissed as a religion practised by morally and culturally inferior gentiles, based on unbelievable claims, which had degenerated into idolatry.

The 1988 Lambeth debate on the Christian attitude towards Judaism was a significant step forward. The discussion shared some of the features of Vatican II – for instance, the prepared document was significantly altered during the conference. The guidelines, which were presented for approval, were called *Jewish–Christian Guidelines for the Anglican Communion*. By the end they had been renamed *Jews, Christians, Muslims: The Way of Dialogue*. Clearly, the conference felt that Christian–Jewish relations could not be commented upon without reference to Christian–Muslim relations.

---

7 Austin Flannery (ed.), 1981, *Vatican Council II: The Conciliar and Post Conciliar Documents*, Dublin: Dominican Publications, p. 741.

We should also not forget the influence of the crisis in Lebanon and the concern over the hostages, one of whom was Terry Waite. In addition, a separate document on Christian–Muslim relations was due to have been published, but the draft for discussion had not been completed in time for the conference. Consequently, there was a danger that nothing would be published. However, as a result of intensive discussions, as well as the support of bishops such as Richard Harries, a compromise was reached.

The final document at the Lambeth Conference in 1988 delivered a scathing denunciation of antisemitism and of the Christian teaching of contempt:

> Through catechism, teaching of school children, and Christian preaching, the Jewish people have been misrepresented and caricatured . . . In order to combat centuries of anti-Jewish teaching and practice, Christians must develop programmes of teaching, preaching, and common social action which eradicate prejudice and promote dialogue and sharing among biblical peoples.[8]

No document had so explicitly argued that there should be a fundamental change in the Christian approach to Judaism. It pointed the way forward and it is now common for statements from Protestant churches and the Roman Catholic Church to acknowledge the legacy of the *Adversus-Iudaeos* tradition and Christian antisemitism, such as the 2001 document *Church and Israel* by the Leuenberg Church Fellowship (consisting of the Reformation churches in Europe), which explicitly acknowledges the Christian contribution to Jewish suffering.

This survey of the Christian awareness of the Christian contribution to antisemitism shows that, over 50 years, significant changes have taken place. We can see that many of the churches have considered the problem not only of antisemitism, but also of Christian antisemitism.

---

8 *The Truth Shall Set You Free: The Lambeth Conference 1988*, London: Church House Publishing, p. 303.

## JEWS, CHRISTIANS AND MUSLIMS IN ENCOUNTER

Unfortunately, the same is not true of the encounter with the Orthodox churches. The changes that have taken place in what may be described as the Western churches find few parallels in the East. The remarkably rapid growth of understanding and trust between Jews and Christians of the Latin tradition, particularly since the 1960s, contrasts with the very slow rate of progress in dialogue between Jews and Christians of the Orthodox tradition.

A few formal meetings of academics and leading figures on both sides have taken place since 1974, initially involving Greek theologians, but since the 1990s this has included Christians from the communist world and the Middle East. In Russia itself, a small number of gatherings have taken place, including one in St Petersburg in January 1997 on 'Theology after Auschwitz and the Gulag'. In October 2000 a conference entitled 'Spiritual Culture Dialogue – Facing Each Other' took place in Moscow. It was addressed by the Patriarch of Moscow and All Russia, Alexej II, who stated that, 'our Church is open to inter-religious dialogue and is interested in its continuation, as it testifies to the ability of believers to make society more healthy and consolidate it'.[9]

Despite these meetings, however, and despite some helpful pronouncements by Orthodox leaders, there is simply no comparison with the current state of play in the Roman Catholic and Protestant churches. To some extent the uneasy relationship of the Orthodox churches with Judaism echoes the state of their involvement in the ecumenical movement too, and it is foolish to expect Orthodox Christians to be more forward in seeking reconciliation with Jews than with their own Christian brethren. Much has to be done before Orthodox Christianity abandons its repository of anti-Jewish polemic.

So where does that leave us? Do we concur with James Parkes, a life-long student of antisemitism, who was once asked how long he thought it would last. His reply was, '300 years'. Or should we believe that we are in the last stages of a millennial malady?

---

9 Interreligious Peace Forum Moscow, November 13–14, 2000, at www.jcrelations.net/Patriarch_of_Moscow_and_All_Russia_to_Conference__Facing_each_other.1308.0.html?page=7

Should we agree or disagree with the central character of *The Plague*, by Albert Camus?

> As Rieux listened to the cries of joy rising from the town, he remembered that such joy could always be imperilled. He knew what those jubilant crowds did not know but could have learnt from books: that the plague bacillus never dies nor disappears for good; that it can lie dormant for years and years in furniture and linen chests; that it bides its time in bedrooms, cellars, trunks, and bookshelves; and that perhaps the day would come when it would rouse up its rats again, and send them forth to die in a happy city.[10]

Or can we be more confident?

I am rather more optimistic. The institutional statements of the Protestant churches and Roman Catholic Church have taken, and continue to take, a strong stand against antisemitism as well as Christian antisemitism. Pope John Paul II firmly condemned it as a sin and called on the faithful to do *teshuva* (repentance) for misdeeds against Jews. This is illustrated by their tackling of the Holocaust.

## *The Holocaust*

While roundly condemning antisemitism, the Vatican until recently largely avoided the question of the Holocaust. In 1987, in the wake of Jewish ire over the Pope's reception of Austrian President Kurt Waldheim, who had been an active Nazi, the Vatican promised to issue such a document and this was affirmed by the Pope at a meeting with Jewish leaders.

The Vatican statement *We Remember: Reflections on the Shoah* was published in 1998. It stresses the evils of antisemitism, concluding 'we wish to turn awareness of past sins into a firm resolve to build a new future in which there will be no more anti-Judaism

---

10 Albert Camus, 1948, *The Plague*, trans. S. Gilbert, London: Hamish Hamilton, pp. 284–5.

among Christians or anti-Christian sentiment among Jews but rather a shared mutual respect.' It incorporates much of Pope John Paul II's forceful criticism of antisemitism. But its treatment of the Holocaust had many disappointing aspects for some Jews, especially those who were over-expectant.

They had unrealistically hoped for a formal apology, on the lines of that issued by the French bishops who stated that 'it is important to admit the primary role played by the consistently repeated anti-Jewish stereotypes wrongly perpetuated by the Christians in the historical process that led to the Holocaust'. *We Remember* speaks of those Christians who helped Jews and those who failed to do so, but implies a balanced picture. It fails to give a plain statement on the role of Christian teachings and stereotypes in motivating those who behaved negatively.

Yet it is a highly significant document and should be recognized as such. It must be remembered that this document is directed to a Christian public, and is primarily a sincere call for the renunciation of antisemitism. Statements such as *We Remember* and Protestant statements that are equally significant reach not only Christians in Western Europe and North America, where dialogue has progressed, but also Christians in regions such as Eastern Europe, Africa, Asia and Latin America, where many have never encountered a Jew in their lives and know little of them except from the New Testament accounts.

Thus as far as the Christian contribution to Jewish suffering is concerned, the Protestant churches and the Roman Catholic Church have now become part of the solution, rather than being part of the problem.

Yet we must notice a danger in these documents on the Holocaust. Notice the following 1996 Methodist statement, *Building Bridges of Hope*, which states:

> Especially crucial for Christians in our quest for understanding has been the struggle to recognize the horror of the Holocaust as the catastrophic culmination of a long history of anti-Jewish attitudes and actions in which Christians, and sometimes the Church itself, have been deeply implicated. Dialogues with Jewish part-

ners have been central for Christians in our process of learning of the scope of the Holocaust atrocities, acknowledgment of complicity and responsibility, repentance, and commitment to work against antisemitism in all its forms in the future.[11]

The Leuenberg document, after having acknowledged the Christian contribution to the Holocaust, states that:

> Irrespective of the particular responsibility of Germany and the Christians in Germany related to the National Socialist period – all the Christian churches in Europe share in the special history of European guilt towards Israel [the Jewish people], wherever they failed clearly to contradict antisemitism or even promoted it directly or indirectly.

The great danger is of building a relationship on guilt, a danger faced by both Jews and Christians. This perhaps lies behind the following statement in *Dabru Emet*, which in opposition to the distrust felt by many Jews states:

> **Nazism was not a Christian phenomenon.** Without the long history of Christian anti-Judaism and Christian violence against Jews, Nazi ideology could not have taken hold nor could it have been carried out . . . But Nazism itself was not an inevitable outcome of Christianity . . . We encourage the continuation of recent efforts in Christian theology to repudiate unequivocally contempt of Judaism and the Jewish people. We applaud those Christians who reject this teaching of contempt, and we do not blame them for the sins committed by their ancestors.[12]

---

11 *Building New Bridges in Hope*, adopted by the 1996 General Conference of the United Methodist Church (USA), at www.archives.umc.org/interior.asp?ptid=4&mid=3301

12 *Dabru Emet: A Jewish Statement on Christians and Christianity*, 2000, at www.jcrelations.net/Dabru_Emet__A_Jewish_Statement_on_Christians_and_Christianity.2395.0.html

While reaction to the Christian contribution to Jewish suffering is an important driving force, Jewish–Christian relations cannot be built solely on responses to antisemitism and Christian feelings of guilt. If recent Christian soul-searching in the aftermath of the destruction of European Jewry leads to a new approach and a repudiation of the *Adversus-Iudaeos* tradition, so much the better. However, the future relationship cannot be built on the foundations of guilt. The sense of guilt is transient and does not pass to the next generation; moreover, it is unstable, inherently prone to sudden and drastic reversal.

We need to move on to a more positive basis for relations, and the institutional documents do exactly that.

## The Jewish Origins of Christianity and the Mission of, and Mission to, Israel

As well as acknowledging the Christian contribution to Jewish suffering, institutional statements illustrate a second revolution in Roman Catholic and Protestant attitudes towards Jews and Judaism. They are reawakening to the Jewish origins of Christianity and are reconsidering the meaning of the mission of, and the mission to, Israel.

They have renounced many of the triumphalist doctrines, most significantly the renunciation of the teaching of the divine rejection of the Jewish people since the time of Jesus – in other words, the divine covenant with the Jewish people is now no longer viewed as having been annulled. According to the 1980 Evangelical Church of the Rhineland statement:

> We believe the permanent election of the Jewish people as the people of God and realize that through Jesus Christ the church is into the covenant of God with his people.[13]

---

13 *Towards Renewal of the Relationship of Christians and Jews*, 1980, Synod of the Evangelical Church of the Rhineland, at www.jcrelations.net/Towards+Renovat ion+of+the+Relationship+of+Christians+and+Jews.2388.0.html?L=3

For its part, *Nostra Aetate* taught Christians that 'the Jews remain most dear to God' who 'does not repent of the gifts He makes nor of the calls He issues'. John Paul II spelled it out in the early years of his pontificate as follows: God's covenant with the Jewish people had never been broken, retains eternal validity; God does not renege on his promises (cf. Romans 11.29). If Jews were not rejected, then Judaism was not a fossilized faith, as had been taught previously, but a living, authentic religion.

The ramifications were manifold. Christians were now told that Jesus, his family and his followers were Jewish and the Jewish background to Christianity was now stressed. Stated first in recent times by the 1947 Seelisberg document, Christians are commended to:

> Remember that Jesus was born of a Jewish mother of the seed of David and the people of Israel, and that His everlasting love and forgiveness embraces His own people and the whole world.
> Remember that the first disciples, the apostles and the first martyrs were Jews.[14]

The rediscovery of the Jewishness of the origins of Christianity led to Christians being taught about the richness of the Jewish context as well as about the perils of relying on the literal text of the New Testament. New subjects for consideration were also broached, which included the closeness of the relationship between Jesus and the Pharisees. Previously, this subject was limited to the consideration of scholars such as George Foot Moore and Travers Hereford. Now, though, Catholics for example learnt (from the 1985 Vatican *Notes*) that Jesus 'had very close relations' with the Pharisees to whom 'he was very near'.

In addition, Christian ordinands were being taught that the final text of the Gospels was edited long after the events described and for example that the authors were concerned with denigrating those Jews who did not follow Jesus. At the same time they were

---

14 *The Ten Points of Seelisberg: An address to the Churches*, 1947, International Council of Christians and Jews, at www.jcrelations.net/60_years_-_the_Ten_Points_of_TSeelisberg.2047.0.html

concerned with vindicating the Romans, whose goodwill they were seeking. This was courageously admitted by the Vatican's 1985 document on the teaching of Judaism, which stated forthrightly:

> It cannot be ruled out that some references hostile or less than favorable to the Jews have their historical context in conflicts between the nascent Church and the Jewish community. Certain controversies reflect Christian–Jewish relations long after the time of Jesus. To establish this is of capital importance if we wish to bring out the meaning of certain Gospel texts for the Christians of today.[15]

There was a realization that too often Christians have pictured Torah as a burden rather than as a delight. Christians were reminded that Jesus was a faithful Jew and 'that from the Jewish people sprang the apostles', the foundation stones and pillars of the Church who 'draw sustenance from the root of that good olive tree onto which have been grafted the wild olive branches of the Gentiles'. Christians therefore became reacquainted with Judaism.

From the Jewish side, individuals such as Martin Buber and Claude Montefiore reminded Jews that Jesus was a fellow Jew (their 'great brother', as Martin Buber described him). But this is rarely stated in Jewish documents. Witness what *Dabru Emet* says and does not say about Jesus. It fails to mention the Jewishness of Jesus, and simply states that 'Christians know and serve God through Jesus Christ and the Christian tradition'.

It is true that *Dabru Emet* recognizes that questions such as the purpose behind the creation of Christianity need to be considered. However, the document does not address the question of whether the fact that Jesus was a Jew has any implications for Jews. It is well known that Jews are very proud of the Albert Einsteins, the Heinrich Heines and the Sigmund Freuds, yet Israel's most famous Jew is generally ignored. Now, in a freer climate as far as Jewish–Christian relations are concerned, is it not time that

---

15 *Notes*, op. cit., 4.21.

there was a greater Jewish interest in Jesus the Jew? I suggest that *Dabru Emet* missed an opportunity in this respect.

For Christians, the tackling of Christian triumphalism illustrates not just a shift from what was, for the most part, an inherent need to condemn Judaism to one of a condemnation of Christian anti-Judaism. It has led to a closer relationship with 'the elder brother' and not, as some have feared from the time of Marcion onwards, to a separation from all things Jewish (who called for a total separation from the Hebrew Bible and much of the Gospel writings).

This shift can be illustrated with a brief discussion of mission, which in many ways is a far more complicated subject than antisemitism. It is easier for Christians to condemn Christian antisemitism as a misunderstanding of the Christian teaching. Mission, however, has been – and still is – central to the Christian faith. This is illustrated by the legacy of the command found in the Gospel of Matthew to 'go therefore and make disciples of all nations'.[16]

In 1948, the WCC did not only condemn antisemitism but also, perhaps incredibly when viewed in hindsight, called for a redoubling of effort at the conversion of Jews. The report recommended that the churches should 'seek to recover the universality of our Lord's commission by including the Jewish people in their evangelistic work'. The conclusion of the WCC was that, in the light of the Shoah, an even greater effort should be made to convert Jews. The report stated that 'because of the unique inheritance of the Jewish people, the churches should make provisions for the education of ministers specially fitted to this task. Provision should also be made for Christian literature to interpret the Gospel to Jewish people.'[17]

It is interesting that the 1948 Assembly linked the two issues: the condemnation of antisemitism with an exhortation to preach the gospel to Jews – on the one hand, a call 'to denounce antisemitism'; on the other, a call for the conversion of Jews.[18]

---

16 Matthew 28.19.

17 *The Christian Approach to the Jews: The Message and Reports of the First Assembly of the World Council of Churches*, 1948, p. 78, at www.jcrelations.net/The_Christian_Approach_to_the_Jews.2584.0.html?searchAutor=First%2BAssembly%2Bof%2Bthe%2BWorld%2BCouncil%2Bof%2BChurches

18 Ibid., pp. 76–7.

At this time, Jews throughout the world were trying to recover from the Shoah. Their view of this report – if they knew it existed – could only have been that the Nazis wanted Jewish bodies, the churches wanted Jewish souls.

As far as the Roman Catholic Church was concerned, there were a number of questions raised that the Secretariat decided not to resolve formally in a conciliar document but to leave until a future time – and one such question concerns mission.

Thomas Stransky explains the dilemma for Catholics – indeed for all Christians – and puts into context the reasons why the subject has, until recently, been avoided. He argues that Christians in their witness should always avoid proselytism (in the pejorative sense); they should shun all conversionary attitudes and practices that do *not* conform to the ways a free God draws free people to himself in response to his calls to serve him in spirit and in truth.

> In the case of the Jewish people, what is Christian proselytism in practice? And what is 'evangelization' – the Church's everlasting proclamation of Jesus Christ, 'the Way, the Truth and the Life'? Is open dialogue a betrayal of Christian mission? Or is mission a betrayal of dialogue?[19]

Interestingly, he also asks the reverse question – that is, what is the continuing mission of the synagogue to the Church? What is the *common* mission of the synagogue and the Church?

The 1985 *Notes* illustrate Stransky's point: on the one hand, 'the Church must preach Jesus Christ to the world'; on the other, it must 'spread their Christian faith while maintaining the strictest respect for religious liberty'. Such a tension is disturbing to many Jews. For example, the belief that salvation can only come through Jesus (or through the Church) relegates not only Judaism but all other faiths to a position of inferiority. Have the changes in doctrine starting with Vatican II robbed this belief of its former

---

19 Thomas F. Stransky, 1988, 'Holy Diplomacy: Making the Impossible Possible', in R. Brooks (ed.), *Unanswered Questions: Theological Views of Jewish–Catholic Relations*, Notre Dame, IN: University of Notre Dame Press, p. 66.

triumphalism? Some Jewish participants in the dialogue remain unconvinced and the publication of *Dominus Iesus* serves only to confuse rather than clarify.

However, we must remember that traditional Jewish eschatology, while not foreseeing the conversion of all to Judaism, does anticipate that all nations will acknowledge the superiority and sovereignty of the God of Israel. Jews and Christians remain adherents of very different faiths and we must recognize that there are beliefs in all religions which characterize that faith and are too fundamental to compromise. This is acknowledged by *Dabru Emet* as follows:

> The humanly irreconcilable difference between Jews and Christians will not be settled until God redeems the entire world as promised in Scripture ... Jews can respect Christians' faithfulness to their revelation just as we expect Christians to respect our faithfulness to our revelation. Neither Jew nor Christian should be pressed into affirming the teaching of the other community.[20]

The 1988 Lambeth Conference confronted the issue of mission to Israel and represents the first occasion when the subject of mission has been tackled by institutional documents.

Although the first time Christian–Jewish relations appeared on the Lambeth Conference agenda was as late as 1988, a report entitled *Witness of the Church to the Jews in London* was produced in 1949. The report stated that the Church must first denounce all forms of antisemitism: 'The first step in presenting the gospel to them [Jews] is the removal of those barriers which pre-dispose them against accepting it ... Very little advance can be made in the matter of proclaiming the Christian gospel unless antisemitism is first attacked.' It advised its readers to convert Jews by 'making friendly contact'; it recommended them to 'invite

---

20 *Dabru Emet*, op. cit.

Jewish neighbours into Christian homes' with the hope that, eventually, Jews would convert.[21]

The report was especially critical of the recent establishment of the Council of Christians and Jews in 1942. First, for creating the impression that the majority of Christians have no other than a humanitarian message for the non-Christian and non-gentile community. Second, for stating that the few in the Church who are missionary-minded towards Jews are irresponsible and isolated individuals. Third, for suggesting to Christians that in fraternizing with their Jewish neighbours they have discharged their Christian duty towards them.

The 1988 Conference took a totally different position. Unlike the other conferences or official documents, Lambeth 1988 emphasized, rather than minimized, the importance of missionary activity for Christian–Jewish relations. It re-examined the understanding of the Christian mission, which was seen not in terms of the conversion of Jews, but rather of a common mission. In the light of Christian–Jewish and Christian–Muslim relations, proselytism was to be rejected and the conference called for 'mutual witness to God between equal partners'.

It stated that although

> there are a variety of attitudes towards Judaism within Christianity today . . . All these approaches, however, share a common concern to be sensitive to Judaism, to reject all proselytising, that is, aggressive and manipulative attempts to convert, and of course, any hint of antisemitism. Further, Jews, Muslims and Christians have a common mission. They share a mission to the world that God's name may be honoured.[22]

This is not to imply that there are no missionary problems today. However, there has been a dramatic downscaling of Christian mission to Jews. For many Christian churches a distinction has been drawn between 'mission' and 'witness'.

---

21 *Mission to London Papers*, 1952 (unpublished), Lambeth Palace, pp. 28–30.
22 *The Truth Shall Set You Free*, op. cit., p. 305.

## JEWISH–CHRISTIAN RELATIONS

Instances of missionary problems come mainly from some evangelical churches (including those 'messianic' movements such as Jews for Jesus). Relations with the evangelical Protestants are especially complex. First of all, they often do not dialogue – even with other Christians. Their fundamentalist views are not to be discussed with others (similar to fundamentalist Jews) and mission is ingrained – as was again exemplified by the recent decision of the Southern Baptist convention, one of the largest groupings in the United States, to intensify mission to Jews in a resolution 'to direct our energies and resources toward the proclamation of the gospel to the Jewish people'.

Nevertheless, the institutional statements illustrate a significant shift in the Christian understanding of the mission of, and the mission to, Israel. They have not only revised the traditional negative assessment of Judaism, but have explained Israel's role in positive terms. This has had a major impact and has resulted in an emphasis on partnership and a common mission rather than the mission of one in contradistinction to the other.

## The Formation of Christian Identity and the Issue of Commonality

The biggest challenge raised by the institutional statements for Christian–Jewish relations today (a far bigger challenge than is appreciated) is illustrated by the following statement of the 1974 Guidelines: 'Christians must strive to learn by what essential traits the Jews define themselves in the light of their own religious experience.'[23] I do not think the Church knew at that time (nor realizes today) how difficult it might be to abide by that principle.

This view is similarly expressed in Protestant churches as, for example, expressed by the Leuenberg document, which states that 'the relationship with Israel is therefore for Christians and for the churches an indispensable part of the foundation of their faith'. Similarly, the latest statement of the WCC, *Christian–Jewish*

---

23 Guidelines, op. cit., p. 744.

*Dialogue Beyond Canberra 1991*, adopted in 1992 by the Central Committee states:

> The WCC will assist the churches to understand the theological significance of living Judaism, to examine contemporary theological affirmations vis-à-vis Judaism . . . and to foster implementation of the churches' recommendations in Christian teaching, mission and liturgical life.[24]

How are these changes in thinking going to be implemented? How are they going to be brought down to grass-roots level? We have seen that Christian theology on Jews and Judaism has been revised drastically.

It is clear that the documents have reached a stage where many of the main divisive issues have been either eliminated or taken to the furthest point at which agreement is possible. The efforts of Catholics and Protestants towards respect of Judaism are reflected in these documents, which project attitudes that would have been unthinkable a few decades ago. Christian theology has been profoundly revised at the official level – all churches are committed to the fight against antisemitism; to teaching about the Jewishness of Christianity; and the problem of mission to Jews has all but disappeared.

There is of course an important agenda for top-level dialogue and consultations, but the emphasis should now shift to filtering to regional and local levels. It is possible today to respond effectively to regional requirements in the new global reality. Consciousness of the changes have been largely confined to the elite (although in certain regions, such as the United States, it has been more widely disseminated). The object now is to get these changes into the everyday understanding of all the faithful, and the fields to be addressed are churches and synagogues, seminaries and yeshivahs,

---

24 *Christian–Jewish Dialogue beyond Canberra 1991*, Central Committee of the WCC, 31/08/92, at www.jcrelations.net/Christian-Jewish_Dialogue_Beyond_Canberra_2585.0.html?page=1

schools and universities, as well as informal education, including the media.

This is where the effects of globalization enter our discussion.

Examples of global phenomena abound in today's world – for example, e-mail and McDonald's are global in that they can extend anywhere on the planet at the same time; BBC broadcasts and credit cards are not restricted by distances or borders; global conditions can surface simultaneously at any point on earth that is equipped to host them – for instance, an internet connection; global phenomena move almost instantaneously across any distance on the planet – for example, telephone calls. Air travel, telecommunications, computer networks and electronic mass media allow us to collect and disseminate information more or less instantaneously between any locations on earth. Technology is crucial since developments in communications and information processing have supplied the infrastructure for global connections.

Yet the extents of the shifts should not be exaggerated. We inhabit a *globalizing* world rather than a completely *globalized* one.

While this process is taking place and resulting in a massive historical shift we must consider the implications for Jewish–Christian relations and set in place new arrangements to help manage this process. Managing globalization means strengthening key international institutions. If our society, economy, politics and so on are becoming global, then Jewish–Christian relations must be global too. And for that we need an effective international system.

We must ensure that the positive developments achieved, particularly the themes identified in this chapter, are properly applied at the regional level. This means attention to education and information (including the media) to ensure that the new teachings are disseminated at grass-roots levels. It involves dealing with the fight against antisemitism in regions such as Russia, and certainly to combat any manifestations within a religious context.

Most importantly, educational guidelines are required – designed for each region. This requirement is equally true of Jews as well as Christians. History has understandably moulded negative Christian stereotypes among Jews and we must now teach the Jewish community about the contemporary changes of attitudes by the churches. The beginnings can be seen in *Dabru Emet*, but this is simply the first step. Claude Montefiore's call for a Jewish theology of Christianity over 75 years ago still waits to be answered.[25]

Yet there is a curious paradox at the heart of globalization. While peoples are being drawn ever more closely together, some forces seek refuge in narrow nationalism and isolation. The demands of nationalist identification have been clearly conveyed in the recent upsurge in nationalism in Central Europe. For instance, witness the following comments by the Croatian writer Slavenka Drakulic:

> Along with millions of other Croats, I was pinned to the wall of nationhood – not only by outside pressure from Serbia and the Federal Army but by national homogenisation within Croatia itself. That is what the war is doing, reducing us to one dimension: the Nation. The trouble with this nationhood, however, is that whereas before, I was defined by my education, my job, my ideas, my character – and, yes, my nationality, too – now I feel stripped of all that. I am nobody, because I am not a person any more. I am one of the 4.5 million Croats.[26]

Thus the threshold upon which we sit provides risk as well as opportunity. Globalization is changing the rules of the game for all of us, and while it has great potential there is also danger. Globalization is with us, and it is here to stay. The challenge for the twenty-first century is to harness the forces of globalization for the good of Jewish–Christian relations. The growing interconnectedness and interdependence of Jewish–Christian relations, supported by the revolution in information technology, is bringing all of us closer together. Globalization affords an unparalleled opportunity to bring about further advances, building on the themes identified in this chapter.

---

25 Claude G. Montefiore, 1923, *The Old Testament and After*, London: Macmillan, pp. 560–1.

26 Vladimir Tismaneanu, 1998, *Fantasies of Salvation: Democracy, Nationalism and Myths in Post-Communist Europe*, Princeton, NJ: Princeton University Press, pp. 89–90.

But there is no guarantee of progress. There are risks, for example, that instability in one part of the world will affect Jewish–Christian relations in another. Globalization is not inherently good or bad – it is a reality, one that we must shape. We must learn to think globally, and act internationally, nationally and locally, to ensure that globalization works *for* us and not *against* us.

We must draw inspiration from the pioneers of Jewish–Christian dialogue who fought so hard and achieved so much in the twentieth century, and build on their work in the global society of today. This is not an optional extra; it simply represents the way in which history is developing. It is challenging all our structures, including the powers and structures of the institutional religions. It does not make them irrelevant but adjusts their role.

What does this mean in practice? It means that our initiatives should come together. Efforts to change theological education, congregational perceptions and interfaith understanding seem on occasions to be the concern of different groups – each of which sometimes hears only part of what was said. Educationalists hear one point; religious leaders another; congregants a third, and so on. The lesson of the global society is that we each need to hear the same points and work together.

Together we can develop programmes that will affect a wide range of areas – social, political, civil, cultural and educational, as well as religious life. This will fulfil the challenge of Jewish–Christian relations today and will help maintain the momentum that has been built up in recent years.

Giant strides have been made, but we are talking of a dynamic and relentless process. We will never be able to sit back and say, 'The work is done. The agenda is completed.' On many major issues, we find ourselves on the same side of the fence, faced with the same challenges. The agenda is changing and new agendas are no less vital and pressing.

So despite great advances, Jewish–Christian relations still face major challenges as well as opportunities. Rising to meet these challenges requires a concerted effort, and in 2001 it requires a global effort.

# 3

# Land and Memory

The apparent constant instability in Palestinian-controlled areas and anti-Israel attitudes of varying intensity in Arab countries, combined with the murder of Yitzhak Rabin by an Orthodox Jew in 1995 and threats from some Orthodox Jews against land for peace initiatives (such as Ariel Sharon's pull-out from Gaza in 2005), are reminders of what seems to be an intractable conflict between Israel and the Palestinians. Yet the military conflict alone does not fully explain why Israel is such a controversial topic in Jewish–Christian relations. Any conversation between Jews and Christians on the significance of the land and State of Israel brims with emotion and passion. Why?

For Jews, the centrality of the land of the Bible, as well as the survival of over a third of world Jewry, is at stake. Christians, for their part, not only disagree as to the place of Israel in Christian theology, but many understandably feel particular concern for Christians who live in Israel and for the future state of Palestine. Indeed, the complexity and sensitivity surrounding Israel means that it is not even easy to choose the appropriate words in discussions. Are we to use the term 'Holy Land', perhaps with a qualifier such as 'Christian' or, alternatively, 'the Promised Land'? Or must we seek ostensibly more neutral terms such as 'Israel and Palestine'? Should we refer to 'Jerusalem', to 'Yerushalayim' or to 'Al-Quds'? Is Hebron, al-Khalil; or Nablus, Shechem? How do we respond to terms such as 'the Zionist entity' rather than the State of Israel?

Although there have been great changes in Christian teaching on Judaism and especially a tackling of the traditional 'teaching of contempt of Judaism', attitudes towards the land and State of Israel continue, from the theological perspective, to be more difficult to tackle, making a Christian reorientation to Israel problematic. Put simply, it has been easier for Christians to condemn antisemitism as a misunderstanding of Christian teaching than to come to terms with the re-establishment of the Jewish State.

## Sacred Space

We begin with a consideration of sacred spaces because most religions recognize the sacredness of space. Holiness attaches to particular places. However, it is not only places that are revered as holy – people, books, art and architecture (among other things) can also powerfully focus the presence of God.

Different types of space can be sacred. Buildings are important to many religions: synagogues to Jews, churches to Christians, mosques to Muslims, temples to Hindus, and so on. These places are hallowed in people's minds, not least by ritual practices. Some religions especially emphasize that, in these buildings, we meet God. In many Hindu temples, for example, you ring a bell when you arrive to remind God that you have come into his presence.

Some religions take the holiness of a place particularly seriously. In several branches of Christianity, for example, a church is consecrated and if it ceases to be a place of worship various ritual acts are done to affirm that this is so. Such places gain holiness over a period of time because ritual acts are carried out, people have come to meet God, and they have met with the 'holy' person (rabbi, priest, imam or whomever).

Religious buildings are also the focus of community life. Many mosques, for instance, are (in hot climates) open to the sky, and people come not only to worship God and be educated in the way of Islam, but to meet and converse – and even to do business.

In the popular mind, 'holy' has come to mean something like 'good' or 'ethically pure'. In fact this is a secondary deduction from its primary meaning. Something that is holy is 'set apart' from the ordinary and mundane, to focus transcendent meaning for devotees. Jews and Christians believe themselves to be a holy people, consecrated to God.[1] The emphasis in that designation is not just upon the ethical quality of Jews and Christians, though that might be hoped for or even insisted upon, but on the call and commitment of God to his people. Although Scripture links God's holiness with his people's obedience, in practice God is believed to keep faith with his followers even when they do not keep faith with him.

Muslims and members of many other religions also see themselves as chosen. A verse in the Qur'an reads, 'Ye are the best of peoples, evolved for mankind, enjoining what is right, forbidding what is wrong, and believing in God' (3.110). Some religions view their chosen status as linked with their tie to a particular land. Examples include Hindus, with their concept of Mother India, Confucianists (and many other Chinese), who regard China as the 'Middle Kingdom', and Sikhs, who have a particular tie to the Punjab.

Religions sometimes seem to play down the sacredness of a particular place. Muslims often delight in pointing out that Muhammad said that 'the whole earth is a mosque' (that is, a place of prostration in worship of God). Even so, Muhammad built a particular mosque in Medina, and Muslims since have built mosques everywhere. Yet such stories may have something to teach us in a religiously diverse world: while sacred spaces focus what is true about the divine presence, they do not exhaust the presence of transcendent reality, which is to be found in all (or most) places.

Is it in fact the case that religions teach that God is to be found everywhere, even if concentrated in various places, people or things? Many religions divide the world into the sacred and the profane. Yet based on sayings of Jesus, Christians initially abandoned food laws and distinctions between what is clean and unclean, or (by extension, and at least to a great extent) sacred and profane (Acts 10). Jesus' radical rejection of at least certain categories of sacred and secular (not just food, but also, for example, notions about the prohibition of work on the Sabbath) might indicate an instinct that they get in the way of what counts.

Other religions (including Judaism, Islam and Hinduism) have highly developed laws of the sacred and profane, in food and in

---

[1] Deuteronomy 28.9; 1 Peter 2.9ff.

other areas of life. In the modern world these laws have, to an extent, broken down for at least some branches of these religions. It is possible to argue over why some things are profane. (For example, are Jews and Muslims forbidden pork simply because God says so or could one deduce, for example, that in a hot climate pigs may not be a safe meat to eat?) However, such reflection should not divert us from a centrally important issue: does affirming that God is particularly somewhere imply that God is not elsewhere?

Every time we go into another's place of worship, it can be regarded as a triumph for interfaith dialogue. Religious thought police have often wanted to ban this, and even today some religious people still try to ban others from their places of worship. The church father John Chrysostom, who became Patriarch of Constantinople in 398 CE, denounced Christians who visited synagogues for Jewish festivals. This implies that some Christians wished to meet and greet their Jewish neighbours, especially at times of religious importance to them. It is gratifying to reflect that such a thing must have been happening to a sufficient extent for Chrysostom to feel the need to denounce it.

Things become more complicated when we look at religious claims to land, as issues around Jerusalem, Mecca and Amritsar illustrate. When an entire land is regarded as holy, this can seem exclusory in ways that are, arguably, unhelpful in a plural world (but note the generosity of Mother India to other faiths).

If dialogue attempts to strip religions down to their bare essentials, it can come at the cost of misunderstanding specific and contextual hopes, grievances and beliefs. A case in point: surely, any resolution of the situation in Jerusalem that Jews, Christians and Muslims can all accept must take into account what the city's sacredness means to the Other, and not assume that one view is paramount. Furthermore, it must recognize that what compels one group does not necessarily persuade another. So, for example, any Muslim conviction that Jerusalem is predominantly a Muslim possession because the Prophet Muhammad made his night journey to the precincts of the sacred mosque there meets with Jewish and Christian objection. Equally, Muslims may reject the claims made by some Jewish groups that only Jews can exert political control over Jerusalem. Divergent views exist among Muslims and Jews but there seems to be no inherent reason why the city cannot be sacred and holy for both, including Christians who venerate the Church of the Holy Sepulchre and other sacred sites in the city.

If one group feels it has the last word on the subject of sacred space (Christians and Muslims are often unreflective supersessionists) or the first (for example, Jews at Sinai), then it is difficult, perhaps impossible, to get that group out of the mindset that *their* way is God's way, which must be obeyed by all right-minded people.

## The Land of Israel in the First Millennium

The destruction of the Second Temple in 70 CE and the dispersion of Jews after the Bar Kokhba revolt of 132–5 CE (when Hadrian built a temple devoted to Jupiter on the Temple ruins) were key moments in the formative period of rabbinic Judaism and Christianity. The rabbis' response to dispossession and powerlessness consisted of the hope of divine restoration when exile would be followed by a time of messianic redemption for all peoples. They also developed the mystical idea that God was exiled with his people and that one purpose of this exile was to bring Torah to the nations of the world so that eventually they would recognize the one God.

By the time of rabbinic Judaism, the land of Israel was much changed from the biblical kingdom of David, but the rabbis reflected on the nature of the command to possess the land, the duty to live in the land, and the promise that after exile would come redemption and return to the land. The fact that the diaspora developed before the exile from the land, and remained in existence after the return of Nehemiah and Ezra to Jerusalem, hardly merited a mention.

The rabbinic writings illustrate how the land of Israel is intricately related to Jewish theology. For example, the covenant between Israel and God cannot be understood without reference to the land. In the Bible, possession of the land of Israel is a key part of the promise given to Abraham by God, and the rabbis considered in detail the meaning of the promise for his descendants.

There was also a view that exile occurred as a result of divine punishment. For Jews, this was understood as a result of their failure to observe God's commands, for example, by fighting each other and failing to live peaceably together. Traditional Christian interpretation also emphasized divine punishment – in this case, as a result of rejecting Christ. This view underpinned the doctrine of replacement theology, the belief that Christians had replaced Jews as the people of God. Replacement theology became dominant in Christian teaching about Judaism, contributing to anti-Judaism and antisemitism. The Church consistently pointed to the historical tragedies of the Jewish people as proof that God had rejected them definitively.

Christian interest in the land of Israel began in earnest in the fourth century, after the conversion of Constantine in 312 CE. A decisive role was played by Helena, Constantine's mother, who made a pilgrimage to Jerusalem. According to folklore, she discovered the True Cross as well as the site of the tomb of Jesus at Golgotha. Large numbers of Christians followed her as they sought to trace the path of the life of Jesus through the year, from his birth in Bethlehem through his ministry in Galilee to Jerusalem, at Holy Week.

The holy land was soon under Christian control and although archaeological records show continued coexistence with Jews through the fourth century, a large number of legal restrictions were enacted, implying that Jews lived on Christian land in sufferance.

In spite of lavish attention, Palestine did not remain at the centre of imperial interests in the centuries that followed. Christian Palestine collapsed in the face of Persian and then Muslim invasion. Thrown into crisis, Palestinian Christianity became more divided than before, with the polemic against Jews being grafted into polemical literature used on all sides of the inner-Christian controversy.

The drive to wrest back control from Muslims gained great momentum, notably in the eleventh century in France and the Lowlands, and resulted in the Crusades. The First Crusade (1095) was in part an expression of the growing power of the Christian West, mobilized by the call of the Byzantine Emperor to defend Constantinople against the Turks, and led to the Crusaders conquering Jerusalem in 1099 for a short period and establishing the Latin Kingdom of Jerusalem, extending across Syria to Armenia.

## The Jewish Response to Exile

Jewish writers, such as the poet Judah ha-Levi, reflected on the future return to Israel. Ha-Levi, a representative of medieval religious Zionism, portrays the 'longing for Zion' and expresses a belief in imminent redemption in the land of Israel. In his poetry, Zion is the feminine allegory for the expression of religious passion, although the commandment to live in the land remained an unrealized ideal. Ha-Levi set off on a journey to the land towards the end of his life, making a concrete allegory for the steps that humanity was to make towards the messianic end-time.

Towards the end of the Middle Ages, leading Kabbalists broke with the passive tradition of waiting for the Messiah before returning to the land of Israel and began to restore a religious–national existence there. For example, sixteenth-century mystic Isaac Luria moved to Safed, where he attempted to re-establish a Sanhedrin. This more active religious Zionism received further impetus from the belief that the suffering of Jews in exile merited the return to the land and the redemption of the whole world.

After many hundreds of years Jews stopped waiting for a divine solution to their predicament and began to take their destiny into their own hands. This was a dramatic change from the earlier diaspora strategy of survival, which advocated endurance of the status quo as part of the covenant with God. By the time of the breakdown of Jewish life in Europe in the late nineteenth and early twentieth centuries, many Jews felt that a Jewish state offered them the best hope not only for survival but also for fulfilment.

In 1862, Moses Hess wrote *Rome and Jerusalem*, which was the first modern and political proclamation of the Jewish national idea. He called for a modern Jewish national revival, based on the ideas of social justice, and was soon followed by Theodor Herzl. From the 1880s onwards, the Jewish goal for self-determination became a key objective. In 1887, the First Zionist Congress adopted Herzl's 'Basle Programme' and declared that 'Zionism seeks to secure for the Jewish people a publicly recognized, legally secured home in Palestine.'[2] Herzl's book *The Jewish State* (1896) called for an independent Jewish state in response to antisemitism. At the same time, religious Zionism played an important role, notably in Eastern Europe, where movements such as *Hovevei-Zion* ('Lovers of Zion') called for the re-establishment of 'the House of Jacob' in the land of Israel. Thus modern Zionism consists of both religious and secular ideologies, and though the State of Israel was ultimately the product of Herzl's secular–political vision, the contribution of religious Zionism was acknowledged in the *Proclamation of Independence* in 1948, which included spiritual phrases such as 'redemption of Israel' and 'with trust in the Rock of Israel'.

However, not all Jews supported a Jewish state, particularly before the Holocaust. Indeed, Zionism resulted in vociferous arguments within and between all Jewish groups, secular and religious, Reform and Orthodox. A common argument was that Zionism encouraged antisemitism by confirming the argument of antisemites that Jews were not committed to the national interests of the countries in which they lived. For their part, many Reform Jews argued that Jewish nationalism undermined their emphasis on universal values and ethical monotheism. Today, only the most ultra-Orthodox Jews, alongside some secular 'hard' left-wing Jews, reject the creation of the Jewish State, arguing that Israel should be a divine and not a man-made creation, relying on traditional rabbinic teaching that eventually God will come, bring the Messiah, and so transform the world.

---

[2] Herzl's speech at the First Zionist Congress (29–31 August 1897) can be found at www.herzl.org/english/Article.aspx?Item=544

## Christians and the Land since 1900

The attitude of Roman Catholicism towards Zionism changed greatly in the course of the twentieth century. In 1904, Pope Pius X famously gave an audience to Theodor Herzl, who asked for support in his endeavour to bring Jews back to the land of Israel. Herzl was told unequivocally by the Pope that because 'the Jews have not recognized our Lord, therefore we cannot recognize the Jewish people'.[3]

However, the Roman Catholic Church has changed its attitude significantly since then, beginning with Vatican II and the 1965 document *Nostra Aetate*, which, while not explicitly mentioning Israel, began the process that eventually led to the Vatican's recognition of the State of Israel in 1994. Increasing awareness among Roman Catholics of the place of Israel became much more noticeable during the papacy of John Paul II, and his acknowledgement of its significance to Jews can be seen as early as 1984, when in his Good Friday Apostolic Letter he wrote: 'the Jewish people who live in the State of Israel, and who preserve in that land such precious testimonies to their history and their faith, we must ask for the desired security and the due tranquility that is the prerogative of every nation and condition of life and of progress for every society'.[4]

Ten years later the State of Israel and the Holy See exchanged ambassadors, and the process begun in 1965 reached another significant landmark with the Pontiff's pilgrimage to Israel in 2000.

Although the papal visit carried theological import, the Vatican was careful to emphasize that its diplomatic policy was rooted in *realpolitik* rather than in theology. The fact that the Holy See signed an agreement with the Palestinian Authority in 2000 that is virtually the same as the one with Israel is one example. The secular diplomatic position is illustrated by the 1985 *Notes*, which states that 'the existence of the State of Israel and its political options should be envisaged not in a perspective which is in

---

3 Marvin Lowenthal (ed.), 1956, *The Diaries of Theodor Herzl*, New York: Dial Press, pp. 429–30.
4 Pope John Paul II, 1995, in *Spiritual Pilgrimage: Texts on Jews and Judaism 1979–95*, E. Fisher and L. Klenicki (eds), New York: Crossroad, p. 34.

itself religious, but in their reference to the common principle of international law'.[5] Nevertheless, the Vatican and the Chief Rabbis of Israel have annual meetings, alternatively in Jerusalem and Rome, demonstrating an overlap between politics and theology. The Archbishop of Canterbury and his interfaith office have similar regular meetings.

In the first years of the twenty-first century, relations between the Holy See and the State of Israel have become strained, epitomized by the lack of agreement between Israel and the Holy See over juridical and tax issues. Occasional bilateral talks have failed to produce agreement over 'the fundamental accord', which has been sought since 1993. The majority of the Holy See's religious communities own large properties and these were purchased in the nineteenth century, when the properties were often deserted; today, they are generally surrounded by modern neighbourhoods. By virtue of a privilege granted by the Ottoman Empire, and then upheld throughout the British Mandate period, these communities were exempted from taxes. Today, there is disagreement about whether these communities should continue to benefit from this exemption or pay the taxes.

Another example of the strained relations is that in 2007 the papal nuncio, Archbishop Franco, threatened not to attend the annual Holocaust Memorial day event at Yad Vashem, Israel's main Holocaust museum, stating that he would not attend unless the museum agreed to remove or rewrite a caption of Pope Pius XII that he found offensive.

Tensions also exist with the Protestant churches, which are deeply divided on Zionism. At one end there are those who make some absolute moral demands on Israel and conclude, like Naim Ateek, that Zionism represents a profane corruption of Judaism's true prophetic mission (Ateek's views are discussed later); at the other end, there are others, like Christian Zionists, who understand the roots of the Church as the people of Israel while the branches are a 'faithful remnant' from Israel. They refer to grafted

---

5 *Notes*, op. cit.

gentile branches of the Church who are reminded not to boast over Israel, because 'you do not support it, it supports you'.[6]

In response to Palestinian suffering, a number of churches have supported boycotts, divestment and sanctions against Israel. For example, the Presbyterian Church (USA) voted in 2004 to initiate a process of phased, selective divestment from multinational companies operating in Israel that do harm to innocent people, whether Palestinian or Israeli. This prompted similar discussions within the Anglican Communion, and in 2005 the World Council of Churches (WCC) Central Committee voted to commend the Presbyterian action and to 'remind churches of the opportunity before them to use investment funds "responsibly in support of peaceful solutions to conflict"'. This remains a cause of controversy because for supporters of Israel – Jew and Christian alike – Israel seems to be made solely responsible for a complex conflict.

When churches adopt divestment initiatives directed against Israel, which is also sometimes likened to the former apartheid regime in South Africa, many see these as attempts to delegitimize Israel's very existence. It recalls the long-standing Arab boycott that was designed to undermine Israel's economy and existence, and that still prevails to no small extent. The fact that the churches do not act similarly regarding human rights abuses and state violence in many other places in the world adds to the strain.

At the other end of the Protestant spectrum are Christian Zionists, whose origins can be traced to the Puritans of the seventeenth century and the desire to study Scriptures in their original texts. Puritan scholars, under the guidance of the rabbis of Amsterdam, not only mastered Hebrew but also developed a new understanding of covenant. They moved from a classical replacement theology to a position in which they believed that God's covenant with his people Israel was eternal. As this was a covenant of both land and people, they came to the conclusion that Palestine was the rightful home of the Jewish people and that God would eventually ensure that they returned to their homeland.

---

6 Romans 11.18.

Christian Zionists grew in number in the nineteenth century, influenced by a dispensational eschatology. They believed that the rejection of Jesus by the majority of Jews only postponed all God's promises for Israel until Christ's second coming. This *parousia* would bring in the millennial reign of Christ during which time all God's plans for Israel, which were thwarted at Christ's first coming, would come to fruition. Influential Christians influenced Lord Balfour to make his declaration regarding the support of the British government for the establishment of a homeland for the Jewish people in Palestine in 1917.

The Declaration consisted of a letter from the Foreign Secretary Arthur James Balfour, which declared the support of the British government for the Jewish claim to Palestine. 'His Majesty's government view with favour the establishment in Palestine of a national home for the Jewish people and will use their best endeavours to facilitate the achievement of this object, it being clearly understood that nothing shall be done which may prejudice the civil and religious rights of existing non-Jewish communities in Palestine or the rights and political status enjoyed by Jews in any other country.'

It would be simplistic to regard the Declaration in terms of religious agendas. Nevertheless, the intersection of religion and politics should not ignore an account of why Britain set aside the interests of the Arab inhabitants of the land, who made up around 90 per cent of the population (10 per cent of whom were Arab Christians), and how she sustained her commitment to a national home for the Jewish people throughout the difficult Mandate period.

Today, Christian Zionists, such as the International Christian Embassy in Jerusalem (ICEJ), are the forebears of the early Christian Zionists and adopt some Jewish customs, notably relating to Sukkot, while maintaining a christological stance. They call for Christian support of Israel (based on the prophecy in Zechariah 14.16) and argue that the modern State of Israel is intrinsically related to the Israel of prophecy and a direct fulfilment of it. Since the 1970s, Christian Zionism has been most evident in American Protestant fundamentalist communities whose interpretation of biblical texts makes them highly supportive of the more conservative elements in Israeli politics, as well as of the concept of a Greater Israel. For these groups, support for the State of Israel is critical to its survival, and ultimately to advance the second coming of Jesus as the Messiah who will be acknowledged by the whole world.

As for the indigenous Christian population in the Middle East, numbers have been declining numerically since the turn of the twentieth century. To a certain extent, the phenomenon has been provoked by the relative improvement in the situation of Arab Christians, whose education, economic position and international connections have often meant they are able to benefit more effectively from the birth of the global village. In the War of Independence, Arab Christians played a prominent role in nationalist movements and were also prominent among those who fled in 1948. Few ended up in refugee camps, and fleeing to Jordan would have placed them in a state with even less experience of a Christian minority, so most left for more cosmopolitan destinations. Those that remained, or who returned, occupied an uncomfortable middle ground. A large part of the Christian population lived in those territories in Galilee that had been marked out to be part of the Arab state that was to have been created by the Partition Plan voted by the United Nations in November 1947, but not accepted by the surrounding Arab states.

Since 1948, a Palestinian theology of liberation has developed, influenced by traditional replacement theology as well as the everyday experiences of Palestinian Christians living in Israel. It is not too extreme to state that the Palestinian Church has faced a major theological crisis since the establishment of Israel, partly due to a view that the Bible has been used as a political Zionist text. Naim Ateek, for example, has argued that since the creation of the state, some Jewish and Christian interpreters have read the Old Testament largely as a Zionist text to such an extent that it has become almost repugnant to Palestinian Christians. In his view, this has resulted in a narrow concept of a nationalistic God, and Zionism represents a retrogression of the Jewish community into the history of its very distant past, with its most elementary and primitive form of the concept of God. 'Zionism has succeeded in reanimating the nationalist tradition within Judaism', he has argued.[7]

A further development took place in 1962 with the Brother Daniel affair. Daniel Rufeisen was a Jewish convert to Christianity and emigrated to Israel under the Law of Return.[8] He argued that his nationality was Jewish although his religion was Catholic. Complicating the issue was the fact that, according to *halakhah*, as the child of a Jewish mother Brother Daniel was indeed Jewish. The Chief Rabbinate ruled that he should be given citizenship as a Jew, regardless of his faith decisions. In 1962 the Supreme Court ruled that, despite this and the unusual circumstances (he had saved many Jews during the Holocaust), it was not possible to be both a Catholic priest and a Jew. While the national term 'Jew' did not necessarily imply the practice of religious Judaism, it could not be applied to someone who practised another faith. Although Brother Daniel lost his case, he was later naturalized as an Israeli citizen and lived in a Carmelite monastery in Haifa until his death in 1998.

In the 1970s, the political shift to the right in Israel threatened a deterioration in relations between Jews and Christians in Israel, particularly in the wake of a series of violent attacks on Christian properties in Jerusalem linked to the new right wing party of Meir Kahane, 'Kach', eventually banned by the government for its overt racism. However, apathy or ignorance of Christianity among Israelis was the norm. Since then, signs of a positive shift in Jewish Israeli attitudes to Christianity became noticeable, especially in the wake of John Paul II's pilgrimage to Israel. To see the Pope at Yad Vashem, demonstrating solidarity, weeping at the suffering of the Jewish people, to learn that he had helped save Jews during the Holocaust and that subsequently, as a priest, he

---

7 Naim Ateek, 1989, *Justice and Only Justice: A Palestinian Theology of Liberation*, Maryknoll, NY: Orbis Books, p. 101.

8 Israel Declaration of Independence states that, 'the State of Israel will be open to the immigration of Jews and the ingathering of exiles from all countries of their dispersion'. The Law of Return was passed by the Knesset in 1950 and gives Jews the right of return and citizenship in Israel. In 1970, this was extended to people of Jewish ancestry (up to and including grandparents) and their spouses.

had returned Jewish children adopted by Christians to their Jewish families, to see the head of the Catholic Church placing a prayer of atonement for the sins of Christians against Jews between the stones of the Western Wall – all of these scenes had a profound effect on many Israelis.

A similar shift can be noticed in the Israeli scholarly community. For example, David Flusser, a pioneering scholar of early Christianity and rabbinic Judaism, influenced a generation of students. The study of Christianity at the Hebrew University is now consciously geared to a scholarly Jewish–Christian dialogue and to the wider interreligious dialogue. A wind of change has also begun to sweep into the religious-nationalist (Modern Orthodox) Bar Ilan University, where scholars have established a collaborative project with Christian theologians from Belgium focusing on 'antisemitism in the Gospel of John'.

Michel Sabbah, Latin Patriarch from 2000 to 2009, commented that Christians in Israel 'are called to be leaven contributing positive resolution of the crises we are passing through'. Sabbah took part in a synod that started in 1995 involving the Catholic churches of the Holy Land, comprising not only the Roman Catholic Church but also the Oriental churches. It lasted five years and reflected on the changes since *Nostra Aetate*. The thirteenth Synod document was entitled 'Relations with believers of other religions' and contains two sections, the first dedicated to Muslims and the second to Jews. The document makes clear that the local Church does not have the same starting point as its European counterparts for it sees itself as free of antisemitic practice, policy and the responsibility for the fate of European Jewry.

David Neuhaus, a Jesuit who is active in Jewish–Christian dialogue in Israel, explains further:

> Christians live as a minority face to face with a Jewish majority (those in Israel), under Israeli military occupation (those in the West Bank) or confronting a regional economic and military power (those in Jordan and Gaza). This is an absolutely unique historical situation. Nowhere else in the world do Christians experience directly the sovereignty and power of a Jewish polity

and never in history have Christians experienced Jewish sovereignty and power (these only having been reestablished in 1948 with the creation of the State of Israel). This unique situation must inform dialogue that takes place in this land between local Christians and Jews, predominantly in Israel. For many of the Holy Land faithful, unfortunately, the Jew is often first and foremost a policeman, a soldier or a settler.[9]

A key factor to reckon with is the Christian status as a minority in the Middle East as a whole. Not only are Christians a minority within the State of Israel – approximately two per cent of the Israeli population are Christian – they are also a minority within the Arab minority. Purely on the psychological level, their church representatives feel under pressure. Yet the Christian Arab and the Muslim Arab, whatever their religious differences might be, live in one society, speak one language and share one culture. Dialogue with Muslims is sometimes a priority for Christians, and in some dioceses it is only the dialogue with Muslims that is real – for example, in Jordan and Gaza (where there are no Jews).

It is perhaps not surprising that Palestinian liberation theologians are accused of being politically partisan, hostile to Jews and Judaism and naive about the possibilities of dialogue with increasingly militant Arab Islam. At the outset of the Intifada in 1987, Christian Arab congregations pressed their hierarchies to demonstrate more solidarity with the Palestinian cause, and in addition to begin to advance Palestinian Christians to positions of leadership. Although integrated in Palestine, Christian Palestinians are clearly concerned at the prospect of the gradual Islamization of the nascent state and of a time when Hamas and other Islamist parties might take over completely. For Christians, the relationship with Jews exists within a framework of a larger dialogue that includes Muslims.

Divisions between Christians sometimes spill over into acts of violence. For example, fights between Catholic and Greek Orthodox

---

9 David Neuhaus and Jamel Khader, 2005, 'A Holy Land Context for Nostra Aetate', 2007, *Studies in Christian–Jewish Relations*, vol. 1, at www.ejournals.bc.edu/ojs/index.php/scjr/article/view/1360

priests in Easter 2005, and Greeks and Armenians in Easter 2008 at the Church of the Holy Sepulchre, illustrate an intra-Christian conflict, which has marked the history of Christianity in the region since its earliest days. The intervention of the state may formally be decried, but the reluctance of Christian representatives to dialogue among themselves on the difficulties means that Israeli intervention is also quietly welcomed.

Finally, some Christians are actively involved in dialogue programmes between Israelis and Palestinians. For example, *Neve Shalom* ('Oasis of Peace') was founded in 1972 by Bruno Hussar (1911–96), a Dominican friar, with the aim of peaceful reconciliation between Jews, Muslims and Christians. Another example is Tantur Ecumenical Institute, located on the border between south Jerusalem and the West Bank. Established by the Vatican, the institute, under the guidance of both Protestant and Roman Catholic rectors, focuses on the relations between the three Abrahamic faiths and the promotion of ecumenical and interfaith dialogue through study and research.

Since the death of Yitzhak Rabin in 1995, the prospects of a negotiated settlement in which part of Jerusalem would become the Palestinian capital have steadily reduced. The collapse of trust between Israel and the Palestinians and the Israeli building programme designed to ring-fence Jerusalem with suburban developments for Jews have made this possibility even less likely. However, as details of the failed agreement between Ehud Barak and Yasser Arafat (2000) emerged, it has become clear that the Old City of Jerusalem was envisaged to be the capital of the future state of Palestine.

Much of the Israeli–Palestinian dialogue since then has sought to bypass religious issues, consisting of secular and intercultural efforts at understanding, designed to underline how much Arabs and Jews have in common. However, the Alexandria Declaration (2002), which consisted of senior Christians, Jews and Muslims pledging themselves to work together for a just and lasting peace, called for religious figures to remain involved in the dialogue. Without their participation, peace will remain as far away as before.

# 4

# Contemporary Questions about Covenant(s) and Conversion: A Public Dialogue

Covenant, mission and dialogue illustrate both the extent of the common ground between Jews and Christians and also many of the difficulties that still need to be addressed. The challenge they bring is demonstrated by *Nostra Aetate*, perhaps the most influential of the recent church documents on Jewish–Christian relations. On the one hand, the document states that 'the church is the new people of God' while, on the other, 'the Jews remain most dear to God because of their fathers, for He does not repent of the gifts He makes nor of the calls He issues (cf. Romans 11:28–29)'. The tension between the two statements is caused by continuing divergence of opinion over the identity of the people of God. Both Jews and Christians claim to be *Verus Israel*, the true Israel, as the core of their self-understanding, and compete to be the heir of all the biblical promises towards Israel.

## Covenant

Covenant (Hebrew, *berith*), a central concept in both Judaism and Christianity, is a subject that has received serious attention in recent years. It refers to God initiating a covenant with a community of people, and that community accepting certain obligations and responsibilities as covenant partners. A covenant is not, as is sometimes mistakenly assumed, a contract or a transaction, but is an agreement dependent upon a relationship. Some exegetes hold to the view that *berith* is better translated by 'obligation' because it expresses the sovereign power of God, who imposes his will on his people Israel: God promises in a solemn oath to fulfil his word to his people Israel, who are expected to respond by faithfulness and obedience. Jonathan Sacks explained this in his address to 600 Anglican bishops at the 2008 Lambeth Conference when he said:

> In a covenant, two or more individuals, each respecting the dignity and integrity of the other, come together in a bond of love and trust, to share their interests, sometimes even to share their lives, by pledging our faithfulness to one another, to do together what neither of us can do alone . . . a contract is about interests but a covenant is about identity. And that is why contracts benefit, but covenants transform.[1]

In the New Testament the concept of the covenant is reinterpreted through the experiences of the early Christian community, and the story of Jesus is seen as a new phase in the covenant-story of Israel. The change in emphasis marked by the translation of *berith* into the Greek *diathèkè* ('decree') in the Septuagint, developed still further in the New Testament, where the concept acquired the meaning of a definitive 'last will and testament' on the part of God. The Vulgate translation used the word *testamentum*, which became the official designation of both parts of the Christian Bible – the Old Testament and the New Testament – with its inescapable implication of supersessionism.

From the Jewish perspective, no change took place in Israel's covenantal relationship with God. The traditional rabbinic attitude is that Judaism remained a community of faith – nothing had been taken away although there was a change in emphasis. The Sinai covenant became more important and there was an increased emphasis on the mutuality of the covenantal relationship between

---

1 Jonathan Sacks's address to the Lambeth Conference can be found at www.rowanwilliams.archbishopofcanterbury.org/articles.php/1063/the-relationship-between-the-people-and-god

God and his people. This is summarized in a well-known midrash, in which God was depicted as travelling around the world asking various peoples to accept his Torah. None was willing to accept its yoke until God came to Israel and the Israelites answered in one voice: 'All that the Lord has spoken we will do, and we will be obedient.'[2]

For Christians, however, a radical break had occurred. Christianity had introduced a new covenant or, at the very least, a radical transformation of the old covenant. According to the New Testament, the relationship between God and his people was mediated decisively through his Son, Jesus Christ. The early Church soon regarded the old covenant of Israel as definitely abrogated; the text on the new covenant in Jeremiah 31.31–34 was interpreted as pointing to fulfilment in Christ:

> Behold, the days come, says the LORD, that I will make a new covenant with the house of Israel, and with the house of Judah. Not according to the covenant that I made with their fathers in the day that I took them by the hand to bring them out of the land of Egypt; which my covenant they broke, although I was an husband unto them, says the LORD. But this shall be the covenant that I will make with the house of Israel. After those days, says the LORD, I will put my law in their inward parts, and write it in their hearts; and will be their God, and they shall be my people. And they shall teach no more every man his neighbour, and every man his brother, saying, Know the LORD: for they shall all know me, from the least of them unto the greatest of them, says the LORD. For I will forgive their iniquity, and I will remember their sin no more.

The question that is absorbing today's Christian theologians, such as Professor Cunningham, concerns the role of the Jewish people after the appearance of Christianity. The traditional Christian teaching is that with the coming of Jesus Christ the Church has taken the place of the Jewish people as God's elect community – this is known

---
2 Exodus 24.7, after *Mechilta BaChodesh* 5.74a.

as replacement theology (sometimes called supersessionism), which implies the abrogation (or obsolescence) of God's covenant with the Jewish people.

After the Holocaust many Christians became aware of the inadequacy of replacement theology, which was perceived to have formed the linchpin of the 'teaching of contempt'. Accordingly, the identification, analysis and repudiation of replacement theology have occupied a prominent place among Christian theologians seeking to put the Church's relationship to the Jewish people on a new theological footing. However, there is less agreement among Christians about what replaces replacement theology.

Clearly, the rejection of replacement theology entails some affirmation of the continuing validity of God's covenant with the Jewish people, that Jews retain a covenantal relationship with God, however the Church might interpret the meaning of the Christ event. But Christian theologians continue to differ about the implications of the rejection of replacement theology for central Christian doctrines, notably christology and the Church's mission. It is for this reason that Professor Cunningham helped initiate a scholarly ecumenical Christian group whose purpose was to explore the new relationship between the Church and the Jewish people. It is based on the assumption that christologies that revolved around the notion that through the Christ event Christianity totally fulfilled (and replaced) Judaism can no longer be sustained. Constructing a new theology of the Church and the Jewish people in the light of the Christ event remains an unresolved and formidable undertaking, perhaps because, as Johann-Baptist Metz argued, the restatement of the Church's relationship with the Jewish people is a fundamental revision of Christian theology.

German scholar Friedrich-Wilhelm Marquardt viewed covenant as the most constructive biblical concept to describe both Christian identity and contemporary Jewish–Christian relations. His conviction is that churches as representatives of the peoples of the earth can only hope to become partners in a covenantal relationship with the people of Israel if they are willing to accept the burden of Israel in sanctifying the name of God in the world, if they join in the calling of Israel to restore the world, and if they are ready to embark with the people of Israel on its journey to the 'new covenant' with God that lies ahead.³

There are at least three possible ways in which Christians may understand the relation between the 'old' and 'new' peoples:

1. Only one (the newer) is truly the 'people of God'.
2. There are two peoples of God, the Jewish and the Christian.
3. The two peoples are really one people of God – identical in some respects and different in others.

The first position states that there is simply only one 'people of God' – Christians. In this case, either Jews convert to Christianity or remain as Jews, a remnant destined to suffer whose lowly position gives witness to the truth of Christ. This Augustinian position, called the witness doctrine, dominated Christian thought until it began to be questioned during and after the Enlightenment.

The second position argues that there are two peoples of God, the Jewish and the Christian. This view is espoused by theologians such as the Jewish writer Franz Rosenzweig, who suggests that both Jews and Christians participate in God's revelation and both are (in different ways) intended by God. Only for God is the truth one, and earthly truth remains divided. Rosenzweig was influenced by Jacob Emden, who viewed Christianity as a legitimate religion for gentiles. In *Seder Olam Rabbah Vezuta* he wrote positively about Jesus and Paul, who did not seek to denigrate Judaism but explained that their teachings were primarily concerned to communicate the Noachide laws to gentiles. 'The Nazarene and his apostles . . . observed the Torah fully', he wrote.

James Parkes also took the two-covenant position and suggested that the Sinai and Calvary experiences provided humanity with two complementary revelations. In his view the Sinai revelation emphasized the aspect of 'community' while Calvary focused on the 'individual'. Parkes remained convinced that the revelation in Christ did not replace the covenant at Sinai and, as a result, Judaism and

---

3 F.-W. Marquardt, 1988, *Von Elend und Heimsuchung der Theologie*, Munich: Prolegomena zur Dogmatik.

Christianity were inextricably linked together. Although there are variations in the views of theologians who follow the two peoples of God (or two-covenant) approach, they tend to share the view that the revelation in Christ was a unique event and resulted in a new sense of intimacy between God and humanity. John Pawlikowski has suggested that the two-covenant approach is particularly close to the New Testament teachings because it emphasizes that as a result of the Christ event, humanity has achieved a deeper understanding of the God–humankind relationship. A challenge for Christians who hold this position is how, after having proclaimed this uniqueness, a special role can be maintained for Judaism in the salvation process.

As for contemporary Jewish supporters of the two-covenant theory, it is an approach shared by myself as well as Israeli scholar David Hartman. A covenant between people and God is predicated on a belief in human dignity. Other religions, it could be argued, especially Christianity and Islam, have their own covenants with God and are called to celebrate their dignity and particularity. A challenge for Jews who hold this position is to what extent Christians can recognize the particular Christian claims about Christ in a two-covenant Jewish matrix.

The third position posits that Jews and Christians represent one people of God who are identical in some respects and different in others. Although both groups differ substantially, they nevertheless share sufficient common ground to make it possible for the same covenant to be applied to both. Christians favouring the one-people (or one-covenant) approach sometimes refer to Ephesians 2.12, which states that to be separate from Christ is to be strangers to the community of Israel. The Roman Catholic Church favours a single-covenant model as does the German Rhineland Synod which, in *Towards a Renewal of the Relationship of Christians and Jews* (1980), declared: 'We believe in the permanent election of the Jewish People as the People of God and realize that through Jesus Christ the Church is taken into the covenant of God with His People.'

Similarly, Catholic scholar Monika Hellwig argues that Judaism and Christianity both point towards a common goal – the same eschatological event. As a result, Christian claims that Jesus had totally fulfilled Jewish messianic expectations must be set aside. In her view, there still remains an unfulfilled dimension awaiting completion. Her words, which were published in an article in 1970,[4] foreshadowed the Pontifical Biblical Commission's 2001 declaration *The Jewish People and their Scriptures in the Christian Bible*, which stated the 'Jewish messianic expectation is not in vain'. In a striking passage dealing with eschatological expectations, the document also stated that Jews, alongside Christians, keep alive the messianic expectation. The difference is that for Christians 'the One who is to come will have the traits of the Jesus who has already come and is already present and active among us'. What Christians believe to have been accomplished in Christ 'has yet to be accomplished in us and in the world'.

The most comprehensive theological study among Protestant theologians is found in the three-volume work by Paul van Buren entitled *A Theology of Jewish–Christian Reality* (1980–8), who argues that the people 'Israel' should be recognized as two connected but distinct branches. The Christian Church represents the gentile believers drawn together by the God of the Jewish people in order to make God's love known throughout the world. Through Jesus, gentiles were summoned by God for the first time as full participants in God's ongoing salvation of humanity. However, the gentiles went beyond God's eternal covenant with the Jewish people and attempted, unsuccessfully, to annul the original covenant. Van Buren argues that both branches must grow together rather than in isolation and that in time they will draw closer while retaining their distinctiveness.

Evangelical scholar David Holwerda, however, argues that Christians are in danger of minimizing the differences between Judaism and Christianity, and in so doing produce a theology that is not true to the New Testament message. Although he recognizes the importance of Christians' reacquaintance with the Jewish Jesus, Christianity still has an implicit argument with Judaism on

---

4 Monika Hellwig, 1970, 'Christian Theology and the Covenant of Israel', *Journal of Ecumenical Studies*, vol. 7, pp. 37–51.

several key issues, but 'the category of election still applies to the Jewish people, even those who do not now believe in Jesus'. The Church is the new Israel, but the old Israel remains elect and in God's faithfulness still has a future. In taking this view, Holwerda bases his argument on Romans 9—11.

Although there are significant differences between proponents of the single-covenant thesis, they all share a number of key features:

- Gentiles can ultimately be saved only through a linkage with the Jewish covenant, something made possible in and through Christ.
- The uniqueness of Christianity consists far more in modes of expression than in content.
- Jews and Christians share equally and integrally in the ongoing process of humanity's salvation.

It is much debated whether the concept of covenant, in its one- or two-covenant version, could function as a bridge between Judaism and Christianity. It has certainly become a common subject for discussion in activist and scholarly circles. Numerous official ecclesiastical statements have in the last few decades declared that the covenant of God with his people was never abrogated, illustrated by the 1985 Vatican *Notes* and the 1992 catechism, which stated that the biblical covenant had not been revoked and that 'Israel is the priestly people of God . . . the older brothers and sisters of all who share the faith of Abraham' (para. 63). It is particularly noteworthy that the present tense is used with reference to the Jewish people.

In recent years a number of scholars have become somewhat dissatisfied with the single- and double-covenant options. These scholars, both Jewish and Christian, have begun to suggest new images of the relationship, such as 'siblings' (Hayim Perelmuter), 'fraternal twins' (Mary Boys), and 'co-emergence' (Daniel Boyarin). These metaphors stress both linkage and distinctiveness between Christianity and Judaism and emphasize a 'parallel' rather than the traditional 'linear' dimensions of the relationship, with Christianity and Judaism, as we know them today, emerging out of a religious revolution in Second Temple Judaism.

## Re-reading Paul

Paul's comments on the identity of the people of Israel and their relationship with God are key to modern Christian interpretations, yet they are complex and sometimes hard to follow and it is unfortunate that they are commonly and misleadingly simplified. He is the New Testament writer par excellence who struggles deeply with the meaning of the covenant of Israel and the election of the Church. Paul is generally viewed as arguing that membership of the true Israel is not determined simply on physical descent from Abraham, but rather on the spiritual affinity to Abraham's trusting relationship with God. In other words, Israel is composed of a combination of Jews and gentiles. The former, due to their spiritual past, include those who have extended their trust in God to a dependence upon Jesus as Lord; the latter includes those gentiles who have entered into the covenantal relationship with God by their acceptance of Jesus. This, however, is a facile interpretation of Paul's assessment, for it simply imputes to him the view that the old becomes new.

A significant re-reading of Paul's writings in modern times began in 1974 when Lutheran scholar Krister Stendahl's book, *Paul Among Jews and Gentiles*, was published. Stendahl showed that Paul could not accept the idea that Jews as a people and religion are totally and forever outside the people of God. According to Stendahl, Paul suggests that both Israel and the Church are elect and both participate in the covenant of God. Paul affirmed that the Jewish people, despite their disobedience towards Christ, are still the elect people of God and that Christian gentiles are honorary citizens grafted on to the rich tree of Jewish heritage. While Paul argued that unbelieving Jews are in a state of disobedience regarding Christ, he nevertheless unreservedly affirmed their continued election.

In his letter to the Romans, Paul asked a controversial question: what of the ongoing validity of God's covenant with his Jewish people? Did the Church, as the New Israel, simply replace the Old as inheritors of God's promises? If so, does this mean that God reneges on his word? If God has done so with regard to Jews, what guarantee is there for the churches that he won't do so again, to Christians this time?

One might argue against Paul by saying that if Jews have not kept faith with God, then God has a perfect right to cast them off. It is interesting that Christians who argue this way have not often drawn the same deduction about Christian faithfulness, which has not been a notable and consistent characteristic of the last two millennia. Actually, God seems to have had a remarkable ability to keep faith with both Christians and Jews when they have not kept faith with God, a point of which Paul is profoundly aware in Romans 9–11. He goes out of his way to deny claims that God has rejected the chosen people, and asserts that their stumbling does not lead to their fall. He also offers a severe warning that gentile Christians should not be haughty or boastful towards unbelieving Jews – much less cultivate evil intent and engage in persecution against them. This critical warning remained almost totally forgotten by Christians, who tended to remember Jews as 'enemies' but not as 'beloved' of God, and took to heart Paul's criticisms and used them against Jews while forgetting Paul's love for Jews and Judaism.

In Paul's view it was impossible for God to elect the Jewish people as a whole and then later displace them. If that were the case, God could easily do the same with Christians. In his view, the hardening took place so that the gentiles would receive the opportunity to join the people of God. The Church's election, therefore, derives from that of Israel, but this does not imply that God's covenant with Israel is broken. Rather, it remains unbroken – irrevocably (Romans 11.29).

The Rhineland Synod document (1980) explained this as follows, referring to the continuing existence of the Jewish people, its return to the land of promise and the creation of the State of Israel as 'signs of the faithfulness of God towards His people'. In the same year, John Paul II referred to 'the people of God of the Old Covenant, which has never been revoked'. As the 1985 Vatican *Notes* stated:

The permanence of Israel (while so many ancient peoples have disappeared without trace) is a historic fact and a sign to be interpreted within God's design. We must in any case rid ourselves of the traditional idea of a people *punished*, preserved as a *living argument* for Christian apologetic. It remains a chosen people, 'the pure olive on which were grafted the branches of the wild olive which are the gentiles' (John Paul II, 6 March 1982, alluding to Rom. 11.17–24).[5]

## Mission

The issue of mission is in many ways far more difficult for the Church to resolve in its relationship with Judaism than, for example, Christian antisemitism, since it is relatively easy to condemn antisemitism as a misunderstanding of Christian teaching whereas mission (in the sense of making converts) has been and still is central to the Christian faith – the legacy of the command found in Matthew 28.19 to 'go therefore and make disciples of all nations'. Initially, the Christian message was preached by Jews to Jews until Paul raised the issue of preaching to the gentiles. The Gospels themselves reflect early controversies over the inclusion of gentiles in Christianity's missionary activity. Mark 7.27 says in this context, 'let the children first be fed, for it is not right to take the children's bread and throw it to the dogs', and similarly in Matthew 10.6 the instruction to 'go nowhere among the Gentiles, and enter no town of the Samaritans, but go rather to the lost sheep of the house of Israel' is ascribed to Jesus. Both verses express the view that the proclamation of Jesus as the Messiah should be expressed to Jews alone. The conclusion of the New Testament authors, however, contradicts this. Not only in Matthew 28.19 but also Acts 28.28, which argues that the 'good news' should also be transmitted to the gentiles: 'let it be known to you then that this salvation of God has been sent to the Gentiles'. Indeed, unlike Jews, the author argues the gentiles 'will listen'.

---

5 *Notes*, op. cit., 6.1.

## JEWS, CHRISTIANS AND MUSLIMS IN ENCOUNTER

For Jews, Christian mission is contentious because it conjures up images of centuries of persecution by the Church, which has failed to understand the Jewish 'no' to Jesus. Some Jews even view Christian missionary activity as no different from Hitler's policies, as for centuries the Church had tried to do spiritually what Hitler had sought to do physically: to wipe out Jews and Judaism. Indeed, the 1948 meeting of the World Council of Churches (WCC) in Amsterdam called for a redoubling of efforts to convert Jews. While acknowledging the six million Jews who perished under the Nazis, the WCC report nevertheless recommended that the churches should 'seek to recover the universality of our Lord's commission by including the Jewish people in their evangelistic work'. The conclusion of the WCC was that, in the light of the Holocaust, an even greater effort should be made to convert Jews.

Much missionary theology rests on Christian claims that salvation is only possible through Christ. The exclusive understanding of salvation is demonstrated by the traditional teaching, *extra ecclesiam nulla salus* (outside the Church there is no salvation), and a discussion of mission and Jewish–Christian relations needs to address the issues of salvation and christology. The Roman Catholic theologian John Pawlikowski strongly argues that *Nostra Aetate* necessitates a rethinking of christology, Christian identity, covenant and mission.

The 2002 document *A Sacred Obligation*, a statement from an ecumenical American Christians Scholars Group on Christian–Jewish relations, argues that with the recent recognition within the Church of the permanency of God's covenant with the Jewish people there automatically comes the realization that the redemptive power of God is at work within Judaism. So if Jews who do not share the Christian faith are indeed in such a saving relationship with God, then Christians require new ways of understanding the universal significance of Christ. This has been the subject of fierce debate and remains highly contested.

Despite the recognition by Christian theologians that the repudiation of the *Adversus-Iudaeos* tradition has profound implications for christology, major problems remain. The Vatican document *Dominus Iesus* (2000) reiterated that all salvation ultimately comes through Christ and that those who do not acknowledge this stand in considerable peril in terms of their redemption. Cardinal Walter Kasper, since 2001 the head of the Holy See's Commission for Religious Relations with the Jews, has advanced the notion that Jews are an exception to the rule in terms of the universality of salvation in Christ because they are the only non-Christian religious community to have authentic revelation from the Christian perspective. Hence Torah is sufficient for Jewish salvation. This thesis remains in its infancy and marginal under the papacy of Benedict XVI, as the 2008 controversy over the revised Tridentine Rite Good Friday prayer demonstrates. The reason the Tridentine Rite touched a raw nerve in Jewish–Christian relations is because the prayer deals with mission and the conversion of Jews, and expressly looks towards their conversion. Since 1965 and until 2008, official Catholic teaching was clear, for, according to the *Catechism of the Catholic Church*, no. 839, 'the Jewish faith, unlike other non-Christian religions, is already a response to God's revelation'. The one prayer for Jews in Catholic liturgy, which before the Second Vatican Council was a prayer for their conversion, previously called the Good Friday Prayer for the Perfidious Jews, had been transformed by the new 1970 English missal into a prayer that Jews will be deepened in the faith given to them by God. It reads: 'Let us pray for the Jewish people, the first to hear the word of God, that they may continue to grow in the love of his name and in faithfulness to his covenant.'

The Tridentine Rite prayer, which retains the pre-Vatican II heading 'prayer for the conversion of the Jews', has been reformulated as follows: 'We pray for the Jews. That our God and Lord enlighten their hearts so that they recognize Jesus Christ, the Saviour of all mankind.'

With the publication of the prayer, the Church now holds contradictory positions on relations with Jews. Pope John Paul II (and Cardinal Joseph Ratzinger, before he became Pope Benedict XVI), among others, regularly used the term 'elder brother' to apply to the relationship with Judaism, and Catholic teaching accepted the irrevocable nature of the covenantal relationship between the Jewish people and God. The new prayer, however, challenges this teaching, and since its promulgation in 2007 a small number of conservative Catholic groups have begun to voice more loudly their desire to seek Jewish converts. This raises a fundamental question: if the Church accepts that the covenant still belongs to the Jewish people, surely there is a less pressing need to convert Jews to Christianity? The revised rite should be seen as part of the growing tension within the Church, which now has no clear consensus in this area. Many Jews expect that if they dialogue with Christians there should be no hidden missionary agenda or secret desire for their conversion.

At the Second Vatican Council, Cardinal Patrick O'Boyle expressed concern should conversion come on to the agenda of Catholic–Jewish relations. 'The word "conversion" awakens in the hearts of Jews memories of persecutions, sufferings . . . If we express our hope for the eschatological union in words that give the impression we are guided by the definite and conscious intention of working for their conversion, we set up a new and high wall of division, which makes any fruitful dialogue impossible.'[6] His words still echo today.

Yet it is a mistake to equate mission with proselytism; rather, mission refers to the sending out of someone to fulfil a particular task, and both Judaism and Christianity have a missionary vocation in the sense that their adherents carry out a specific witness in the world. Christian missionary activity has traditionally been understood as converting non-Christians to belief in Christ, and that has included Jews. Generally, Jews have not understood their mission as converting others to Judaism but as faithfulness to Torah and the covenantal obligations, sometimes described in terms of 'being a light to the nations' (Isaiah 42.6); therefore non-Jews are not targets for conversion because the righteous of all nations will have a share in the world to come if they keep the Noachide Laws.

Of course, there has always been ambiguity in the Church's understanding of mission and Jews: on the one hand, it sought to

---

6 John Oesterreicher, 1986, *The New Encounter: Between Christians and Jews*, New York: Philosophical Library, pp. 199–201.

bring as many Jews as possible into the fold, at times by force; and on the other, it had respect for the tradition that was at the root of Christian faith. The Church sought to preserve the identity of the Jewish people because Jews were the recipients of God's providential care as the chosen people and eschatologically they had a role in the final act of redemption. This raised a tension between belief that the conversion of Jews was an essential part of Christian mission and not wanting to thwart God's final salvific plan.

This tension remains – as demonstrated by those who seek the conversion of all Jews, because there is no exemption from the need for salvation in Christ; others who witness to faith in Christ, without targeting Jews specifically, and believe in sharing the Christian faith with all people (including Jews); and finally, those who have no conversionary outlook towards Jews, where mission is understood as mutual and joint ethical witness in an unredeemed world (sometimes called 'critical solidarity' or 'mutual witness').

It has been argued that the Church alone is the theological continuation of Israel as the people of God, and mission to the Jewish people is necessary, as illustrated by missionary organizations such as the Christian Mission to the Jewish People; on the other hand, Jews were still the elect of God, demonstrated by the Leuenberg document (2001), which rejected the need to actively seek the conversion of Jews.

Put slightly differently, if the main emphasis is on the concept of the Church as the body of Christ, the Jewish people are seen as being outside. The Christian attitude to them would be in principle the same as to adherents of other faiths and the mission of the Church is to bring them either individually or corporately to the acceptance of Christ so that they become members of this body. However, if the Church is primarily seen as the people of God, it is possible to regard the Church and the Jewish people together as forming the one people of God – separated from one another for the time being, yet with the promise that they will ultimately become one. Consequently, the Church's attitude towards Jews is different from the attitude it has to all others who do not believe in Christ.

Mission is therefore understood more in terms of ecumenical engagement in order to heal the breach, than of seeking conversion.

The 1988 Lambeth Conference was the first Anglican conference to reflect on the issue of Christian mission and Judaism. It explained mission not in terms of the conversion of Jews, but rather of a *common mission*. In the light of Christian–Jewish and Christian–Muslim relations, proselytism was to be rejected and the conference called for 'mutual witness to God between equal partners'. It stated that although

> there are a variety of attitudes towards Judaism within Christianity today . . . All these approaches, however, share a common concern to be sensitive to Judaism, to reject all proselytizing, that is, aggressive and manipulative attempts to convert, and of course, any hint of antisemitism. Further, Jews, Muslims and Christians have a common mission. They share a mission to the world that God's name may be honoured.

In contrast, some evangelical Christian leaders, such as de Ridder, firmly believe that it is the divinely mandated mission of the Church to preach the gospel to Jews, as well as to everyone else. Alongside the missionary activity, it is also suggested that Christians should re-examine their relationship with Judaism by increasing their understanding of the Jewish roots of Christianity. This has led to some intriguing social and political alliances between evangelical Christian organizations and Orthodox Jewish groups, particularly in the United States – for example, working together to form joint opposition to abortion.

According to this view, embraced by many Southern Baptist churches in the United States, Christians would be false to their faith if they failed to try to bring Jews into Christian fellowship. The 1996 Southern Baptist Convention reaffirmed the need to direct 'energies and resources towards the proclamation of the gospel to the Jewish people', and the Jews for Jesus movement also exemplifies active mission towards Jews – its charter states that 'we believe in the lost condition of every human being, whether Jew or

Gentile, who does not accept salvation by faith in Jesus Christ, and therefore in the necessity of presenting the gospel to the Jews.'

For evangelicals in particular, the question of Christian mission to Jews is not a practical problem as to whether Christians should witness their faith to Jews; rather, it is *how* Christians should witness their faith to Jews. At the heart of the tension between evangelism and dialogue lies conversion and conversation. One evangelical Anglican, Roger Hooker, argued that evangelism (in other words, conversion) and dialogue (in other words, conversation)

> have to walk together but always as uneasy partners. If they are not walking together, there can be no tension between them. If there is no tension, then the proponents of each caricature the others in order to enjoy the phony security of always being right. When that happens we stop asking questions and so no longer grow.[7]

---

7 Roger Hooker, 1997, 'Christian Faith and Other Faiths: The Tension Between Dialogue and Evangelism', in *Common Ground*, vol. 3, at www.jcrelations.net/Mission_and_Salvation_III__Christian_Faith_and_Other_Faiths.2252.0.html?page=5

# PART 2

# Jews, Christians and the Bible

# 5

# 'Whom do men say that I am?' (Matthew 16.13)

Scholars have spent an impressive amount of energy on the study of the historical Jesus, and much of it has revolved around his Jewishness. The cleavage between Jews and Christians in the first century was determined by the fact that Christians accepted Jesus as God's Messiah. Jews did not – not then and not now.

'Whom do men say that I am?', Jesus once asked his disciples (Matthew 16.13). The varied answers reveal how even then there was little consensus over his identity.

Yet it can be agreed that Jesus was born a Jew, raised a Jew, taught as a Jew and died a Jew. He was indicted by Pilate as 'king of the Jews' and was condemned to death as such.

There were many ways to be Jewish in the first century. Josephus mentions four groups: Pharisees, Sadducees, Essenes and Zealots. With which of the groups did Jesus have dealings? The Gospels never mention the Essenes, although – like the Essenes – John was also an ascetic.

Jews referred to as Zealots were active from the time of the Maccabees until the last Jewish revolt against Rome in 135 CE. Josephus accuses them of destroying the Temple in the war against Rome and during the first century CE, kidnapping Jews as hostages and killing their own people whom they regarded as traitors. The Zealots are hardly mentioned in the New Testament, although Luke includes Simon the Zealot among the 12 disciples.

The Gospels make clear that Jesus' major dealings were with Pharisees and Sadducees. The Sadducees are mentioned in the New Testament in polemics with Jesus (e.g. Mark 12.18–27 and parallels), and as members of the Sanhedrin that tried Paul (Acts 23.7–8). They became a powerful faction in Judean politics, but seem not to have survived the destruction of Jerusalem in 70 CE. Sadducees were mainly wealthy aristocrats, but the assumption that they were all priests or that all priests were Sadducees (a traditional extrapolation from Acts 5.17) has now been largely discarded. For example, Josephus, a priest, was a Pharisee. Thus the Sadducees were associated with worship at the Temple in Jerusalem and collaborated with Greek rule, and then Roman rule.

The Pharisees – other than the Jewish followers of Jesus – were the only major Jewish group to survive the Jewish rebellion against Rome. After the Temple was destroyed in 70 CE, they began to reconstruct the Jewish faith and so became known as the fathers of rabbinic Judaism. They placed a heavy emphasis on the Oral Torah, as well as the Written Torah, and developed interpretations that ordinary people could observe in whatever context they lived.

The conflict between Jesus and the Pharisees generally centres on the interpretation of the Torah, especially in terms of observing the Sabbath, dietary laws and issues of purity. Interestingly, however, the Pharisees are notable by their absence from the Passion narratives.

It is important to know that, for all the differences within the divergent interpretations of Judaism at that time, there was also much in common. Two convictions especially bound Jews together. The first was a belief in the one and only God, who accepted no rivals. God made behavioural demands of his people, so Jewish faith could be described as ethical monotheism. The second was that God had entered into a special covenantal relationship with Jews. In the call of Abraham, the Exodus from Egypt and the giving of the Torah on Sinai, God had elected and chosen his own people.

There is also limited but relevant evidence outside the Gospels of Jesus. For example, Tacitus' brief reference in the *Annals* (15.44) mentions his title, *Christus*, and his execution in Judea by order of Pontius Pilate. The only clear non-Christian Jewish reference in this period is from Josephus in a passage from *Jewish Antiquities* (28.63–4), called the *Testimonium Flavianum*. Virtually all scholars are agreed that the received text is a Christian rewriting, but most are prepared to accept that in the original text Josephus did offer a brief account of Jesus (although a reconstruction of what Josephus wrote is necessarily speculative).

## The Messiah

Naturally, the question as to why Jews rejected Jesus as the Messiah became a fundamental preoccupation of the New Testament writers, who insisted, one way or another, on continuity between the Church and Israel. In time, the interpretation of Old Testament texts became the subject of debate, because while Jews and Christians accepted that some passages referred to the coming of the Messiah, the latter believed them to be fulfilled by Jesus and the former did not. In addition, Christians referred to other texts, which had not previously be viewed as messianic, to explain why the Messiah, who had been expected to bring a Jewish triumph over Rome, suffered and was crucified. An example of this can be seen in the messianic interpretation of Psalm 118.22–23, found in Acts 4.11 ('He is "the stone you builders rejected, which has become the cornerstone"').

Jesus shared many of the central convictions of the Pharisees, but the beliefs of his early followers that he was the Messiah and Son of God led to a parting of the ways with them, as well as with other Jewish groups, which helps to explain why the pages of the Gospels are charged with hostility towards the Pharisees.

There is much debate about whether, and what sort of, a Messiah was expected in the first century. It has often been argued – for example, by Jacob Neusner – that the concept of the Messiah was not a well-known one in the Jewish world at the time of Jesus. Yet messianic movements are mentioned by Judas the Galilean and Theudas in the first century CE; in Acts 5.36–37 Gamaliel compares them with the activity of Jesus. The Dead Sea Scrolls seem to have envisaged two Messiahs (King and Priest), including the Davidic messiah fulfilling the prophecy of the lion of Judah mentioned in Genesis 49.10.

The Gospel of Mark begins with the declaration of faith: 'The beginning of the good news about Jesus, the Messiah, the Son of God'. Paul, in his earliest writing, 1 Thessalonians, which dates from about year 50, calls Jesus the Messiah in his opening greeting (1.1). Yet only once, in the fourth Gospel, does Jesus claim in so many words to be the Messiah, privately to a Samaritan woman (4.25f.). On two other occasions he accepted the designation, but on neither does he do so forthrightly.

The first occasion is recorded by the Synoptic Gospels.[1] Jesus asked his disciples what people were saying about him. He then asked what they thought. Peter replied, 'You are the Messiah'. After this, Matthew differs from Mark and Luke. They record that Jesus gave them strict orders not to tell anyone, but Matthew maintains that Jesus welcomed Peter's statement but then went on (as in the two other accounts) to warn them against broadcasting this view. It is followed, in Mark and Matthew but not by Luke, by Jesus rebuking Peter as 'Satan' for not believing that the Messiah must suffer many things and be put to death. This is a mysterious scene. Did Jesus actually accept the title or not? Yes, though with reservations, if we follow Matthew; in the other accounts, the most we can say is that he did not straightforwardly refuse it.

The second occasion takes place after Jesus is arrested and brought before the High Priest, who asks him, 'Are you the Messiah?' Mark records that Jesus said 'I am' (14.61f.), whereas according to Matthew he replied, ambiguously, 'You have said so' (26.63f.). In Luke's account, the whole assembly asks Jesus the question, which he refuses to answer at all by saying, enigmatically, 'If I tell you, you will not believe' (Luke 22.67f.). Here, again, ambiguity and enigma prevail.

The puzzling fact that Jesus was, early on, called Messiah, and yet seems to have used it of himself only cautiously and rarely, if at all, is compounded when we look at the world of Judaism in his day. Popular imagination holds that many people believed in a coming Messiah, but the evidence suggests that some did whereas others did not. Some scholars believe that the titles 'Son of Man'

---

[1] Mark 8.27-31; Matthew 16.13-21; Luke 9.18-22.

and 'Son of God' shed light on Jesus' messiahship. 'Son of Man' has its origin in a christological explanation of Daniel 7.13, where it refers to a vision of the figure 'like a son of man' coming with the clouds to the Ancient of Days (God). Here the term should be understood as apocalyptic, rather than messianic.

However, 'Son of God' is likely to have been a messianic title (on the basis of 2 Samuel 7.14 and Psalm 2.7 and their interpretation in Qumran). In Jewish tradition, 'son of God' was used to refer to the people of Israel and was associated with election and obedience. In Christianity, 'Son of God' as a title for Jesus has been used to express Jesus' divinity and his special relationship with God. Interestingly, rabbinic Judaism seems to have deliberately avoided the phrase 'son of God', perhaps due to the fact that Christians made extensive use of this concept in their christological reflection.

One important story indicates that Jesus did believe he was the Messiah: his entry into Jerusalem at the beginning of the last week of his life.[2] Scholars accept the historicity of this account, because it is similarly recorded by all the Gospels, although Bultmann warns about its 'fairy tale motif'. The description of the entry is both messianic and kingly. For example, the journey from the Mount of Olives is reminiscent of the expected Last Days (Zechariah 14.1–4). Matthew certainly understands Jesus' entry in this way, as his quotation of Zechariah 9.9 makes clear ('Say to the Daughter of Zion, "See, your king comes to you, gentle and riding on a donkey, on a colt, the foal of a donkey"'), but all the Gospels identify Jesus as king, whose actions legitimate his claim to authority. The cries of 'hosanna ['help' or 'save now'] to the son of David' also indicate that Jesus' entry was viewed by the crowds as the entry of a king and messiah who was expected to redeem his people.

To claim to be the Messiah, if it was an offence against Judaism at all, was certainly not (as the Gospels contend) an offence against Jewish law for which Jesus could have been put to death. The Gospels say that Jesus' claim to be the Messiah was blasphemy,

---

2 Mark 11.1–10; Matthew 21.1–11; Luke 19.28–38.

but in Jewish law, blasphemy was to revile and curse God using God's sacred name. Jesus did nothing of the sort. There were others who claimed to be a Messiah and Josephus mentions some of them. But they were not tried by a Jewish court nor sought out by any Jewish authority. The religious rulers were not disturbed by them, but the political rulers were. The Romans sought out and executed these 'Messiahs' as rebels or potential rebels. The Romans had reason to fear anyone who was, or might be regarded as, the Christ (= Messiah). To the Jews of Jesus' time, 'Christ' referred to the king of the Jews who would deliver them from Rome.

## Polemic

The problem of polemic concerning relations between Jesus and his Jewish contemporaries provides one of the major challenges in Jewish–Christian relations. The traditional Christian teaching of contempt ('énseignement du mépris', a term coined by Jules Isaac, a French historian, who explored the Christian roots of anti-semitism, of Jews and Judaism) fostered an abuse of the Scriptures, both Old and New, and has been used to justify anti-semitism. Christian biblical interpretation may have been used to promote hatred, discrimination or superiority, but is anti-semitism to be found within the pages of the New Testament?

This question is complicated by the fact that Jesus was a Jew who taught his fellow Jews, some of whom followed his teaching, while others did not. Most of his contemporaries, of course, had never heard of him. After his death, his Jewish followers, encouraged by their experience of the resurrection, argued for the validity of his teaching and their own against their fellow Jews, who had not been persuaded. To complicate the position even further, Jesus' Jewish followers argued among themselves about the conditions under which gentiles might be admitted to this new Jewish movement. In addition, some of the Jewish communities within the Jesus movement – with or without gentile members – found themselves further at odds with other Jews over issues such as Torah observance and claims about Jesus.

The New Testament bears witness to the debates and arguments that were taking place. These disputes were serious, vigorous and often bitter. Nevertheless, what has often been forgotten or neglected is the fact that the arguments were primarily between Jews, about a Jew or about Jewish issues (even when they concerned gentile converts). The problem of polemic is magnified when passages are read as if they were 'Christian' arguments against Jews. To read them in this way is to misread them and to ignore the context of the ministry of the earthly Jesus: first-century Palestinian Judaism.

This misreading contributed to the development of the 'teaching of contempt'. Yet the Christian Bible shares an intrinsic problem that is common to the Jewish Tanach and the Qur'an – namely, that polemic against a named other, once enshrined in documents venerated as Scripture, carries a weight and authority throughout history. Moreover, such texts are constantly available for use or abuse, to justify the most appalling actions in the name of God. Their very existence is, and remains, the problem, for they cannot simply be expurgated or interpreted out of existence.

However, it can be useful to juxtapose texts from the same Scripture that offer a contrasting approach. For example, when dealing with New Testament accounts of arguments between Jesus and the Pharisees, one might turn to passages that demonstrate their close relationship, such as Luke 13.1. One might compare verses such as 'No one comes to the Father except through me' (John 14.6) or 'neither is there salvation in any other; for there is no other name under heaven given among men, by which we must be saved' (Acts 4.12) with passages such as 'other sheep I have, which are not of this fold' (John 10.16). Nevertheless, this approach neither removes the existence of problematic texts, nor their availability. They can always return to haunt the inheritors of such revelations and provide potential new victims, despite the worthiest of efforts. In other words, while contextualization is essential in understanding and reinterpreting a text, it will not erase the polemic.

Thus although reading difficult texts within their proper historical context will help to avoid 'false' readings – for it *does* make a difference if the reader understands something of the background, and develops a keener awareness of the context from which these texts came – this cannot always render a text innocent. The text's original context is not the only necessary source of its meaning or effect. To 'solve' the problem at a historical level does not change the history of a text's effect and interpretation.

The 'history of effects' of texts represents a shift away from the traditional historical critical quest for the original meaning of a text, towards its reception history (*Wirkungsgeschichte*) – that is to say, the history of a text's impact on Jewish–Christian relations. It is one of the striking features of powerful texts that they can be read anew in different contexts – for good of course, but also for ill. So even if texts can be found to be part of an intra-Jewish debate at a specific time, this is not how they have always been read since, and not how – in some places – they are still read now.

## Jewish Scholarly Studies of Jesus

In recent times, Jews have begun to read the New Testament in a more positive light. There is of course no reason intrinsic to their faith why they should do so, since it is not sacred Scripture for them. Indeed, there is every reason why they should ignore it, since it has been used to justify, and may even be the source of, anti-semitic actions by Christians. Yet an increasing number of Jewish scholars have turned their attention to studies of Jesus. The pioneers in this field in the early twentieth century include Abraham Geiger, Joseph Klausner and Claude Montefiore. In more recent years, the most significant studies have been produced by Geza Vermes, David Flusser and A.-J. Levine.

Abraham Geiger, leader of German Reform Judaism in Germany in the nineteenth century, dealt with Jesus in several large sections of his *Judaism and its History* (1866). He concluded that Jesus was a Pharisee, who walked in the ways of Hillel but expressed no new ideas. According to Susannah Heschel's biography (*Abraham Geiger and the Jewish Jesus*, 1998), Geiger wanted to find the place of Jesus in Jewish history. Judaism could therefore claim Jesus as one of its own, a Pharisee who lost his bearings. But what

Jesus did himself was not nearly as pernicious, Geiger says, as what his followers did with their understanding of Jesus. Many of the themes that have emerged repeatedly in modern Jewish–Christian discussions and in the debate about the Jewishness of Jesus were first broached by Geiger.

One of the first modern studies by a Jewish scholar, Joseph Klausner, was entitled *Jesus of Nazareth*, published in English in 1925 (Hebrew original 1921). Klausner observed that

> in his [Jesus'] ethical code there is a sublimity, distinctiveness and originality in form unparalleled in any other Hebrew ethical code; neither is there any parallel to the remarkable art of his parables. The shrewdness and sharpness of his proverbs and his forceful epigrams serve, in an exceptional degree, to make ethical ideas a popular possession. If ever the day should come and this ethical code be stripped of its wrappings of miracle and mysticism, the Book of the Ethics of Jesus will be one of the choicest treasures in the literature of Israel for all time.[3]

Klausner suggests that Jesus surpassed Hillel in his ethical ideals, by changing the golden rule from a negative form ('What thou thyself hatest, do not unto thy neighbour') to the positive form ('What thou thyself wouldest that men should do unto thee, so do thou also unto them'). Even so, Klausner observes that Jesus' ethical teaching has not proved possible in practice. One can notice an apologetic strand running through Klausner's work for he argues, as do a number of other Jewish writers, that Paul distorted the message of Jesus by Hellenizing it, and that Judaism is more fitted to be the bearer of monotheism to a needy world. As Claude Montefiore put it, Paul was no rabbinic Jew.[4]

For his part, Montefiore expressed the view that it was time for Jews to abandon a negative attitude towards Christianity. The appropriate moment had arrived for a Jewish reappraisal of Christianity and a Christian reappraisal of Judaism. It was time for

---

3 Joseph Klausner, 1925, *Jesus of Nazareth*, London: Macmillan, p. 414.
4 Claude G. Montefiore, 1911, *Judaism and St Paul*, London: M. Goshen.

these two religions to stop judging each other from their defects; instead they should examine the positive qualities. Previously, it was the norm for Jews to look for defects in Christian works or for parallels in rabbinic writings. 'What was true could not be new and what was new could not be true.'[5] This phrase summarized many Jewish attitudes towards Christianity, but Montefiore sought to take a more balanced approach. As far as Christians were concerned, he did not feel that he must assume that Jesus was always right; with Jews he did not feel obligated to defend the ancient rabbis. As a result, Christian scholars attacked him for being too Jewish and Jewish scholars for being too Christian.

Montefiore admired enormously the figure of Jesus, and in *The Synoptic Gospels* (1909) suggested that his teaching was a revival of prophetic Judaism and in some respects pointed forward to Liberal Judaism. Jesus emphasized precisely those values that Liberal Judaism wanted to bring out – for example, inward goodness at the expense of outward forms. Jesus, Montefiore argued, should be viewed as a great and wise teacher, but in no sense God. Part of the significance of Jesus lay in the fact that 'he started the movement which broke down the old barriers and brought about the translation of Judaism into the Gentile world – the translation of Judaism with many modifications, curtailments, additions both for the better and worse, good and evil'.[6]

Among more recent Jewish writings on the New Testament, one of the most interesting is Pinchas Lapide's *The Resurrection of Jesus* (1983). He believes that the resurrection actually happened, though he is a practising Orthodox Jew. He is unconvinced by the 'strange paraphrases' of many modern Christian theologians about the resurrection. He believes them 'all too abstract and scholarly to explain the fact that the solid hillbillies from Galilee who, for the very real reason of the crucifixion of their master, were saddened to death, were changed within a short period of time into

---

5 Claude G. Montefiore, 1923, *The Old Testament and After*, London: Macmillan, pp. 561ff.
6 Claude G. Montefiore, 1911–12, *Hibbert Journal*, vol. 10, p. 773.

a jubilant community of believers'. Only resurrection could have accomplished that.[7]

Lapide, building on the thought of Franz Rosenzweig, suggested that Christianity is the '*judaizing*' of the pagans. Lapide refers approvingly to Clemens Thoma, a Catholic theologian, who argued that, through the resurrection of Jesus, an access to faith in the one (until then unknown) God of Israel was opened to the gentiles. In other words, Jesus is the way for the gentiles, but Jews, who already know God, do not need Jesus. This conviction has not gained wide acceptance among either Jews or Christians, though it is an intriguing one.

Martin Buber, who in *I and Thou* (1937) interpreted the Bible and relations with God in a personal and existential fashion, has had a huge impact on modern Protestant theology, though he has been rather less influential in Jewish circles. He argued that Jewish faith, *emunah*, is in the history of a nation, whereas Christian faith, *pistis*, is in that of an individual. Buber wrote that 'from my youth onwards I have found in Jesus my great brother. That Christianity has regarded and does regard him as God and Saviour has always appeared to me a fact of the highest importance which, for his sake and for my own, I must endeavour to understand ... I am more than ever certain that a great place belongs to [Jesus] in Israel's history of faith.'[8]

The most significant Jewish scholars of the New Testament in the latter part of the twentieth century are Geza Vermes and David Flusser. In *Jesus the Jew* (1973), Vermes opened the eyes of many to the Jewishness of Jesus, whom he depicted as a Galilean Hasid, holy man. In his careful examination of titles claimed for Jesus (such as prophet, lord, Messiah, Son of Man, and Son of God) he concluded, controversially, that none of the claims and aspirations of Jesus link him with the Messiah, that no titular use of 'Son of Man' is attested in Jewish literature, and that 'prophet', 'lord' – or even, figuratively, 'Son of God' – could be easily applied

---

7 Pinchas Lapide, 1984, *The Resurrection of Jesus: A Jewish Perspective*, London: SPCK, p. 125.

8 Martin Buber, 1951, *Two Types of Faith*, London: Routledge & Kegan Paul, pp. 12–13.

to holy men in the Judaism of Jesus' day. As far as Vermes is concerned, Jesus was a charismatic teacher, healer and prophet.

He compares Jesus to his contemporary, Hanina ben Dosa, another charismatic leader and healer. Vermes concludes:

> The main finding of this exploration of the historical and linguistic elements of the Gospels . . . is that whereas none of the claims and aspirations of Jesus can be said definitely to associate him with the role of the Messiah . . . everything combines . . . to place him in the venerable company of the Devout, the ancient *Hasidim* . . . [This] means that any new enquiry may accept as its point of departure the safe assumption that Jesus did not belong among the Pharisees, Essenes, Zealots or Gnostics, but among the holy miracle workers of Galilee.[9]

Jesus died, said Vermes, because he was perceived as a potential threat to the authorities. The real Jesus, Jesus the Jew, challenges traditional Christianity as well as traditional Judaism. In his view, Jesus cannot be viewed as the founder of Christianity. The significance of Vermes's work can be illustrated by the effect of the title of his first major book, *Jesus the Jew*, which seemed revolutionary at the time but is now almost taken for granted in New Testament scholarship. A synthesis of his writings on Jesus can be found in *The Changing Faces of Jesus* (2000).

Around the same time, another Jewish scholar of the study of Jesus stands out – David Flusser. In his biography *Jesus* (1968), Flusser accepts Jesus fundamentally as he is portrayed in the Gospels (with some preference for Luke), recognizes him as a charismatic figure and respects his teaching and his extraordinary sense of mission. He invites his readers to listen to Jesus himself and wonders out loud whether the responses that Jesus gave in connection with human conflict may not still be the best that anyone has proposed. Flusser commends Jesus for remaining aloof from the zealotism that destroyed the Temple and Jerusalem.

---

9 Géza Vermes, 1973, *Jesus the Jew*, London: SCM Press, p. 223.

Jesus instructed his disciples not to resist authority, as it would only make the behaviour of the civil authorities worse.

The recognition that Jesus was a Jew and had to be understood in his Jewish context represents one of the most important changes in the study of Jesus. Not all New Testament scholars take this point as seriously as they should, and many of those who do are unable to master the languages and customs of first-century Judaism. A small number, unfortunately, prefer to ignore and even to minimize the Jewishness of Jesus by categorizing Jesus as a 'peasant' or as a 'Cynic'.

Finally, we briefly consider Amy-Jill Levine, Professor of New Testament at Vanderbilt University in Nashville, whose most well-known book on the subject – *The Misunderstood Jew: The Church and the Scandal of the Jewish Jesus* (2006) – puts Jesus in the historical context of his time.

Her thesis for this book is that Jesus was a 'good Jew', who taught Jews in a Jewish land. Levine is particularly concerned with anti-Jewish interpretations that arise from the Gospels and Epistles. This particularly happens when, in attempting to set aside Jesus as unique, the Jewish people and/or leaders of his time are depicted as monolithic, obsessively rule-following, unconcerned with the poor and outcast and particularly oppressive to women. The danger is that such polar views create dangerous stereotypes of Judaism in the first century CE and today.

Chapter 3 of Levine's book – 'The New Testament and Anti-Judaism' – explores and comments on various offending passages: 'The Jews, who killed the Lord Jesus and oppress everyone' (1 Thessalonians 2.14–16); 'His blood be on us and on our children' (Matthew 27.25); and 'You are from your father the devil' (John 8.44). Our modern assumptions about what Jesus (and Paul) meant in their original settings are deeply entrenched, often serving agendas of which we are not even aware. She argues these texts demonstrate, regardless of authorial intent or historical context, that the plain meaning of the New Testament is often virulently anti-Jewish. However, she also encourages Jews to appreciate Jesus in continuity with other leaders and prophets of Israel. She describes how Jesus dressed, ate, taught and prayed like a Jew, argued like a Jew with other Jews and amassed Jewish followers. She also notes that the Nicene and Apostles' creeds contain no indication that Jesus was a Jew.

The work of Vermes, Flusser and Levine, built on the work of other scholarly Jewish studies of Jesus, should encourage everyone, Jew and Christian alike, to take the Jewishness of Jesus seriously. It is time to recognize fully the contribution of Jewish scholars in the same way as Christianity has reawoken to the fact that Jesus was born, lived and died a Jew.

# 6

# Mary – The Jewish Mother

Although Christians (and Jews) now take for granted that Jesus was born, lived and died a Jew, Mary, the mother of Jesus, is rarely viewed in the same way. The first Christians were Jews, and in its origins Christianity was one of a number of Jewish groups in the first century. Hardly ever, though, do we think about Mary as a Jewish mother.[1]

Mary and her family were Torah-observant Jews and, for example, would have observed Shabbat; circumcised male babies on the eighth day after birth; attended synagogue; obeyed purity laws in relation to childbirth and menstruation; and kept kosher. The New Testament is a witness to this observant Jewish mother, who brought up her son as a Jew: 'when the days of her purification according to the law [*nomos*=Torah] of Moses were accomplished, they brought him to Jerusalem, to present him to the Lord; As it is written in the law of the Lord "Every male that openeth the womb shall be called holy to the Lord"' (Luke 2.22–23).

Yet Christianity soon forgot its Jewish roots and rejected its Jewish origins, condemning Jews and Judaism in the process. Known as the *Adversus-Iudaeos* writings, Christian anti-Judaism was commonplace, demonstrated by the regular appearance of anti-Jewish polemical texts from the second to the eighteenth

---

1 One exception is a chapter in Johnson's *Truly Our Sister*. I would like to thank Mary Boys for pointing this out. See Elizabeth A. Johnson, 2006, *Truly Our Sister: A Theology of Mary in the Communion of Saints*, London: Continuum, pp. 162–84.

century.[2] Some of these appeared in Christian interpretations about Mary.

In recent decades, the Church has sought to re-establish positive relations with its 'elder brother' and has rediscovered a respect for its Jewish sibling and an awareness of the significance of the Jewishness of Jesus. Christian theologians and leaders now regularly assert the Church's debt to its Jewish heritage. The Church's 'rediscovery' of Judaism has continued unabated since then, exemplified by the pontificate of John Paul II, who was the first pope in modern times to visit the main synagogue in Rome in 1986 and Jerusalem in 2000, to weep at Yad Vashem (Israel's national Holocaust Memorial), and to stand in silent prayer at the Western Wall. In May 2009, his successor – Pope Benedict XVI – also made a successful visit to Israel and in January 2010 delivered a significant address in the Rome synagogue.

These moments demonstrate a fundamentally new relationship in the Catholic–Jewish encounter as well as a repudiation of anti-Judaism. (Similar changes, it should be noted, can be seen in the Protestant–Jewish encounter, but much less so in the Orthodox-Christian/Jewish relationship.) Although there have recently been a number of 'bumps in the road', less and less do we come across the anti-Jewish sentiment that had for so many centuries pervaded the pews and pulpits of the churches, the halls and lecture rooms of the seminaries, and the citadels and courts of the religious authorities.[3]

Since Christians and Jews have reawoken to the Jewishness of Jesus, surely it is well overdue to reconsider Mary in Jewish terms? Why should her Jewishness be ignored? As a Jewish theologian and teacher of Jewish–Christian relations, I occasionally have to remind my students that Mary was a first-century Palestinian Jewish woman from Galilee, not a Roman Catholic from Christian Europe.

---

2 For further details, see James Carleton-Paget's entry, 'Adversus Iudaeos', in Edward Kessler and Neil Wenborn (eds), 2005, *A Dictionary of Jewish–Christian Relations*, Cambridge: Cambridge University Press, pp. 6–8.

3 Examples include the Bishop Williamson affair, the revised Tridentine Rite prayer for the conversion of the Jews, tensions between the Vatican and the State of Israel over implementing the Fundamental Accord of 1993 and disagreements over the actions of Pope Pius XII during the Holocaust.

The 2001 document *The Jewish People and their Sacred Scriptures in the Christian Bible*, issued by the Pontifical Biblical Commission, mentions Mary only five times in 56,000 words – but not once with reference to Judaism, even though Mary was a Jewish woman not only in an ethnic sense, as part of the Jewish people, but also in a religious sense. Her faith in God was shaped by the covenant at Sinai, nourished by Jewish narratives about God's saving deeds in history, expressed by the prayers, rituals and practices of Judaism, as well as by observance of Torah.

There are tentative signs in some of the most recent Christian institutional writings that Mary is beginning to be depicted as a bridge between Christians and Jews. For example, in 2004, the Pontifical Council for Promoting Christian Unity and the Anglican–Roman Catholic International Commission issued a joint statement, which acknowledged that 'the New Testament speaks not only of God's preparation for the birth of the Son, but also of God's election, calling and sanctification of a Jewish woman in the line of those holy women, such as Sarah and Hannah, whose sons fulfilled the purposes of God for his people'.[4] Later, the same document stated that 'the scriptural witness summons all believers in every generation to call Mary "blessed"; this Jewish woman of humble status, this daughter of Israel living in hope of justice for the poor, whom God has graced and chosen to become the virgin mother of his Son through the overshadowing of the Holy Spirit'.[5]

## Mary and First-century Judaism

Diversity was a hallmark of the first-century Judaism of Mary. There were many ways to be Jewish and Josephus mentions four groups: Pharisees, Sadducees, Essenes and Zealots.[6] The Gospels make clear that, most of all, Jesus and Mary encountered the

---

4 *Mary: Grace and Hope in Christ*, 2004, Anglican–Roman Catholic International Commission, at www.anglicancommunion.org/ministry/ecumenical/dialogues/catholic/arcic/index.cfm. A.11.

5 Ibid., A.30.

6 Josephus, *Antiquities*, 18.9.

Pharisees and Sadducees. Both groups were in existence by the second century BCE, and Josephus lists the Sadducees as one of the 'three philosophies' (alongside Pharisees and Essenes).[7]

In the New Testament, the Pharisees are prominent as the main rivals of Jesus, yet they had more in common with Jesus and Mary than other contemporary Jewish groups. They shared many beliefs – such as the coming of the Messiah, life after death and the resurrection of the dead, immortality and a Day of Judgement. The harsh criticism of the Pharisees in the Gospels is recognized as having as much to do with rivalry between the communities in which the texts were written (especially the Matthean community) as with anything that happened during the lifetime of Jesus and Mary. To consider that Jesus dismissed the whole of Pharisaic Judaism is to attribute to him an impossibly superficial approach. Indeed, the level of overlap and coherence between the teachings of Jesus and the Pharisees probably outweighs the areas of difference of opinion.[8]

When picturing Mary's religious world, it is not enough to say that Jewish belief and practice formed a mere 'background' to her observant Jewish household in Galilee. Christian memory of Mary risks multiple distortions if the deeply Jewish roots of her piety are forgotten. Judaism was the religion of Jesus and Mary, which neither son nor mother ever repudiated. Mary worshipped the one God; she made pilgrimages to the Temple; she prayed the *shema* morning and evening; and she obeyed Torah in the spirit of the covenant. Just as New Testament scholarship no longer seeks to divorce Jesus from the Judaism of his day, so Christian studies of Mary should portray her as a Jew, not as an intruder into first-century Palestine.

Of course, while being aware of the intimacy of the relationship between Jews, Mary and the Jesus followers, they were distinguished from their fellow Jews by their relationship to Jesus of

---

7 Josephus, *Jewish Wars*, 2.108–166.

8 See, for example, Anthony J. Saldarini, 1989, *Pharisees, Scribes and Sadducees in Palestinian Society*, Edinburgh: T & T Clark; P. Sanders (ed.), 1992, *Judaism: Practice and Belief, 63 BCE–66 CE*, London: SCM Press; Günter Stemberger, 1995, *Jewish Contemporaries of Jesus: Pharisees, Sadducees, Essenes*, Minneapolis: Fortress Press.

Nazareth. This, of course, continues to be the main division between Jews and Christians today. Following him in his lifetime, agonizing over his death, Mary and these Jewish followers of Jesus developed certain rituals that identified them as a distinctive movement – but it remained a distinctive movement within Judaism.

For example, the last glimpses in Scripture of the historical Mary depict her as remaining a practising Jew. Acts 1.14 states, 'all of these [male disciples] with one accord devoted themselves to prayer, together with the women and Mary the mother of Jesus and his brothers'. Mary and the early post-resurrection Jesus followers continued to observe Jewish practice, most notably, 'continually in the Temple blessing God' (Luke 24.53). Reawakening to the Jewishness of Mary not only sheds light on the origins of Christianity, but has implications for the formation of Christian identity and for contemporary Christian self-understanding.

Let us take as an example the influence of the Jewish understanding of the *Shekhinah* on Christian interpretations of the Holy Spirit. This *Shekhinah* refers to God's presence, and Jewish interpretations always portrayed it in the feminine form. In the Hebrew Bible, the *Shekhinah* refers to God's glory 'dwelling' over the tabernacle and indicates both divine presence and continuity.[9] It continues even when in exile or in the desert, and in post-biblical times was understood to be present after the fall of the Temple in 70 CE. The midrash states that 'when they [Israel] went into Egypt, the *Shekhinah* went with them; in Babylon the *Shekhinah* was with them'.[10] Later, in kabbalistic writings, the *Shekhinah* is identified as a bride – either as the bride of God (equating the *Shekhinah* with Israel) or as the bride of Israel.[11]

Perhaps influenced by the Jewish interpretation, Mary was commonly depicted, especially in Syriac writings, as a holy virgin

---

9 Exodus 40.35.
10 Babylonian Talmud (BT), Megillah 29a.
11 Gershom Scholem, 1977, *On the Kabbalah and its Symbolism*, New York: Schocken, pp. 138–51.

bride and described as a 'bridal chamber'.¹² Could the *Shekhinah* provide a Jewish context to the Christian understanding of a woman – Mary – providing a dwelling place for God?

It has even been suggested that the influence was reciprocal. Jewish scholar Arthur Green has argued that 'the unequivocal feminization of "Shekhina" in the kabbala of the thirteenth century is a Jewish response to, and adaptation of, the revival of devotion to Mary in the twelfth-century Western Church'.¹³ His argument is reinforced by recent studies that show the extent to which rabbinic literature adapted some Christian teaching and interpretation, which was digested into the mainstream Jewish literary corpus.¹⁴

The two-way encounter between Judaism and Christianity continues to this day, and some Jewish theologians, such as Michael Wyschogrod, have identified the *Shekhinah* as the closest analogue to the Christian understanding of the incarnation.¹⁵ Christian theologians have also given this topic some thought. John Pawlikowski, for example, in a study of the interaction between Jewish and Christian biblical theology, has suggested that incarnational christology might provide the best possibility

---

12 See Sebastian Brock, 2005, 'Syriac Tradition', in James Leslie Holden (ed.), *Jesus in History, Culture and Thought: An Encyclopedia*, Oxford: ABC-Clio, pp. 824–9. Syriac writings are especially rich in examples of exegetical encounters with Jewish interpretations because of close geographical and theological relations between Jews and Syriac Christians, demonstrated by shared interpretations and language but also by sharp antagonisms. See Helen Spurling, 2008, 'Genesis 49:10: Ephrem and Jewish Exegesis', *The Harp: A Review of Syriac, Ecumenical and Oriental Studies*, vol. 23, pp. 85–102.

13 Arthur Green, 2002, 'The Shekhina and the Virgin Mary and the Song of Songs', *Association for Jewish Studies Review*, vol. 26, pp. 1–52.

14 See Edward Kessler, 2004, *Bound by the Bible: Jews, Christians and the Sacrifice of Isaac*, Cambridge: Cambridge University Press.

15 Kendall Soulen, 2005, *Abraham's Promise: Judaism and Jewish–Christian Relations*, London: SCM Press, pp. 1–22; Kendall Soulen, 2004, 'Michael Wyschogrod and God's First Love', *The Christian Century*, vol. 121, pp. 22–7; Kendall Soulen, 1996, 'A Jewish Perspective on Incarnation', *New Theology*, vol. 12, pp. 195–209. For further details, see Edward Kessler and Hans Herman Henrix, 2006, 'Gottes Gegenwart in Israel und die Inkarnation: Ein christlich–jüdischer Dialog: I. Inkarnation: Die Trennungslinie zwischen Judentum und Christentum; II. Inkarnation: Tiefster Glaubensunterschied und stärkstes Bindeglied', *Freiburger Rundbrief*, vol. 1, pp. 6–25.

for preserving the universalistic dimensions of the Christ Event while opening authentic theological space for Judaism.[16]

The influence of the *Shekhinah* can also be noticed in the prologue to John's Gospel, which includes a reference to the 'dwelling' or 'tabernacling' of the Word. Drawing upon a pun in Greek where the word for 'tent' is similar to the Hebrew for 'to dwell', Jesus, the Word of God, is depicted as encamping with the people of the world: 'and the word became flesh and dwelt (lit. tabernacled) among us'.[17]

The Gospel accounts of Jesus' birth provide relatively little detail about Mary. In the infancy narratives, both Matthew and Luke name the parents of Jesus as Mary and Joseph, but the circumstances of conception later became the subject of contention. Geza Vermes has argued in his study of the infancy narratives that midrash and theology profoundly influence the Gospel accounts, and what they omitted became the source of speculation and argument between Jewish Christians, gentile Christians, Jews and pagans. Vermes also points out that the miraculous birth of Jesus resonates with biblical accounts of other miraculous births, such as the birth of Isaac and rabbinic interpretations of the birth of Moses.[18]

Rather than comparing with Moses, a more relevant comparison could be made with his sister, Miriam. Mary's Hebrew name is Miriam, and both Miriam and Mary are both associated with music: Mary sings a psalm of praise, the Magnificat, and the Song

---

16 John T. Pawlikowski, 2001, *Christ in the Light of Christian–Jewish Dialogue*, new edn, Eugene, OR: Wipf & Stock. See also John T. Pawlikowski, 2005, 'Reflections on Covenant and Mission', in Edward Kessler and Melanie J. Wright (eds), *Themes in Jewish–Christian Relations*, Cambridge: Orchard Academic, pp. 273–99.

17 John 1.14. See James Aitken's entry, 'Shekhina', in *A Dictionary of Jewish–Christian Relations*, op. cit., p. 403.

18 Geza Vermes, 2006, *The Nativity: History and Legend*, London: Penguin, pp. 58–9. See also Edward Kessler, *Bound by the Bible*, op. cit., pp. 100–7. Interestingly, in *The Posterity and Exile of Cain* (134), Josephus' near contemporary, Philo of Alexandria, describes Sarah as a virgin at the time she conceives Isaac.

of Moses probably belonged originally to Miriam.[19] They are both portrayed as women of faith, demonstrated in Mary's case by the Magnificat, in which Mary praises God for exercising divine justice and compassion on behalf of the lowly, both for herself and for Israel as 'God's servant'. Mary's obedience puts her alongside other leaders of Israel such as Moses. Just as Miriam appeared at the beginning of the Moses story and at the end of the Exodus story, so did Mary in Gospel accounts of Jesus, beginning with the Magnificat and ending at the cross. The annunciation scene also has similarities. Just as Mary was informed about Jesus by an angel, the second-century CE writer Pseudo-Philo recounts Miriam's dream in which an angel tells Miriam of the miraculous birth of her brother Moses.[20] Miriam and Mary seemingly converge again in the Qur'an, where Mary/Maryam is described as the 'sister of Aaron'.[21] Finally, just as contemporary Jewish women and feminists try to recover the spiritual legacy of Miriam, so Christian women past and present appeal to Mary's example.

We do not know how long Mary remained part of the Jerusalem community; perhaps she lived out her final years there – the Church of Dormition claims the honour of the place where she 'fell asleep in Christ'. One tradition suggests she went to the city of Ephesus with John the Apostle, and its Church of St Mary honours the place where she died.[22] There is simply no evidence. But Elizabeth Johnson depicts Mary in her old age in Jerusalem, helping to alleviate the poverty that existed in the Jewish community

---

19 Luke 1.46–55; Exodus 15.1–18. See Luke 1.20–21. Miriam is the first woman in Scripture to be called a prophet (Exodus 15.20). Micah implies that Miriam, no less than Moses and Aaron, led the Children of Israel out from Egypt: 'I brought you up out of Egypt and redeemed you from the land of slavery. I sent Moses to lead you, also Aaron and Miriam' (Micah 6.4). See Mhairi Macmillan, 1991, 'Miriam: Wilderness Teacher, Priestess Ancestor of Mary', in Alix Pirani (ed.), *The Absent Mother: Restoring the Goddess to Judaism and Christianity*, London: Mandala Books, pp. 74–81.

20 Pseudo-Philo, *Biblical Antiquities* 9.10.

21 Sura 3 (*House of 'Imran*'), Sura 19.29 and 66.11–12.

22 Pope John Paul II on his visit to Ephesus in 1979 declared the church a place of pilgrimage for Christians, and Pope Benedict XVI held a Mass there in November 2006.

at the time.[23] Johnson's depiction of the poverty of Jerusalem is supported by rabbinic writings and also by Paul in his letters.[24] (Hillel is said to have lived in such poverty that he was sometimes unable to pay the admission fee to study Torah and, because of him, that fee was abolished.)[25]

Although there is no evidence, it is very doubtful whether Mary lived to the year 70 CE and witnessed the destruction of the Temple. However, it is reasonable to assume that she continued to live out her life as a Jew who believed in the God of Israel and that Jesus would soon return. Although Mary and the other Jewish followers of Jesus began to develop their own traditions and after Jesus' death increasingly diverged from other Jewish groups, they not only preserved their Jewish identity but also faced the same challenges as their fellow Jews. The greatest challenge to face the Jewish community as a whole was the destruction of the Temple in 70 CE.

## Christian and Jewish Polemic

Although the Jewishness of Mary is taken for granted in the New Testament, we now move to post-biblical Christian writings, which either ignored her Jewishness or adopted anti-Jewish interpretations. The centuries following the New Testament saw growing and vehement Christian anti-Judaism, and the *Adversus-Iudaeos* tradition became central to Christian self-understanding and interpretation. As we shall shortly see, Jews were accused of attempting to sabotage Mary's funeral, desecrating Marian images as well as deriding her cult. Jews responded with their own polemic, notably against the belief that Jesus was born of a virgin.

Lying behind the polemic is a tension that continues to exist today. On the one hand, a realization that Jesus was a Jew; that Mary and the first Christians were Jews; that Christianity, at its birth, was a Jewish group whose teaching is rooted in the Old

---

23 Elizabeth Johnson, *Truly Our Sister*, op. cit., p. 181.
24 Galatians 2.10; 1 Corinthians 16.1–4; Romans 15.25–26.
25 BT, Yoma 35b.

Testament. On the other, an awkwardness among Christians at the Jewish 'no' to Jesus, and at the refusal of the majority of Jesus' fellow Jews to recognize Jesus as the Messiah; as God incarnate in human flesh.

The Jewish rejection was extremely embarrassing, in particular, for the early Church and led to some harsh accusations from pagans as well as Jews. Romans especially considered new cults as suspicious and dangerous. Critics, such as the second-century pagan Celsus, were quick to exploit Jewish rejection of Christianity in their polemical writings and accused Christians of deserting Jewish tradition even though they claimed to be faithful to their Jewish heritage. Celsus placed the following criticism into the mouth of a Jew, 'Why do you Christians take your origin from our religion and then, as if you are progressing in knowledge, despise these things, although you cannot name any other origin for your doctrine than our law?'[26]

In response to pagan, as well as Jewish, criticism, the writings of the church fathers demonstrate a hardening of attitudes towards Jews and Judaism. The Jew, as encountered in the pages of many of the church fathers, is not really a human being at all; rather he is, at best, an opponent and, at worst, a monster.

This anti-Jewish portrait can also be found in patristic writings about Mary, such as those of Proclus, a fifth-century priest in Constantinople, who led a movement in favour of adopting the term *theotokos* (Bearer of God) to describe Mary, rather than *christotokos* (Bearer of Christ). This title was the cause of controversy at the Council of Ephesus in 431 and, in his homily two years earlier, Proclus argued that Mary's enemies were not to be found only among heretical Christians but also among the Jews of Constantinople:

> There may chance be a Jew in our midst
> Like the fox of Judah lurking in the vineyard of Christ
> After the congregation is dismissed
> He might stand outside and mock our words

---

[26] Origen, *Contra Celsum* 2.4. See Judith Lieu, 1996, *Image and Reality: The Jews and the World of Christianity in the Second Century*, Edinburgh: T & T Clark, pp. 103–54.

Say such as these:
'Why do you Christians invent such novelties
And boast of things which cannot be proved.
When did God ever appear on earth?'[27]

From the year 500 onwards, a period that coincided with the establishment of Christian rule in the Roman Empire, a number of Christian texts reflected on Mary's end, known as the dormition, and her assumption to heaven. The earliest and most well-known of these, *Transitus Mariae*, dates from the fifth century and, in its praise of Mary, disparages Jews as her enemies. It states how 'the Jews hated Lady Mary greatly'.[28] Miri Rubin's recent study of Mary describes medieval stories of the apostles carrying Mary for burial and being attacked by Jews. They were protected by a miraculous wall of fire, which at the same time blinded the Jewish attackers. When they realized their error, many converted.[29]

Ora Limor recounts a sixth-century account by the traveller Antoninus whose travels bring him to Nazareth. There he discovers that two brothers, Galbius and Candidus, had come across Mary's robe in Nazareth in the house of an old Jewish woman with whom they were lodging. She told them that the robe, entrusted to a female acquaintance before Mary's assumption, had been safely kept in her family. The robe was stolen (described as *furta sacra*, 'a holy theft') by the two brothers and then brought to the Church of Blachernae in Constantinople, where it became one of the most important relics of the seventh century and was credited with various miracles, including the protection of the city. When the old woman discovered the theft, she died of sorrow.[30]

---

27 Miri Rubin, 2009, *Mother of God: A History of the Virgin Mary*, London: Allen Lane, p. 45.

28 Steven Shoemaker, 1999, '"Let Us Go and Burn Her Body": The Image of the Jews in the Early Dormition Tradition', *Church History: Studies in Christianity and Culture*, vol. 68, p. 778.

29 Miri Rubin, *Mother of God*, op. cit., pp. 228–36. She also includes a medieval image from the parish church of St Mary, Chalgrove, Oxfordshire, which depicts the story in art.

30 Ora Limor, 2006, 'Mary and the Jews: Story, Controversy, and Testimony', *Historien*, vol. 6, pp. 55–71.

Jewish writings that depict Mary are rare, and of what little energy the rabbis spent on refuting Christianity, most was directed to Jesus. Three aspects about Jesus are particularly mentioned: his illegitimate birth; his skills as a magician (which led Israel astray); and his trial and crucifixion. The miraculous birth is most relevant to this study. The following passage discusses the names ben Stada and ben Pandira, which sometimes allude to Jesus:

> 'He who cuts upon his flesh.' It is tradition that Rabbi Eliezer said to the Wise, 'did not ben Stada bring spells from Egypt in a cut, which was upon his flesh?' They said to him, 'he was a fool, and they do not bring a proof from a fool.' Ben Stada is ben Pandira. Rab Hisda said, 'the husband was Stada, the paramour was Pandira.' The husband was Pappos ben Jehudah, the mother was Stada. The mother was Miriam, the dresser of women's hair (miriam m'gaddela nashaia [a pun on Mary Magdalene]), as we say in Pumbeditha, 'such a one has been false (stat du) to her husband.'[31]

The Talmudic passage deals, at the literal level, with remembering magical spells. It begins with the premise that since ben Stada (Jesus) brought magical spells from Egypt in an incision in his flesh, the practice might be allowable. However, the response is that since ben Stada is a fool his case proves nothing. An explanation of the name ben Stada is offered, and he is identified with ben Pandira for Stada is described as the name of the husband of his mother and Pandira the name of her lover. However, Hisda's opinion is questioned because her husband's name is Pappus ben Jehudah and, therefore, Stada must have referred not to the father but the mother. Again, the opinion is questioned because the mother was called Miriam, 'the dresser of women's hair'. The conclusion is that Miriam is the proper name and Stada the nickname because *stat du* means 'she has gone astray' from her husband.

---

31 BT Sanhedrin 67a and Shabbat 104b. See Peter Schäfer, 2007, *Jesus in the Talmud*, Princeton: Princeton University Press, pp. 15–19.

The rabbinic description of Miriam (in other words Mary) as a 'dresser of women's hair' appears to be a confused reference to Mary Magdalene, as the Aramaic words are *miriam m'gaddela nashaia*. The rabbis seem to be aware that the figure of Mary Magdalene was somehow related to the figure of Jesus, although they show little knowledge of her. Overall, the rabbinic writings have preserved only a very vague recollection of Jesus, who was seen as a dangerous heretic and deceiver, but extremely little was known of the historical figure – and even less of Mary.

Another example is found in *Toledot Yeshu* ('The generations of Jesus'), a polemic against Christianity perhaps written as early as the sixth century. Mary's pregnancy is described in terms of deception by a neighbour, Joseph Pandera, who pretends to be her husband, Yohanan. Mary is portrayed as an unwilling and innocent sexual victim and such that the doctrine of the Virgin Birth simply masked her adulterous pregnancy. 'At the close of a certain Sabbath, Joseph Pandera, attractive and like a warrior in appearance, having gazed lustfully upon Miriam, knocked upon the door of her room and betrayed her by pretending that he was her betrothed husband, Yohanan. Even so, she was amazed at this improper conduct and submitted only against her will.'[32]

For Christians, Jewish polemic reinforced the view of Jews as particular enemies of Mary. This is reflected in the Marian miracle tales, which depict Mary watching over all Christians and willing to intervene on their behalf. Marian tales commonly contain an anti-Jewish motif because, as well as defending Christianity, Mary was a bulwark against heretics and Jews. The sixth-century Syrian monastic writer John Moschus tells the story of a Jewish boy who lived with his family in Constantinople among Christians and went to school near Hagia Sophia. On one occasion, a great deal of bread and wine was left over from the Eucharist ceremony, and the school children, including the Jewish boy, ate what was superfluous. When the boy returned home, he told his father that he

---

32 A translation of *Toledot Yeshu* can be found at www.ccat.sas.upenn.edu/~humm/Topics/JewishJesus/toledoth.html. See Miri Rubin, *Mother of God*, op. cit., p. 74; Miri Rubin, 1999, *Gentile Tales: The Narrative Assault on Late Medieval Jews*, New Haven and London: Yale University Press, pp. 7–29.

had eaten communion bread and his father was seized with such anger that he threw him into a furnace. When his mother returned home, she found him in the fire and brought him out of the flames unharmed. The son told his mother that a woman dressed in purple told him not to be afraid, and both converted to Christianity, while the father, who refused, was burned.[33]

The miracle of the Jewish boy illustrates Mary's power over Jewish violence and contrasts her mercy against Jewish cruelty. The story also depicts the eventual Jewish acknowledgement of Christian truth by the conversion of the boy and his mother, a theme that became popular in many Marian stories and extended into later English literature (illustrated by the conversion of Shylock's daughter Jessica at the end of *The Merchant of Venice*).

The role of Jews as protagonists in English Marian miracle tales is also found in Geoffrey Chaucer's *The Prioress's Tale*. Although written in the fourteenth century, when in theory no Jews lived in England, the *Tale* demonstrates that the *Adversus-Iudaeos* tradition had become ingrained in contemporary English Christian culture. It recounts the story of a boy murdered by 'cursed Jews' who are eventually punished following Mary's miraculous intervention. Chaucer describes how a Christian boy was singing a hymn to Mary while walking through the Jewish quarter on his way to school. This chanting upset Jews who decided to have him killed:

And as the child gan forby for to pace,
This cursed Jew hym hente and heeld hym faste,
And kitte his throat, and in a pit hym caste.[34]

Music continued to rise from the boy's severed throat, and when his mother discovered him – still singing the hymn – she called on Christians to take vengeance. As the child was buried, thanks to Mary he rose to heaven.

---

33 Miri Rubin, *Mother of God*, op. cit., pp. 74–5.
34 Geoffrey Chaucer, *The Prioress's Tale*, at www.fordham.edu/halsall/basis/canterbu.txt

The depiction of Mary as *mater dolorosa*, the suffering mother, also provided an outlet for the *Adversus-Iudaeos* tradition as Jews were portrayed as responsible for Mary's suffering. Miri Rubin gives a number of examples, such as the following thirteenth-century Provençal poem in which Mary cries out to the Jew:

O Jew, cruel and criminal!
You have killed my good and beautiful son
Put me in the earth, we will both die.[35]

Yet not all medieval interpretations were polemical. Anselm, the eleventh-century Archbishop of Canterbury, differs from other medieval theologians, who ridicule the views of their usually fictional Jewish opponents. He addresses in *Cur Deus Homo?* Jewish objections such as how Mary remained a virgin after the birth of Jesus by answering with a question of his own. 'How is a crystal filled with the brightness of the sun without cracking?' he answered. Although it is unlikely that Anselm had contact with Jewish thinkers and his objections are literary devices, they are serious and sophisticated, and he treats Jews with respect.

Likewise, although most medieval Jewish writings about Christianity were also polemical, Judah ha-Levi's *Kuzari* was an exception. Ha-Levi, who lived around the same time as Anselm, wrote a fictitious dialogue between the king of the Khazars and a representative each from Aristotelianism, Christianity, Islam and Judaism. When the Christian stated his faith to the king, ha-Levi simply has the Christian say, 'the very last of the revelations was one in which the Divinity took a physical form. This form first manifested as a fetus in the womb of a virgin. She was from a family of Jewish royalty and she later gave birth to this entity. The child was visibly human but secretly divine.' Although the treatise allows ha-Levi to demonstrate the superiority of Judaism, he grants Christianity and Islam a place as *praeparatio messianica*, because they contain authentic Jewish elements.

---

35 Miri Rubin, *Mother of God*, op. cit., p. 255.

More emotional and polemical were the *piyyutim*, poetry of lament, that articulated Jewish suffering during the Crusades (eleventh to sixteenth centuries). The Jewish Chroniclers, who recounted the Crusaders' massacres, occasionally referred to Mary as they poured scorn on Jesus. Much of the Jewish polemic focused on the idea of God taking on flesh, experiencing gestation, birth and childhood. As the twelfth-century writer Joseph Kimhi wrote in *The Book of the Covenant*, 'How can I believe in a living God who is born of a woman, a child without knowledge and sense, an innocent who cannot tell his right from his left, who defecates, urinates and sucks from his mother's breast out of hunger and thirst, and cries when he is thirsty and whom his mother pities; and if she would not, he would die of hunger as other people do?'[36]

## Marian Bridges between Jews and Christians Today

Having examined the New Testament accounts as well as post-biblical Christian and Jewish writings, we will conclude with a brief reflection on how 'this Jewish woman' and 'this daughter of Israel' (as depicted by the 2004 document *Mary: Grace and Hope in Christ*) could remind Christians today of their close relationship with Jews and Judaism. A clue lies in the Christian liturgical calendar, in which the celebration of Mary on traditional holy days retains its original Jewish context and depicts her Jewishness. I will briefly offer three examples:

*The Presentation of Jesus* demonstrates Mary's observance of Judaism by her redemption of Jesus as her first-born. She presents Jesus in the Temple and, according to Luke, she is purified by the prayer of Simeon the Just.[37] The presentation of Jesus is attested to in the fourth century by the pilgrim Egeria and is generally

---

36 Miri Rubin, *Mother of God*, op. cit., p. 167. See also the thirteenth-century *Sefer Nizzahon Yashan* ('The Old Book of Polemic'), which advised its Jewish readers to 'know with certitude that Joseph had relations with her [Mary] in a normal manner and she bore his child'. See David Berger, 1979, *The Jewish–Christian Debate in the High Middle Ages: A Critical Edition of the Nizzahon Vetus*, Philadelphia: Jewish Publication Society of America.

37 Luke 2.22ff. See also Numbers 18.15.

celebrated on 2 February (although Armenian Christians observe the feast on 14 February).

*The Feast of the Circumcision*, on 1 January, takes place eight days after Christmas Day, but tends to be overlooked today because of its timing on New Year's Day (and perhaps also because of a focus on circumcision, which may seem unfamiliar to Christians). Yet this festival was popular for medieval and renaissance preachers and emphasizes Mary's willingness to accept Jewish tradition by having her son circumcised (as other Jewish mothers).

A third example is *The Presentation of the Blessed Virgin Mary*, which commemorates an event recounted not in the New Testament, but in the apocryphal Infancy Narrative of James. Mary's parents, Joachim and Anne, who had been childless, received a heavenly message that she would bear a child. In thanksgiving, they brought their daughter to the Temple to consecrate her to God. Mary remained there until puberty, at which point she was assigned to Joseph as guardian. This festival reminds Christians of Mary's close connection with the Temple in Jerusalem which, as we have seen, continued even after the crucifixion of Jesus.

These three examples illustrate that throughout her life Mary was an observant Jew and brought up Jesus as a Jew. He was the Jewish child of a Jewish mother, raised in a Jewish home and reared among Jewish traditions. The New Testament witnesses that throughout their lives, mother and son lived as Jews and among Jews.

Reawakening to the Jewishness of Mary will remind Christians (and Jews) of the Jewish origins of Christianity. Mary may have lived on the cusp of the divide between Judaism and Christianity, but however much Jews and Christians may differ about her significance, it is well overdue that they acknowledge that she was Jewish like her son, Jesus of Nazareth, that she lived her life as a Jew, among Jews, and followed a Jewish way of life. Mary was a Jewish mother.

# 7

# Bound by the Bible: Jews, Christians and the Binding of Isaac

### Introduction

As a Jewish scholar engaged in the study and teaching of Jewish–Christian relations for over 12 years, I have thought a great deal about the past history of Jewish–Christian relations, especially in relation to the Bible. During that time, I have noticed increasing interest being shown to both the Jewish context of the New Testament and to the influence of Jewish biblical interpretation on the formation and development of Christianity.

For understandable reasons, it has generally been assumed that Judaism influenced Christianity, but relatively little attention has been given to the other side of the same coin – the question of Christian influence upon Judaism. Did Christian teaching and interpretation influence the Jewish commentators? Did a two-way encounter develop? On the basis of a study of the Binding of Isaac, I will examine evidence for a meeting between Jewish and Christian interpreters during the first seven centuries CE.

You might ask what relevance this has to our impending discussion on covenantal identity. The answer is this: the existence of a two-way encounter provides a context to Jewish–Christian dialogue today and sets the scene for our conversation about covenant. At the foremost of our minds, of course, is the important and challenging *A Sacred Obligation*. Yet this document, as so many that have preceded it since the historic 1947 Seelisberg meeting, is based first on a Christian rediscovery of the fact that Christianity emerged from Judaism, and second (and more recently), an increasing reflection, particularly prevalent in the Roman Catholic Church, on the fact that the Jewish people remain part of God's covenant.

Today, Jewish–Christian dialogue takes for granted – thankfully – that Jesus, his family and his followers were Jewish; that he was born, lived and died a Jew; that the first Christians were Jews; that the New Testament is, for the most part, a Jewish work. We take this as our starting point, not as our goal. In other words, the emergence of Christianity from Judaism has become a platform upon which we open new conversations about the significance of shared values and teachings, many of which we have in common. The meaning and significance of covenant is one example.

My concern in this chapter is not to draw attention to one-covenant or two-covenant theories. Frankly, I am not sure how much this matters – what matters is exploring the *significance* of commonality and difference. In other words, to what extent do Jewish and Christian understandings of covenant shed light on Jewish–Christian relations? In this chapter, I will apply the same question to Jewish and Christian understanding of Scripture, and the answers will, I hope, provide an insight into Jewish–Christian relations in ancient times – and now.

This is significant for us because the Jewish–Christian encounter – what Paul calls the 'Mystery of Israel' – continued after the formative first couple of hundred years and still continues today. It continued (and continues) not only in terms of the Jewish influence on Christianity, but the Christian influence on Judaism. This influence is nowhere more apparent than in our approaches to Scripture.

The story of Abraham's attempted sacrifice of Isaac is one of the most well-known stories of the Bible. It has been an important passage for Judaism and Christianity from an early period. For Jews, from at least as early as the third century CE, the passage has been read on Rosh ha-Shana, the Jewish New Year. For Christians, from around the same period, the Sacrifice of Isaac was mentioned in the Eucharist prayers, and the story is read in the period leading up to Easter.

The focus of the biblical story concerns Abraham's relationship with God and how his faith in, and commitment to, God was demonstrated by his willingness to sacrifice his long-awaited son at God's command. Little attention was given to Isaac. Both the rabbis and the church fathers reflect a great deal on the story. Indeed, it is the central thesis of this chapter that neither Jewish nor Christian interpretations can be understood properly without reference to the other.

A study of biblical interpretation sheds light on Jewish–Christian relations because both Jews and Christians lived – and continue to live – in a biblically orientated culture. There are a number of similarities between Jewish and Christian approaches to Scripture. These include an insistence on the harmony of Scripture and an emphasis on the unity of the text. Consequently, many Jewish and Christian interpretations were understandable to adherents of both religions. This situation provides the context for the decision of exegetes, such as Origen and Jerome, to turn to Jewish contemporaries for help in translating biblical texts. Although it goes without saying that the rabbis and the church fathers developed their own distinctive literary methods, their approaches would not have prevented particular interpretations from being understood in both communities.

We will now consider some examples of Jewish and Christian interpretations of the Binding of Isaac, known in Hebrew as the Akedah.

### Genesis 22.1–2: God Tests Abraham

> **v. 1** And after these things God tested Abraham, and said to him, 'Abraham!' And he said, 'Here am I.' **v. 2** He said, 'Take your son, your only son Isaac, whom you love, and go to the land of Moriah, and offer him there as a burnt offering upon one of the mountains which I shall tell you.'

The church fathers shared with the rabbis a number of interpretations that explain the reasons for the test and illustrate a common exegetical framework in Jewish and Christian biblical interpretation. Examples include patristic and rabbinic concern with, and a desire to respond to, the charge that God desired human sacrifice.

Another shared interpretation explains that the Akedah enabled Abraham to be honoured throughout the world. Both the church fathers and the rabbis explained that the purpose of the Akedah was to exalt Abraham. For instance, the rabbis stated that the Akedah educated the world about the excellence of Abraham. One interpretation declares that the Akedah took place to 'make known to the nations of the world that it was not without good reason that I [God] chose you [Abraham]'.[1]

The election of Israel and rabbinic concern about the ongoing nature of God's covenant – this was a cause of anxiety for Jews as well as Christians! – provide the context for another interpretation, which considers whether the Akedah implied that God would be willing to break his covenant with Israel. If God were willing to ask Abraham to sacrifice his son, would God be willing to break his covenant with Abraham's children, the Jewish people?

The rabbis argue that God would not break his covenant with Abraham or his seed by quoting Psalm 89.35, 'I will not defile my covenant'. God's covenant with Abraham and his children (the Jewish people) will endure in perpetuity. This psalm was chosen because verses 30–39 describe how God ensures that David's seed will endure for ever. Even if Israel transgresses and is punished, 'My mercy will I not break off from him . . . My covenant will I not profane.' This rabbinic interpretation parallels the words of Pope John Paul II, who declared that Jews are the people of God of the Old Covenant, which has never been revoked by God, and are partners in a covenant of eternal love.

Another similarity shared by the church fathers and rabbis is that they sometimes asked the same questions of the biblical text.

---

1 Tanhuma Buber (TanB) Va-yera 46; Tanhuma Yelamdenu (TanY) Va-yera 22. Cf. TanB Behuktai 7; TanY Behuktai 5.

This occurred because both the rabbis and the church fathers were very close readers of the biblical texts and interested in the detail of Scripture. This is illustrated by Origen, who commended his community to 'observe each detail of Scripture, which has been written. For, if one knows how to dig into the depth, he will find a treasure in the details, and perhaps also the precious jewels of the mystery lie hidden where they are not esteemed.'[2] It is not entirely by chance that Origen uses the metaphor of 'digging' beneath the text to make sense of it. The metaphor also aptly describes rabbinic hermeneutical methodology and seeks to derive meaning from the detail of Scripture. For example, the term 'midrash' is derived from the verb 'to enquire'. Origen is representative of both the patristic and rabbinic traditions when he writes that 'the wisdom of God pervades every divinely inspired writing, reaching out to each single letter'.[3]

Both the rabbis and the church fathers were interested in God's choice of words, 'your son, your only son, whom you love, Isaac'. They asked the same question – Why did God not simply say 'Isaac'? – and came to the same conclusion, agreeing that the purpose of the drawn-out description of Isaac was to increase Abraham's affection. According to the rabbis, God's words not only indicated the extent of Abraham's love for Isaac, but also made the test even more severe. Their purpose was 'to make Isaac more beloved in his eyes'.[4] Gregory of Nyssa offered a similar interpretation, which can also be found in the writings of a number of church fathers: 'See the goads of these words, how they prick the innards of the father; how they kindle the flame of nature; how they awaken the love by calling the son "beloved" and "the only one". Through these names the affection towards him [Isaac] is brought to the boil.'[5]

Another example of a shared interpretation is the common use by Jewish and Christian exegetes of dialogue as a means of inter-

---

2 Origen, Homilies on Genesis (Hom in Gen) 8.1.
3 Origen, On the Psalms 1.4.
4 For example, GenRab 55.7; Pesikta Rabbati (PesR) 40.6. Cf. GenRab 39.9.
5 Gregory of Nyssa (Greg of Nys), On the Son of God and the Holy Spirit; Chrysostom (Chry), Homilies on Genesis (Hom in Gen); Romanos, On Abraham v. 2; Origen, Hom in Gen 8.2.

preting the verse. Both the rabbis and the church fathers used dialogue to explain the reason for God's command. The church fathers created an imaginary account of what Abraham might have said to God, but did not. The rabbis, on the other hand, constructed a conversation that Abraham did have with God. The shared use of dialogue offered a number of benefits, not least of which was to add a theatrical dimension to the sermon, which helped to retain the interest of the congregation. Chrysostom, known as the 'golden mouth' because of his skill as a preacher, emphasized the importance of maintaining the interest of a congregation, who tended 'to listen to a preacher for pleasure, not for profit, like critics at a play or concert'. He warned that if the sermon did not match their expectation, the speaker would leave the pulpit 'the victim of countless jeers and complaints'.[6]

The joint use of dialogue provides another example of a shared approach to Scripture. Gregory of Nyssa proposed the following imaginary words, spoken by Abraham to God:

Why do You command these things, O Lord? On account of this You made me a father so that I could become a childkiller? On account of this You made me taste the sweet gift so that I could become a story for the world? With my own hands will I slaughter my child and pour an offering of the blood of my family to You? Do you call for such things and do you delight in such sacrifices? Do I kill my son by whom I expected to be buried? Is this the marriage chamber[7] I prepare for him? Is this the feast of marriage that I prepare for him? Will I not light a marriage torch for him but rather a funeral pyre? Will I crown him in addition to these things? Is this how I will be a 'father of the nations' – one who has not produced a child?

Did Abraham say any such word, or think it? Not at all![8]

---

6 Chry, On the Sacrifices, 5.
7 This is one of many examples of imagery borrowed from Euripides' Antigone. Like Abraham, Antigone lamented the fact that she would have no wedding-song and that her marriage chamber would be her tomb.
8 Greg of Nys, On the Son of God.

The dialogue enabled Gregory to force the fathers in his congregation to consider what their reaction might have been had they received such a command. He suggests that, had Abraham hesitated and challenged God, his reaction would have been representative of that of the fathers in his congregation. However, as befits a theatrical performance, Gregory brings Abraham's imaginary questioning to an end with the closing statement that, unlike the fathers, Abraham said no such thing. He did not complain nor think similar thoughts. The dialogue enabled Gregory to exalt Abraham and promote him as a model to follow.[9] While fathers in Gregory's congregation would 'argue with the command', Abraham 'gave himself up wholly to God and was entirely set on [fulfilling] the commandment'.[10]

The rabbis also used dialogue in their interpretation and, like Gregory, developed an element of theatre:

God said to Abraham: 'Please take your son.'

Abraham said: 'I have two sons, which one?'

God: 'Your only son.'

Abraham: 'The one is the only son of his mother and the other is the only son of his mother.'

God: 'Whom you love.'

Abraham: 'I love this one and I love that one.'

God: 'Isaac.'[11]

The purpose of the rabbinic dialogue was quite different from that of Gregory. In addition to arousing the amusement of the audience,

---

9 Cf. Origen, Hom in Gen 8.7.
10 Greg of Nys, On the Son of God.
11 GenRab 39.9 and 55.7; BT Sanhedrin 89b; TanY Va-yera 22, TanB Va yera 44; PesR 40.6 and 48.2.

the interpretation reveals that Abraham either deliberately misunderstood the command or attempted to delay its implementation. While the rabbis offered a similar hermeneutical method – in other words, the use of dialogue – its purpose is in marked contrast to the conclusion of the church fathers, who did not once question Abraham's desire to fulfil God's command.

Fittingly enough, the value of comparing rabbinic and patristic commentaries is discussed in the recent Catholic document (2001) published by the Pontifical Biblical Commission entitled *The Jewish People and Their Sacred Scriptures*. Significantly, the document calls for Christians to learn about Judaism and how it retained its vitality and continued to develop for over 2,000 years after the birth of Jesus and, as far as Jewish interpretation of Scripture is concerned, it radically calls for the use of Jewish commentaries by Christians.[12] This continues the emerging trend noted in the Introduction that the Church has identified a need for Christians to learn about Judaism as it developed in post-biblical times. Interpretations of the Akedah serve as a good example.

The next interpretation we shall consider deals with the subject of priesthood, a well-known source of controversy between Jews and Christians. This disputed subject was central to the interpretations of both the church fathers and the rabbis although, not surprisingly, their conclusions were diametrically opposed. We will shortly see how interpretations of Genesis 22 illustrate significant differences between Judaism and Christianity in terms of covenantal identity.

The rabbis considered the subject of priesthood in a discussion of Abraham's response to God's command. In the following interpretation, Abraham asks God whether he had the authority to sacrifice Isaac and is told that he had already been appointed a priest as affirmed in Psalm 110.4:

---

12 *The Jewish People and Their Sacred Scriptures in the Christian Bible*, 2001, A.7.22, para 4, at www.vatican.va/roman_curia/congregations/cfaith/pcb_documents/rc_con_cfaith_doc_20020212_popolo-ebraico_en.html

> He [Abraham] said to Him, 'Sovereign of the Universe, can there be a sacrifice without a priest?' 'I have already appointed you a priest' said the Holy One, Blessed be He, 'as it is written "You are a priest forever"' (Ps. 110:4).[13]

The rabbis also considered Abraham's suitability for kingship as well as priesthood, concluding that he fitted the position of both:

> On two occasions Moses compared himself to Abraham and God answered him, 'do not glorify yourself in the presence of the king and do not stand in the place of great men' (Prov. 25:6). Now Abraham said, 'Here I am' – ready for priesthood and ready for kingship and he attained priesthood and kingship. He attained priesthood as it is said, 'The Lord has promised and will not change: you are a priest forever after Melchizedek' (Ps. 110:4); kingship: 'you are a mighty prince among us' (Gen. 23:5).[14]

The reason why Melchizedek is important to the rabbis is because the priesthood was taken away from him and bestowed upon Abraham.

The interpretations of Origen provide an interesting contrast. Origen begins by describing Isaac not only as the victim but also as the priest,[15] because whoever carried the wood for the burnt offering must also have borne the office of priest. Origen's interpretation was probably influenced by Philo, who stated that Abraham began 'the sacrificial rite as priest with a son as victim'.[16] Origen suggested that, as a result, Isaac was like Christ, yet Christ was a priest 'forever, according to the order of Melchizedek' (Psalm 110.4).[17]

Interestingly, in direct contrast to Origen's description of Isaac as equal to Abraham in terms of the sacrificial function, the rabbis

---

13 GenRab 55.7.
14 LevRab 25.6, BT Nedarim 32b; Midrash Tehellim on Psalm 76.3.
15 Origen, Hom in Gen 8.6.
16 Philo, On Abraham, 198.
17 Origen, Hom in Gen 8.9.

paid no attention to Isaac's suitability as priest. Rather, they emphasized his role in the sacrifice in terms of the offering itself and described him as 'a burnt offering without blemish' in accordance with the requirements of a burnt offering.[18]

Origen's reference to Psalm 110.4 is significant; it parallels the rabbis' quotation and, at the same time, emphasizes Melchizedek, an important figure in the early Church. Melchizedek's significance is illustrated by the fact that he is mentioned on nine occasions in the Letter to the Hebrews and highlights the superiority of Christ's priesthood over the Levitical priesthood.[19] Hebrews (followed closely by Cardinal Dulles) also quotes Psalm 110.4 to reveal the obsolete character of Jewish worship and ritual that followed the Levitical order. Since Christ was viewed as high priest 'after the order of Melchizedek' and 'not after the order of Aaron', Christ's priesthood was superior to that of the Levites.

The significance of Melchizedek and of Psalm 110.4, especially its apologetic overtones, would not have been lost on either Origen or the rabbis. As far as Origen was concerned, the eternal priesthood of Christ was foreshadowed by the priesthood of Abraham and Isaac, while in contrast the rabbis argued that Abraham, rather than Melchizedek, was a priest for ever and that this authority could not be transferred elsewhere. The rabbinic interpretation is a riposte to Christianity because if Moses, the greatest prophet of all, was not worthy to be called king and priest, no one else (i.e. Christ) could be king and priest.

As well as quoting Psalm 110.4, Origen also made the same comparison as the rabbis between Abraham (and Isaac) and Moses. Abraham, he stated, was superior to Moses because, among other reasons, he was not asked to remove his shoes when God gave him the command to sacrifice Isaac, whereas Moses was asked to remove his shoes when God spoke to him in the burning bush.[20] The rabbis, on the other hand, used the comparison to show that Abraham was suitable not only for priesthood but also for kingship, implying

---

18  GenRab 64.3.
19  Hebrews 7.1–11 and 17–21.
20  Exodus 3.5.

presumably that no other person could be chosen. Abraham, and by extension Jews, would retain this authority for ever – in other words, it could not be taken away or appropriated by another figure.

We can be confident in assuming these patristic and rabbinic interpretations illustrate an exegetical encounter because:

- the same scriptural quotations are used (i.e. Psalm 110.4; Exodus 3.4–5);
- the same literary form is used (i.e. a comparison between Moses and Abraham);
- the opposite conclusions are reached (i.e. Abraham is priest for ever; Christ replaces Abraham as priest);
- a well-known controversial theme is discussed (i.e. priesthood and authority).

This implies that a proper understanding of either Jewish or Christian interpretations, even in areas of disagreement, is dependent upon knowledge of both. This is symptomatic of the unique relationship between Judaism and Christianity – am I being too provocative to suggest that you cannot understand the one without the other?

## Genesis 22.6–8: Abraham's and Isaac's Journey to Moriah

> **v. 6** And Abraham took the wood of the burnt offering, and laid it on Isaac his son; and he took in his hand the fire and the knife. So they went both of them together. **v. 7** And Isaac said to his father Abraham, 'My father!' And he said, 'Here I am, my son.' He said, 'Behold, the fire and the wood; but where is the lamb for a burnt offering?' **v. 8** Abraham said, 'God will provide himself the lamb for a burnt offering, my son.' So they went both of them together.

In the interpretations of the church fathers, Isaac reverts back to the youth of the biblical story and is no longer the adult portrayed by the earlier post-biblical writings. This change is particularly noticeable when the patristic interpretations are compared with the rabbinic writings, which still consistently portray him as an adult. Jewish and Christian discussion concerning Isaac's age represents a clear example of an exegetical encounter. We begin with the church fathers.

Isaac was described by a number of church fathers as childlike. Cyril, for example, emphasizes Isaac's youth by describing him as 'small and lying in the breast of his own father'.[21] Origen explains how, during the tortuous three-day journey, Abraham viewed Isaac as 'the child who might weigh in his father's embrace for so many nights, who might cling to his breast, who might lie in his bosom . . .'[22] Eusebius comments that Genesis 22.3 'did not say, "a lamb", young like Isaac, but "a ram", full-grown, like the Lord'.[23] Each of these interpretations depicts Isaac as a boy.

Other church fathers, such as Chrysostom, portray Isaac as slightly more mature, but who nevertheless retained his youthfulness: 'Isaac had come of age and was in fact in the very bloom of youth.'[24] Gregory of Nyssa states that Isaac was old enough to be considered for marriage, when God commanded him to sacrifice his son. According to Gregory, Abraham had believed that when God summoned him (Genesis. 22.1), he was about to be told to prepare a marriage and the wedding chamber.[25]

Thus two opinions existed in the writings of the church fathers. The first saw Isaac as a child and the second viewed him as a youth or young man. It is clear that although there is a discrepancy between the two, the church fathers agreed that while Isaac

---

21 Cyril of Alexandria (Cyril of Alex), Glaphyrorum in Genesim (Glaph in Gen).
22 Origen, Hom in Gen 8.4.
23 Catena no. 1277. F. Petit, 1985, *La Chaîne sur la Genese*, Louvain: Peeters, pp. 236–7.
24 Origen, Hom in Gen.
25 Greg of Nys, On the Son of God. Although it is outside of our timescale, it is worth noting the description in the medieval collection of rabbinic interpretations, *Midrash Ha-Gadol*, which portrays Abraham preparing the altar like a bridegroom's father.

played an important role, he remained young and had not yet reached full adulthood.

The rabbinic position was quite different. The rabbis stated that 'Isaac was 37 years of age, when he was offered upon the altar'.[26] Another interpretation gave his age as 26 years,[27] and a third proposed 36 years.[28] It is significant that, while the precise age varied, the rabbis were consistent in their portrayal of Isaac as an adult. None of the rabbinic interpretations, in direct contrast to those of the church fathers, hinted that Isaac might have still been a child. For the rabbis, perhaps influenced by the portrayal of Isaac's age in the earlier post-biblical writings, Isaac was a fully developed and mature adult.

The figure of Isaac is a key by which to unlock the exegetical encounter. Not only was Isaac's age of interest, but Jewish and Christian exegetes also explored the significance of Isaac carrying the wood. The interpretations of the church fathers consider this in some detail. Unsurprisingly, they viewed it as a model of Jesus carrying the cross. Evidence of an exegetical association between the wood of the Akedah and the cross of Christ can already be seen at least as early as the second century CE. This is illustrated in the writings of Melito, bishop of Sardis, who lived in one of the oldest and possibly largest Jewish communities of Asia Minor. Melito points to a large number of parallels between Isaac and Jesus:

- Isaac carrying the wood to the place of slaughter was understood as a reference to Christ carrying the cross.
- Both remaining silent indicated their acceptance of the will of God.
- Isaac 'carried with fortitude the model of the Lord'.
- Isaac, like Jesus, knew what was to befall him.

---

26 GenRab 55.4, 56.8; TanB Va-yera 42 and 46; TanY Va-yera 23.
27 GenRab 56.8.
28 Targum Pseudo-Jonathan (Tg Ps Jon).

- Both Isaac and Jesus were bound.[29]
- Both were led to the sacrifice by their father, an act that caused great astonishment.
- Neither was sorrowful at their impending sacrifice.

Melito exhibits a twofold typological approach to interpreting the Akedah. First, the Akedah foreshadows the sacrifice of Christ, and second, the Akedah is incomplete. Isaac represents Christ and is a model of Christ, who was going to suffer. On the one hand, Isaac paralleled Christ; on the other, he looked forward to Christ.

For the church fathers, the Akedah represented a sketch that was required before the completion of the 'final picture'. Examples of typological interpretations are commonly found and Isaac's carrying of the wood is one of the most frequently mentioned. For instance, Irenaeus exhorted Christians to carry their cross with the faith of Abraham and like Isaac who carried the sacrificial wood,[30] and Origen commented 'that Isaac who carries on himself the wood for the sacrifice is a figure, because Christ also himself carried his own cross'.[31]

One of the consequences of the typological approach is an increasing emphasis on the figure of Isaac. This does not result in Abraham's significance being diminished, for he remains the model of faith par excellence; rather, Isaac's significance dramatically increased. While Abraham remained the model of faith, Isaac became the model of Christ. Thus, for example, Barnabas's brief reference to the Akedah is to Isaac, not Abraham, since Jesus 'fulfilled the type' that was established in Isaac.[32] Another example of an increasing emphasis on Isaac is found in the interpretation of Cyril of Alexandria, who explained that it was the promise

---

29 It is interesting that Melito used the Jewish description of Isaac being bound, which may be an example of his use of Jewish categories of thought as well as of exegetical influence.

30 Catena no. 1233, F. Petit, *La Chaîne sur la Genese*, op. cit., pp. 206–7; Irenaeus of Lyons, *Against the Heresies* 4, 5.4.

31 Hom in Gen 8.6.

32 Barnabas 7.3.

given to Isaac, not Abraham, that was fulfilled through the cross of Christ.[33]

The typological approach not only provided parallels between Isaac and Christ but also contrasts. The church fathers offered interpretations that stressed the anti-type, or the dissimilarities, between Isaac and Christ. Isaac pointed forward to the even more amazing deed in the sacrifice of Christ. These contrasts, such as Melito's comment that 'Christ suffered, [but] Isaac did not suffer', demonstrate, first, that the sacrifice of Isaac was not complete, and second, that the Akedah prefigured the future sacrifice of Christ. What is important is that Isaac was not sacrificed and remained only the model, waiting to be fulfilled by Christ.

Typology, then, was the reason why the church fathers viewed Isaac as a child. He represented an outline, an immature image of what lay ahead. The child (Isaac) was to be fulfilled by the adult (Christ). The rabbis, on the other hand, maintained that Isaac was an adult. His action was not to be interpreted in the light of any later event, but had significance in its own right.

Like the church fathers, the rabbis also commented on Isaac carrying the wood, and the following interpretation appears remarkably similar to those mentioned above:

'And Abraham placed the wood of the burnt-offering on Isaac his son.' Like a man who carries his cross (*Tzaluvo*) on his shoulder.[34]

What is even more surprising is that this interpretation is not found in a relatively unknown collection, but in one of the best-known rabbinic texts – Genesis Rabbah – which is also one of the oldest exegetical midrashim. Most unusually, no additional interpretation was offered by the rabbis to elucidate the brief comment. This was undoubtedly deliberate and surely betrays an exegetical encounter. This Christian interpretation, appropriated and modified by the rabbis, reminds me of the recent Jewish statement

---

33 Cyril of Alex, Easter Homilies, 5.
34 GenRab 56.3.

on Christianity, *Dabru Emet*, and particularly the assertion that 'Jews and Christians seek authority from the same book (Bible)'. An awareness of shared sacred Scriptures is not simply a modern phenomenon.

The reference to a cross (*tzaluv*) is an explicit reference to Christianity and represents one of the few occasions when a short comment was not expanded on. Concern about Christian reaction or censorship might explain why no further detail was provided; alternatively, much of the material in Genesis Rabbah was extremely popular, which might explain why such a controversial statement was retained: it was too well known to be easily deleted.

The rabbis depict Isaac as a mature adult who was willing to give up his life at God's command. Although he was associated with those who suffered, it was Isaac's willingness to suffer that was important. Even when the rabbis use the term the 'ashes of Isaac', they often preceded the discussion with the proviso 'as if it were possible'; in other words, as if Isaac had been sacrificed, but had not actually been. The emphasis was not on whether Isaac had actually been sacrificed, but on his willingness to be sacrificed; not on martyrdom, but on self-offering.

We notice another remarkable similarity between the rabbinic emphasis on Isaac willingly offering himself to his father and the interpretations of the church fathers in their interpretations of the Akedah. In their view, Jesus, like Isaac, was not forced by human hand to carry the cross but carried it freely. For example, Cyril of Alexandria stated:

> And the child, Isaac, was loaded with the wood for the sacrifice by the hand of the father until he reached the place of the sacrifice. By carrying his own cross on his shoulders outside the gates (John 19:17–21) Christ suffered, not having been forced by human strength into His suffering, but by His own will, and by the will of God.[35]

---

35 Cyril of Alex, Glaph in Gen.

The rabbis also emphasized that Isaac was not forced to offer himself as a sacrifice, but willingly gave himself to Abraham. For example, in one interpretation, the rabbis portray Isaac speaking to God as follows:

> Sovereign of the Universe, when my father said to me, 'God will provide for Himself a lamb for the burnt offering', I raised no objection to the carrying out of Your words and I willingly let myself be bound on top of the altar and stretched out my neck under the knife.[36]

Other interpretations suggest that because he was concerned that his fear of the knife would invalidate the sacrifice, he told his father to bind him well. Once again, the voluntary nature of Isaac's actions is emphasized.[37] It is Isaac's willingness to give up his life that provides the basis for this interpretation and appears to be a rabbinic response to the Christian teaching that Christ was willing to give up his life for Israel.

The willingness of Isaac to give up his life is reinforced by the rabbis' suggestion that he was informed in advance of the sacrifice and continued the journey with Abraham. 'One to bind and the other to be bound, one to slaughter and one to be slaughtered.' Unlike the church fathers, who laid stress on the fact that Abraham did not tell his son of the impending sacrifice, the rabbis argued that Isaac's awareness of what was to happen served to emphasize his full participation in the Akedah. According to the church fathers, however, Abraham gave no indication to Isaac of the impending sacrifice.

The emphasis on Isaac's self-offering led the rabbis to associate the Akedah primarily with Isaac rather than with Abraham (who remained the central figure for the church fathers). As a result, the biblical story became known in the Jewish tradition as 'The Binding of Isaac' rather than, for example, 'The Test of Abraham'. The rabbis suggested that because Isaac was a fully grown adult, in contrast to his father who was an old man, he must have meta-

---

36 Lamentations Rabbah, proem (LamRab Pr) 24
37 GenRab 56.8.

phorically 'bound himself' for, if he had so desired, he could have prevented his elderly father from binding him. Isaac's request to his father to bind him implied that he was not forced into it.

As I have shown, the church fathers applied this description to Christ, who willingly offered himself to be sacrificed. Isaac was a child, guided by his father and eager to fulfil the divine command, while Christ was a grown man who obeyed his Father, willingly gave up his life, and was not forced by human strength into the sacrifice.

Thus both the church fathers and the rabbis emphasized the importance of the principle of voluntary self-offering. It was their interpretation of the significance of the self-offering, rather than the fact of whether or not it took place, that was important and which accounted for differences in their interpretations. For the church fathers, the child Isaac was an outline of the adult Christ and, therefore, the self-offering of Isaac merely foreshadowed the saving action of Christ. For the rabbis, the self-offering of the adult Isaac was sufficient to provide benefit to Isaac's children (Jews) for future generations.

In their view, so willing was Isaac to give up his life that they described the Akedah in terms such as 'the blood of the binding of Isaac' (or 'the ashes of Isaac').[38] This is startling because the biblical account explicitly states that the angel stopped Abraham from harming his son and commanded him 'not to do anything' to Isaac.[39] An illustration can be found in the Mekhilta de Rabbi Ishmael:

> 'And when I see the blood, I will pass over you' (Exodus 13:12 and 25) – I see the blood of the Binding of Isaac. For it is said, 'And Abraham called the name of that place (the Lord will see)'. Likewise it says in another passage, 'And as He was about to destroy the Lord beheld and repented Him' (I Chronicles 21:15). What did He behold? He beheld the blood of the Binding of Isaac, as it is said, 'God will for Himself see to the lamb.'[40]

---

38 For example, GenRab 49.11; 94.5; LevRab 36.5; NumRab 17.2; Mekhilta de Rabbi Ishmael (MdRI) Pisha 7 and 11.
39 GenRab 56.7.
40 Pisha 7 and 11.

This interpretation clearly suggests that Isaac's blood was shed – an opinion repeated in the Mekhilta de Rabbi Shimon ben Yochai, which states that Isaac 'gave one fourth of his blood on the altar'.[41] The use of the terms 'the blood of the binding of Isaac' and 'the ashes of Isaac' imply that Isaac actually was sacrificed. Indeed, ashes would be all that remained of a burnt offering. According to the rabbis, blood and ashes were an intrinsic aspect of atoning ritual since biblical times,[42] and their adoption in rabbinic interpretations of Genesis 22 consequently link the Akedah to fasting, atonement[43] and the Temple. For example, there is a tradition that states the Temple was rebuilt where Isaac's ashes were found.[44]

Did the rabbis go so far as to suggest that Isaac died? Yes! The eighth-century CE Pirkei de Rabbi Eliezer states that Isaac did die and, soon after, experienced resurrection:

> When the sword touched his neck the soul of Isaac took flight and departed but when he heard the voice from between the two cherubim saying, . . . 'do not lay a hand' his soul returned to his body and [Abraham] set him free, and he stood on his feet. And Isaac knew the resurrection of the dead as taught by the Torah, that all the dead in the future would be revived. At that moment he opened [his mouth] and said, 'Blessed are You, O Lord, who revives the dead.'[45]

Like the rabbinic reference to carrying a cross, the interpretation of the death and resurrection of Isaac is clearly influenced by Christianity. The rabbis viewed the Akedah as redemptive and as illustrative of God's miraculous life-saving power, and cited the story in connection with the resurrection of the dead. 'Through the merit of Isaac, who offered himself upon the altar, the Holy One, Blessed be He, shall raise the dead.'[46]

---

41 Mekhilta de Shimon ben Yochai (MdRSbY) Va-yera 6.
42 For example, Jonah 4.6; Isaiah 58.5; Lamentations 3.16.
43 For example, GenRab 49.11; BT Ta'anit 16a; Targum 1 Chronicles 21.15.
44 BT Zebulun 62a.
45 Pirkei de Rabbi Eliezer, cht. 31.
46 Pirkei de Rav Kahana, Supplement, 1.20.

## Conclusion

Even though Jewish and Christian biblical interpretations are often put to different uses, we have seen that some interpretations offer examples of mutual awareness, influence and even encounter. The Binding of Isaac provides us with a text that is of significance for both Judaism and Christianity, and also therefore a text that helps us discover an exegetical encounter that took place many centuries ago, the echoes of which may still be heard and that continue to influence the Jewish–Christian encounter today.

Interestingly, Jewish and Christian interest in the Binding of Isaac remains as strong today as it was in the first six centuries CE. The biblical story continues to attract significant attention in theological writings as well as in the arts and literature. Modern writers have somewhat different concerns from those in late antiquity, but they ask similar questions of the biblical narrative and their writings demonstrate a continuing exegetical encounter. They are to a certain extent interrelated, which reinforces my main thesis: that Jews and Christians share not only a common biblical text, but also a common exegetical tradition.

For example, one the most prominent post-enlightenment Christian theologians, Søren Kierkegaard, wrote *Fear and Trembling*, a title chosen to describe Kierkegaard's feeling about Genesis 22. He describes Abraham as the 'knight of faith', because he was willing to carry out God's will. Kierkegaard has influenced generations of Jewish as well as Christian writers. Eliezer Berkovits refers to Kierkegaard when he addresses the challenge to faith posed by the Holocaust. Abraham makes not a leap of faith, he argues, but shows trust in God and in the continuing covenantal relationship between God and Israel. In his view, the 'very essence of trust consists not in "leaping" but in standing firm'.[47] He suggests that the Akedah is a story of faithfulness, because Abraham retains his faith in the covenant with God, which mirrors those Jews who retained their faith in God when they were forced to live in ghettoes and concentration camps.

---

47 Eliezer Berkovits, 1979, *Crisis and Faith*, New York: Sanhedrin Press, p. 124.

The Akedah has also been given attention by Israeli authors who view it as a metaphor for the sacrifice by fathers of their children to ensure the survival of Israel. The story illustrates the failure of fathers to protect their children. Yehuda Amichai wrote a poem called 'The True Hero of the Akedah', in which he identified the ram as the true hero of the biblical story, because it was the only figure in the biblical narrative that died. The angel and Isaac had gone home, and 'Abraham and God had long since gone'.

It has been suggested that Amichai might have been influenced by the First World War poet Wilfred Owen. In his famous poem, 'The Parable of the Old Man and the Young', Owen describes how the angel was too late to save Isaac. Commenting on the moment, when the angel called out to Abraham to stop the sacrifice, Owen writes, 'But the old man would not so, but slew his son – and half the seed of Europe, one by one'.

The exegetical encounters in late antiquity have consequences for contemporary Jewish–Christian relations. The writings of the rabbis and the church fathers provide the foundation for today's Christianity and Judaism, both of which are heavily influenced – if not dependent – upon the teachings and literature of the rabbis and the church fathers. When Jews and Christians read post-biblical interpretations, they discover a shared emphasis on the importance of certain biblical texts as well as a willingness to be open to, and to engage with, each other's teachings.

Is it too bold to suggest that the exegetical encounters that took place so long ago point the way forward today?

# 8

# The Sacrifice of Isaac (the Akedah) in Christian and Jewish Tradition: Artistic Representations

## Introduction

As we have seen, the Sacrifice of Isaac in Genesis 22 has been, and still is, the subject of much discussion in Christian and Jewish literature. It is generally examined from a literary perspective, but the focus of this chapter is to consider the story from the perspective of the artist. We should, of course, consider first whether the artist has been allowed to play a role at all in interpreting the story. In the past, scholars turned to Exodus 20.3–4:

> You shall not make for yourself a graven image, or any likeness of anything that is in the heaven above, or that is in the earth beneath, or that is in the water under the earth; you shall not bow down to them or serve them; for I the Lord your God am a jealous God.

This command has been interpreted to mean that Jews and Christians would automatically have opposed every form of figurative visual representation.

In support, scholars referred to Josephus, who was clearly hostile to images,[1] as well as to Tacitus, Pliny and others, who remarked on the absence of statues and images in Jewish cities and synagogues. Yet their writings were not necessarily typical.

---

[1] Josephus, *War*, 2.195; *Jewish Antiquities*, 17.151.

Even Josephus reported that there existed groups, such as the Hasmonean family in the first century BCE, who produced human representations.

As far as the rabbis were concerned, there were, as so often, differing views. For instance, there is the well-known story about R. Gamaliel II, head of Yavneh, who was criticized for going into a bath-house that boasted a statue of Aphrodite.² Many rabbinic passages make reference to the widespread existence of Jewish figurative art, but opposing views existed.³ The Targum mentions that figurative art in synagogues was approved as long as it was used not for idolatrous purposes but only for decoration:

> You shall not set up a figured stone in your land, to bow down to it, but a mosaic pavement of designs and forms you may set in the floor of your places of worship, so long as you do not do obeisance to it.⁴

Figurative art was also a significant part of everyday life in the early Church. Like the rabbis, the church fathers were concerned about the idolatrous nature of art in places of worship. For example, at the Council of Elvira in approximately 300 CE, the thirty-sixth canon stated that there should be no pictures in a church in case the object of worship was depicted on the walls (*picturas in ecclesia non debere, ne quod colitur et adoratur in parietibus depingatur*). Nevertheless, the early Church was not as hostile to art as has been almost universally assumed. Tertullian, like Rabban Gamaliel II,

---

2 Mishnah, *Avodah Zarah* 3.4: '"Why does thou bathe in the Bath of Aphrodite?" He answered, "One may not make an answer in the bath". And when he came out he said, "I came not within her limits: she came within mine!" They do not say, "Let us make a bath for Aphrodite", but, "Let us make an Aphrodite as an adornment for the bath". Moreover, if they would give thee much money thou wouldest not enter in before thy goddess naked or after suffering pollution, not wouldest thou make water before her! Yet this goddess stands at the mouth of the gutter and all the people make water before her. It is written, *their gods*, only; thus what is treated as a god is forbidden, but what is not treated as a god is permitted.'

3 Rabbinic acceptance of figurative art is found in Jerusalem Talmud (JT), *Avodah Zarah* 3.3, 42d and 3.2. Rejection is illustrated by the MdRSbY, *Ki Tisei* 31.

4 Tg P's Jon (to Leviticus 26.11).

states that figurative representation was not forbidden because it was not idolatrous.[5] Murray shows how later commentators misrepresented the church fathers by either ignoring or minimizing comments about the acceptability of figurative art.[6]

The first extant examples of Christian imagery appear as early as the beginning of the third century CE in funereal art such as the catacomb frescoes. The Dura-Europos chapel makes it clear that other forms of art, such as Christian iconographic paintings, appear from the mid-third century. Thus already a century before the Edict of Tolerance, art was an important element of Christian life and consequently artistic interpretations of the Bible became a significant feature of Christian exegesis. We can be certain, therefore, that figurative art plays an important role in the study of both Judaism and Christianity in late antiquity, and evidence exists to show that it fulfilled an important function in everyday life.

The Sacrifice of Isaac was one of a small number of popular biblical images found on glass, jewellery, amulets, seals and even ivory. However, this chapter will focus on representations depicted on mosaics and frescoes, in synagogues and churches, and in chapels and catacombs.

## The Sacrifice of Isaac in Christian Art

### The Sacrifice of Isaac in the Christian tradition

The Sacrifice of Isaac was a very popular subject for early Christian art and is found among a small number of selected biblical images. These include Noah, Daniel and Jonah, as well as the Raising of Lazarus and the Good Shepherd. It appears in many forms, including frescoes, sarcophagi and mosaics. In the classical writings of the church fathers there are a number of references to its portrayal. Gregory of Nyssa, for instance, wrote:

---

5 Tertullian, Against Marcion, 2.22.
6 Charles Murray, 1977, 'Art and the Early Church', *Journal of Theological Studies*, vol. 28, pp. 313–45.

> I have seen many times the likeness of this suffering in painting and not without tears have I come upon this sight, when art clearly led the story before the sight.[7]

Augustine also discussed this subject:

> The deed is so famous that it recurs to the mind of itself without any study or reflection, and is in fact repeated by so many tongues, and portrayed in so many places, that no-one can pretend to shut his eyes or his ears from it.[8]

For many years, scholars of early Christian art, like those of Jewish art, have been excessively influenced by trends in the *written* tradition. As a result, images were understood primarily in terms of the crucifixion of Christ. Scholarly debates centred on whether the artistic representations should be understood in terms of typology or in terms of deliverance. Some scholars suggested that because patristic writings do not offer a detailed typological understanding of the relationship between the figures of Isaac and Jesus until after the conversion of Constantine (312 CE), typological representations could not appear in art before then. They therefore placed an emphasis on deliverance[9] and pointed out, for example, that Isaac was never portrayed as bound on the altar until the mid-fourth century. More recently Jensen, who has offered a critique of the existing scholarship, has questioned the validity of arguments based on a few existing pre-Constantinian images

---

7 Greg of Nys, On the Son of God.
8 Augustine, Reply to Faustus the Manichean, 22.73.
9 Isabel van Woerden, followed by other scholars, argued that 'since the greater part of the early monuments has to do with death and burial the emphasis seems to lie on "deliverance in need" . . . From 313 onwards it appears transformed'. Isabel van Woerden, 1961, 'The Iconography of the Sacrifice of Abraham', *Vigiliae Christianae*, vol. 15, pp. 214–55.

and challenged the accuracy of their dating. Jensen also suggested typology could be discovered in early Christian literature.[10]

The weakness of all these arguments is that they are based upon the literary tradition. They do not begin from the image but from the word, implying that the image supports the word rather than the word supporting the image. None of the works I have read examine artistic interpretation in its own right, as illustrated by Jensen, who suggests that 'homilies and liturgies were the most important sources from which early Christian imagery derives meaning for its audience'.[11] While I agree that it is important to evaluate the context of the image, I would suggest that this is already the third stage. The first stage is to examine the image on its own; the second is with reference to the biblical story; the third is with reference to the context. After these three stages are completed, we are then in a position to offer a full and thorough examination of the artistic interpretation.

Before we discuss Christian artistic representations of the Sacrifice of Isaac, it is worthwhile to summarize the views expressed in the writings of the church fathers. This will enable us to see the similarities as well as the differences between artistic and literary interpretation. There are a number of important developments in the interpretation of the Sacrifice of Isaac in early Christian literature. First, it is worth noting that there are only a few explicit references to the story in the New Testament, suggesting that it does not play an important role. Abraham's faith is seen in terms of obedience and trust in response to suffering; the significance of the Sacrifice of Isaac lies in supporting the authors' exhortations to remain faithful to the Christian gospel. From the end of the first century onwards, we find the development of a typology. Beginning with the Epistle of Barnabas, developed in detail by Melito (Bishop of Sardis

---

10 Robin Jensen states that the altar was a place not where the victim was killed but where the offerings were laid – that is, after the killing. 'By the late fourth century the illustrators may simply have forgotten the earlier practices or sensed no need to make the scene look familiar or correct to their audience.' Robin Jensen, 1994, 'The Offering of Isaac in Jewish and Christian Tradition', *Biblical Interpretation*, vol. 2, p. 105.

11 Ibid., p. 106.

160–70 CE) and Origen (185–251 CE), the story of Isaac was compared to the story of Jesus. Typology was used by Christians to support a number of assertions, such as the view that biblical events foretold the coming of Christ. Similarities between Isaac and Jesus were highlighted: both carry wood to the place of slaughter; both assent to the will of God; both are led to the sacrifice by their father. In sum: Isaac was a model of the Christ, who was going to suffer.

Typology did not solely link Isaac to Christ, but also Christ to the ram. According to Melito, there was a parallel between the sacrifice of the ram in substitution for Isaac and the sacrifice of Christ as a ransom for mankind. The deliverance of Isaac by the slaughter of the ram foreshadowed the deliverance of mankind by the death of Christ.[12] Origen developed this further and, in a discussion on the verse 'a ram was caught by its horns' (Genesis 22.13), suggested that the ram represented the flesh, which suffered, while Isaac represented the Word, that is the Spirit, which remained incorruptible.[13] This verse lent itself to christological interpretation. Typical are the words of Basil of Seleucia (Bishop of Seleucia 440–68 CE), 'the ram caught in the plant was like Christ on the Cross'.[14] Other fathers such as Tertullian (200 CE) interpreted the bush to represent the crown of thorns.[15]

In Christian literary tradition, there is an emphasis on the fact that Jesus did die while Isaac did not. The Sacrifice of Isaac was itself a model of the sacrifice to come, a pale shadow of the future event. Jesus died; Isaac was saved. This type of exegesis emphasized the efficacy of the Christian gospel and, at the same time, replied to Jews who emphasized the Akedah as atoning in its own right. In addition, the Sacrifice of Isaac became bound up with early Christian liturgy. It was (and still is) used in the Eucharist ceremony, in the Easter liturgy and in the prayer for the dying. Finally, there exists a modest literary tradition, which portrays Sarah in a more significant role. This tradition is found primarily

---

12  Melito, 'Fragment 10', in S. Hall (ed.), 1979, *Melito*, Oxford: Clarendon Press, p. 76.
13  Origen, Hom in Gen 8.
14  Basil of Seleucia, Oration 7.
15  Tertullian, Against the Jews, p. 13.

in Syriac writings where she is described by Ephrem, for example, as willing to give up her son. Ephrem compares Sarah to Mary and points to a number of parallels, including both questioning God, both having miraculous births and both giving up their sons.[16]

## *The Sacrifice of Isaac in funereal art*

Funereal art does not simply consist of imagery associated with the fears and sorrows surrounding death. The images illustrate examples of divine intervention and express the desire that God may show the same favour to the deceased. Funereal art is divided into two sections – sarcophagi and catacomb paintings. Both proclaim the same hope – that the deceased may find happiness beyond the grave.

The earliest catacomb frescoes illustrate the theme of deliverance. For instance, the Callixtus catacomb in Rome (**Plate no. 1**) is dated from the first half of the third century CE. Abraham and the child Isaac are offering thanks for their deliverance. In the foreground, to their right, stands the ram, erect and proud. Quite clearly, the three main characters are Abraham, Isaac and the ram. Behind the ram are an olive tree and the wood for the sacrifice.

Another (late) third-century fresco located in the Catacomb of Priscilla in Rome (**Plate no. 2**) illustrates the same theme. It shows the boy, Isaac, carrying wood, and Abraham, according to van Woerden,[17] pointing to the fire on an altar. I would suggest, however, that Abraham is pointing to a tree. Nearby (presumably) stands the ram. Abraham is looking up to the heavens, perhaps hearing the word of God.

Two other fourth-century frescoes have very similar images. Although the similarity between them has not been noticed, I would suggest that there is a link. In the late third- or early fourth-century fresco in the Catacomb of Peter and Marcellinus (**Plate no. 3**), Abraham holds a knife in his raised right hand and

---

16 See S. Brock, 1974, 'Sarah and the Aqedah', *Le Muséon*, vol. 87, pp. 67–77.
17 Isabel van Woerden, 'The Iconography of the Sacrifice of Abraham', op. cit., p. 222.

at his feet is the child Isaac – naked, kneeling and bound for the sacrifice. The ram appears on the far side of the altar, which is alight, and the image is above a scene of the paralytic carrying his bed. Cubiculum C in the Via Latina (**Plate no. 4**), from the late fourth century, reproduces this image almost exactly. The altar has wood burning upon it; to the left is the ram, which appears to be looking for Abraham, who has a sword in his hand. Abraham is looking at something (an angel? the voice of God?) while Isaac is kneeling with his hands behind his back. Below is a representation of a servant with a donkey, possibly at the foot of the mountain.

All the examples of catacomb art emphasize the aspect of deliverance and do not indicate typology. This artistic interpretation either parallels, or perhaps even precedes, the early Christian prayer for the dead, which contained a cycle of deliverance. The earliest reference to this prayer is from the seventh century, although it is believed to have originated much earlier.

In addition to frescoes, we commonly find images of the Sacrifice of Isaac in early Christian sarcophagi. The Mas d'Aire Sarcophagus from the third century is the earliest. It shows the child Isaac, bound and kneeling. Abraham grasps his hair from behind and raises the knife to strike. Abraham's eyes are not on Isaac but the ram, which is standing at his side (almost nuzzling him). The ram appears eager to be sacrificed. Sarcophagi provide a variety of altars – sometimes Isaac is bound upon an altar, sometimes next to the altar, and sometimes, as at Mas d'Aire, there is no altar. Sarcophagi also fail to portray the ram caught by its horns or caught in a bush. Thus the evidence suggests that the christologically interpreted ram was not of importance to the artists. None of the sarcophagi show Isaac carrying wood as a model of Christ carrying the cross. The concern of the artist is significantly different from that of the literary exegete as there is little interest in typology.

Many of the sarcophagi, which are dated from the fourth and fifth centuries, provide evidence of post-biblical interpretation that cannot be found in contemporary Christian literature. For instance, a number depict two or three assistants or onlookers, which implies that the Sacrifice of Isaac did not take place in secret. This may also indicate that artistic interpretations contain traditions that would have otherwise been lost. For example, in a Luc-de-Bearn sixth-century sarcophagus, a man and woman are watching the sacrifice. The woman, who has her hand to her mouth to indicate dismay, may be Sarah. The appearance of Sarah at the sacrifice is mentioned in the poems of Ephrem of Syria and other Syriac writings but rarely in the Greek or Latin fathers. She is also portrayed in the chapels of the El Bagawat (Egypt) necropolis, which are dated from the fourth century CE.

In El Bagawat the story is depicted several times. It is found in the chapel of Exodus, where Abraham stands next to an altar, which is already alight. On the other side of the altar stands Isaac with his arms crossed, while his mother Sarah stands at his side under a tree and lifts her arms to the sky in an act of prayer. The ram also stands under a tree, and the hand of God is seen to the right of the name Abraham. In the fifth-century Chapel of Peace (also known as Byzantine Museum), we find the Sacrifice as one in a number of images (**Plate no. 5**); these include the symbols of peace, justice and prayer, alongside Adam and Eve, the ark with Noah and his family, Jacob, Daniel and the lions, the annunciation and Paul and Thecla (described in the apocryphal *Acts of Paul* as a convert and companion of Paul).

In the image of the Sacrifice of Isaac a hand (of an angel?) is throwing two knives in the air and another is held by Abraham. Isaac, a child, is unbound and his arms are outstretched, perhaps in supplication. Archaeologists have suggested that mother and son are holding incense.[18] Sarah has a halo around her head, and Abraham, Isaac and Sarah are all identified. A tree/plant with flowers is drawn on the right-hand side, probably to balance the tree on the left. As a result of the inclusion of Sarah in the representation of the Sacrifice of Isaac, the artists of El Bagawat expand the biblical story and portray its significance for the whole family. They do not follow the biblical account, which depicts the story in terms of a father–son relationship, but offer their own interpretation.

---

18 A. Fakhry, 1951, *The Necropolis of El-Bagawāt in Kharga Oasis*, Cairo: Services des Antiquités de l'Égypte, p. 73.

## The Sacrifice of Isaac in church mosaics

There are two famous Byzantine mosaics in sixth-century Ravenna – San Vitale and San Apollinare in Classe. Both associate the Sacrifice of Isaac with the offerings of Abel and Melchizedek, which are linked to the liturgy of the Eucharist. For example, in San Vitale we find a portrayal (**Plate no. 6**) of the mosaics of Cain and Melchizedek sharing a church altar, near which are placed the bread and wine. Nearby are the three angels announcing the promise of a son while Abraham offers them a calf and Sarah stands in the doorway of a tent. To the right is a representation of the Sacrifice of Isaac.

Isaac is kneeling on the altar and Abraham's sword is raised, but the hand of God appears to prevent the sacrifice. At Abraham's feet is the ram looking at Abraham, striking a typical christological pose. These mosaics flank the real church altar where the Eucharist was celebrated. The biblical figures are linked by the following prayer:

> Be pleased to look upon these offerings with a gracious and favourable countenance, accept them even as you were pleased to accept the offerings of your just servant Abel, the sacrifice of Abraham, our patriarch and that of Melchizedek, your high priest – a holy sacrifice, a spotless victim.

This prayer and its reference to the Sacrifice of Isaac came into use by the fourth century CE, and it is clear that artistic interpretation paralleled the liturgical development. In early Christian liturgy, the Sacrifice of Isaac is mentioned during the offertory prayers, associated with the epiclesis (a petition for the descent of the Holy Spirit upon the bread and wine), alongside Abel, Noah, Moses and Aaron, and Samuel. The reading of Genesis 22 was an important element of the lectionary cycle and was mentioned by Egeria during her visit to Jerusalem in the late fourth century CE.[19]

---

19 J. Wilkinson, 1971, *Egeria's Travels: Newly Translated (from the Latin) with Supporting Documents and Notes*, London: SPCK.

The Easter cycle was the major feature of the liturgical year and Genesis 22 was commonly read on the Thursday before Easter. Considering that readings were often quite different from church to church, this consensus is quite remarkable. We should also note that the homilies of Melito (*Peri Pascha*) as well as the interpretations of Gregory of Nyssa (*In Sanctum Pascha*) and Athanasius (Epistle Six), each of which discuss the Sacrifice of Isaac, were all composed at Easter.

Thus in early Christian art, the Sacrifice of Isaac focused on deliverance and the Eucharist as represented by images of the communion and divine deliverance. Images are found in funereal art because the story was understood in relation to death and resurrection. The ram is significant in artistic interpretation, not because of any christological significance, but because of its allusion to deliverance. The Isaac–Christ typology is rarely found in artistic interpretation during this period, and when it is found it is associated with liturgy, not literature.

## The Akedah in Jewish Art

### The Akedah in the Jewish tradition

In classical rabbinic thought, there are a number of significant developments in the interpretation of the Akedah. First, Isaac becomes a central character and is no longer a passive victim. For the rabbis, he is a grown man and joins Abraham and God as a principal actor. Isaac allows himself to be offered upon the altar and such is his stature that he is able to 'view the perfection of the heavens'. He becomes the paradigm of martyrdom as he voluntarily offers himself to be sacrificed.

Second, in Jewish thought, the Akedah was linked to Passover as well as Rosh ha-Shana. Jubilees, the targums and the Mekhilta link the Passover lamb with Isaac's sacrifice. Isaac is placed on the same theological level as the Passover lamb. 'By a lamb Isaac was redeemed; by a lamb Israel was redeemed.' In a comment on Exodus 12.13, 'And when I see the blood (of the Passover lamb), I will pass over you' we are asked, 'What does God see?' We are told, 'The blood of Isaac's Akedah'.[20] The association with Rosh ha-Shana eventually triumphed and the Akedah became part of the new-year liturgy. In the Mishnah, it is closely associated with the concept of human atonement and divine forgiveness.[21] Indeed, in the targums (and elsewhere) we are told that whenever the children of Israel ask for forgiveness, God will remember the Akedah.

Third, even though Isaac was not sacrificed, the Akedah is regarded by the rabbis as a true sacrifice and wholly acceptable to God. The reason why the sacrifice was not completed was because the son was exchanged for the ram – in the words of the rabbis, 'although the deed was not carried out He accepted it as though it had been completed'.[22] For the church fathers, the son was exchanged because Isaac was not acceptable and it was not yet time to complete the test. In the words of Melito, 'Christ suffered, whereas Isaac did not suffer for he was the model of the Christ who was going to suffer.'[23]

Fourth, Mount Moriah is linked to the Temple. Following 2 Chronicles 3.1, Josephus and the rabbis associate the site of the Akedah with the site of the Temple.[24]

## The Akedah at Dura-Europos

When the Dura-Europos synagogue was uncovered in 1932, a new era in the study of Jewish art began, because the synagogue contained the earliest known cycle of biblical images (244–5 CE). Externally, Dura-Europos was modest in the extreme, being located in a private house and not comparing architecturally with Sardis. However, its uniqueness lay in its interior, for its wall decorations were second to none (**Plate no. 7**). The city itself was founded by Seleucus I in approximately 300 BCE and remained a

---

20 MdRI, Pisha 7. Cf. Targum to the Song of Songs, 1.13.
21 Mishnah, *Ta'anit* 2.4, 'He who answered Abraham on the mountain of Moriah, may He answer you and hearken this day to the voice of your pleading.'
22 GenRab 55.5.
23 Melito, 'Fragment 9', in S, Hall (ed), 1979, *Molito*, op. cit., p. 74.
24 Josephus, *Jewish Antiquities*, 1.226; 7.333; GenRab 55.7.

Seleucid outpost until the mid-second century BCE, when it was captured by the Parthians. For the next three centuries, it flourished as a centre for east–west trade. In the second century CE, it was captured by the Romans, until it was destroyed by the Persians in 256 CE and never resettled.

Dura-Europos contained 16 temples catering to the needs of an eclectic pantheon of Roman, Greek and Persian gods. It also contained a modest Christian chapel. In the synagogue there are more than 30 scenes covering the four walls of a 40-ft room. Several images surround the Torah shrine (on the base level):

- Esther;
- Elijah restoring life to the son of the widow of Zarephath (1 Kings 17);
- Samuel anointing David (1 Samuel 16);
- Moses as a baby floating in the Nile and rescued by the daughter of Pharaoh (Exodus 2).

To illustrate the elaborateness of the paintings, I have selected part of the Ezekiel Cycle (**Plate no. 8**). The painting is based on Ezekiel 37 and the description is of the resurrection of the dead. God is symbolized by the hand and Ezekiel is depicted three times, as he receives divine commission. At the prophet's feet lie numerous body parts instead of the bones mentioned in the biblical text, and beside him the mountain has split in two with an olive tree on each peak. To the right is a fallen house, illustrating an earthquake during which the resurrection would occur, and to the right of one mountain stands Ezekiel, whose right hand is raised to the hand of God stretched out to him. His left hand points to the three lifeless bodies beside which stands a female figure who probably represents the *pneuma* providing the *ruah* (both terms mean 'breath' or 'spirit') to revive the dead. Further right stands Ezekiel, again pointing to the three *psychai*, butterfly-winged goddesses, who renew the lifeless bodies.

In addition to the richness of the painting, I would emphasize two features that are depicted elsewhere – the hand of God and the gesture of Ezekiel's right hand. In this gesture, the palm is turned outward and the second and third fingers are held extended while the thumb, the fourth and fifth fingers are doubled back against the palm. The most familiar analogy is the Christian gesture of benediction, found commonly in Byzantine art. The archaeologist Kraeling associates this gesture with general pagan practice,[25] and Goodenough links it with the Sabazius cult, suggesting that it was a cultic gesture – just as Sabazius brought immortality to his followers, so Ezekiel worked a comparable miracle by bringing life to the corpses.[26]

The image of the Akedah (**Plate no. 9**) is found over the opening for the ark, the Torah shrine. This was the most prominent feature of the synagogue and was always built on the Jerusalem orientated wall. The ark of the scrolls (*aron*), which housed the Torah, stood inside the shrine and several images and inscriptions refer to it. This feature became so well known that John Chrysostom accused Jews of exaggerated veneration for their 'Holy Ark'. In Dura-Europos, the Torah shrine belonged to a phase of synagogue decoration that was distinct from, and earlier than, the other paintings and must therefore be examined separately. Unlike the other images, which were replaced during repainting, it was retained and not touched.

Our eye moves from left to right, focusing first on the menorah, the palm branch (*lulav*) and citron (*etrog*). At the centre we see the Temple, and to the right the Akedah. The symbols of Sukkot and the Temple suggest a vision of a future feast of Tabernacles to be celebrated in Jerusalem by all nations as described in Zechariah 14.

The Temple could be viewed as much in terms of the future as well as the past, and could represent a new Temple to be built on the site of the destroyed Temple. The synagogue building had been dedicated 170 years after the destruction of the Second Temple,

---

25 Kraeling refers to two Roman senators who made the gesture when they addressed magistrates before a tribunal. C. H. Kraeling, 1956, *The Synagogue: The Excavations of Dura-Europos Final Report VIII, Part 1*, New Haven: Yale University Press, p. 194.

26 E. Goodenough appears to have been the first to make this suggestion. See E. Goodenough, 1953–68, *Jewish Symbols in the Greco Roman Period*, vol. 10, Princeton: Princeton University Press, p. 184.

and restoration was a realistic dream, as Julian the Apostate would make clear 120 years later.

Let us examine the characters in more detail. A primitively drawn Abraham, knife in hand, stands resolutely with his back to the onlooker, as does the little bundle of Isaac lying on the altar. This is emphasized by the shock of black hair that we see on both figures rather than facial features. Isaac is clearly a child and appears unbound. In the distance a tiny figure, also with a shock of black hair, stands before a tent, with an opening on the top. This figure has been variously interpreted as Abraham's servant,[27] Ishmael,[28] Abraham himself in his house,[29] and Sarah.[30]

However, arguments are readily available to render each proposal unlikely. For instance, the figure appears to be wearing a man's clothing and is therefore unlikely to be Sarah; he is not wearing the same clothes as Abraham (and therefore unlikely to be him); the traditions concerning hostility between Isaac and Ishmael were influenced by the rise of Islam (seventh century) and so rule out Ishmael. My own opinion is that the character is Isaac. The tent is touching the altar and is thus linked to Isaac. The figure is the same size as Isaac and both have black hair. We should also remember that Sarah died after the Akedah and that the first time Isaac was comforted was when Rebecca was brought to him and taken into his mother's tent (Genesis 24.67). The open hand of God appears beside the tent. This representation of the hand is the earliest surviving image. The hand symbolizing the *bat kol*, the divine voice, is mentioned in many literary works, including both rabbinic and non-rabbinic writings.[31]

Although I have pointed out a number of developments and changes to the biblical story, such as Isaac being unbound, the

---

27 C. H. Kraeling, 1956, *The Synagogue*, op. cit., p. 343.
28 P. Prigent, 1991, *Le Judaisme et l'Image*, Tübingen: Mohr, p. 116.
29 Du Mesnil du Buisson, 1939, *Les Peintures de la Synagogue de Doura-Europos*, Rome, pp. 24–7.
30 E. Goodenough, 1991, *Jewish Symbols*, op. cit., vol. 4, Princeton: Princeton University Press, p. 189.
31 For example, Josephus, *Jewish Antiquities*, 1.13; 4.233; Philo, *On Abraham*, 32, 176; TanB Va-yera 23; Pirkei de Rabbi Eliezer (PRE), ch. 31.

third character and the presence of the hand of God, the representation of the Akedah at Dura-Europos is closer to the biblical text than many other representations. For instance, the ram is behind Abraham and Isaac is lying on the altar.

In the lower foreground, the rather large ram waits patiently, tethered to a tree. The Hebrew text is probably the source for this illustration for, unlike the Septuagint, it describes the ram as 'behind' Abraham. It is centrally located, which emphasizes its importance to the artist. Although the rabbis suggested that the ram had been created on the sixth day of creation and had been waiting since for its moment of destiny,[32] they did not give a great deal of attention to it, nor did they describe it being tethered to a tree. There appears no Jewish literary source for this artistic interpretation. However, the fourth-century Coptic Bible mentions a 'ram tied to a tree',[33] which may indicate the existence of a Jewish artistic interpretation retaining a tradition no longer found in Jewish literature. This suggestion is supported by artistic evidence elsewhere, both Jewish and Christian, which depicts the ram tied to a tree.

## The Akedah at Beit Alpha

In 1929, an excavation in the eastern Jezreel valley, just south of Galilee, unearthed a mosaic floor of a sixth-century synagogue. A sequence of three scenes, bordered like a carpet, make their way to the Torah located in a wall orientated towards Jerusalem (**Plate no. 10**). These scenes are:

- the Akedah;
- the zodiac with Helios and his four horses;
- the ark.

---

32  Tg Ps Jon, Mishnah, *Pirkei Avot* 5.6; PRE, ch. 31.
33  A. Ciasca (ed.), 1885, *Sacrorum Bibliorum Fragmenta Copto-Sahidica*, I, Rome: Musei Borgiani, p. 22.

At the entrance, a mosaic lion and a bull flank bilingual inscriptions, which in Greek acknowledge the artists and in Aramaic thank the donors. These inscriptions date the synagogue to the reign of Justin (518–27).

The narrative plane (**Plate no. 11**) moves from left to right, from the donkey to the ram to Isaac; from the accompanying youths to Abraham. The Hebrew, naturally, moves from right to left identifying Isaac, the ram and the command issuing from the hand of God. Abraham throws Isaac into the fire on the altar while the hand of God, as at Dura-Europos, prevents the sacrifice. A large ram is tied to a tree and is standing erect. The ram, following the biblical story, is caught by one horn and tied to a tree.

The ram is significant for it is even bigger than the tree, emphasizing the importance of the ram to the artist – in contrast to Jewish literary tradition. The fact that early literary tradition, except in a few instances, does not refer to the role of ram is especially noteworthy, when we see that later rabbinic writings such as Pirkei de Rabbi Eliezer of the eighth century discuss the ram in detail. This development might be viewed as having been influenced by artistic interpretations such as depictions of the ram looking for Abraham (see below). Since this literary development occurred much later than the artistic representations, we could justly argue that the literary interpretation is based upon the artistic.

In the mosaic, two servants, one of whom has a whip in his hand, hold the ass, which has a bell around its neck. Above, the hand of God presents some interesting features for it extends from a dark area, which looks like the end of a sleeve and is described by archaeologists as a 'cloud'.[34] Perhaps the most remarkable figure is the child Isaac, floating beyond Abraham's fingertips. Does Abraham hold him close, or at arm's length in preparation for the loss? Isaac is suspended and his arms are crossed but not bound, swinging precariously between the flames of the sacrifice and his obedient father. The trial is still Abraham's – but not unequivocally, for we focus on the helpless, dangling figure of the son.

---

34 E. Sukenik, 1932, *The Ancient Synagogue of Beith Alpha*, Jerusalem, p. 40.

The ambiguity of the mosaic raises the question of Isaac's willingness. As mentioned earlier, the Jewish literary tradition emphasizes Isaac's voluntary obedience by describing his maturity and giving his age as 37 years.[35] The artistic portrayal of Isaac as a child suggests that he has little active role in the sacrifice. It is even possible to view him as a reluctant participant. Once again, we can see that artistic interpretation possesses its own emphasis, significantly different from the literary interpretation.

## *The Akedah at Sepphoris*

In 1993, a well-preserved early fifth-century synagogue was discovered in the city of Sepphoris, capital of Galilee. Judah ha Nasi lived in Sepphoris in the early part of third century, bringing with him institutions of Jewish leadership, and the city enjoyed a renaissance. Sepphoris had 18 synagogues at the time of Judah ha Nasi and remained the capital of Galilee until the end of the third century CE, when the Sanhedrin and Patriarchate moved to Tiberias. A general overview shows that it was a Jewish city similar to the pagan cities of the region – there were no clear separate neighbourhoods on the basis of religious, social or economic criteria.

The mosaic floor is the most important part of the synagogue that has survived, covering the building's entire floor and consisting of 14 panels. The central band depicts the zodiac. Each of the 12 signs, which surround the sun, is identified with the name of the month in Hebrew. Most have images of young men, the majority clothed but some naked; the four seasons are depicted in the corners accompanied by agricultural objects characteristic of each season.

The Akedah is depicted in two panels and the first (**Plate no. 12**) has a Greek inscription, 'be remembered for good, Boethos (son) of Aemilius with his children. He made this panel. A blessing upon them. Amen.' The word 'amen', written in Hebrew, ends

---

35  GenRab 56.8.

the benediction. The archaeologists Weiss and Netzer suggest that the panel shows the two servants, who remain at the bottom of the mountain with the ass. One holds a spear while his other hand is raised slightly in a gesture we have already seen made by Ezekiel in Dura-Europos. The other servant sits under a tree, at the foot of the mountain, holding the ass.[36]

There is no other instance of a servant making the special sign and I would suggest an alternative explanation is required. Rather than a servant, I propose that the figure is Abraham instructing the servant to remain behind. The shoes of Abraham appear to be exactly the same as those portrayed in the right-hand panel (**Plate no. 13**). This panel is badly damaged and depicts the head of an animal tethered to the tree by its left horn; below are two upturned pairs of shoes – a small pair for Isaac and a large pair for Abraham. In another small section of the panel, Weiss and Netzer suggest, there exists the blade of a vertically held knife with traces of a robe to its right.

The small pair of shoes again emphasizes that, for the Jewish artistic exegetes, Isaac was not the youth of the biblical story nor the adult of rabbinic literary interpretation. His shoes indicate that he was a boy. The idea of removing shoes is probably derived from other biblical passages such as Moses at the burning bush (Exodus 3.5) and Joshua in the presence of the Lord's Host (Joshua 5.15). The artist has clearly decided that when Abraham and Isaac reached the sacred spot they would have removed their shoes out of respect for the sanctity of the site. Once again we notice an artistic interpretation that is not found in the literary tradition. The artistic interpreter provides evidence for an alternative tradition, perhaps in a debate about the significance of the removal or non-removal of shoes.

In conclusion, the first point to make is that the Akedah was part of an extensive tradition of synagogue decoration. It is highly unlikely that the existence of the Akedah in three synagogues was mere chance. Second, in artistic interpretation, far more than in

---

36 Zev Weiss and Ehud Netzer, 1996, *Promise and Redemption: A Synagogue Mosaic from Sepphoris*, Jerusalem: The Israel Museum, pp. 30–1.

literary interpretation, the Akedah is linked to the Torah and the Temple. Artistic interpretation associated the Akedah with the Jewish people's redemption and reminded God of his promise to Abraham and his children. Third, Isaac is always portrayed as a child. Artistic interpretation does not follow literary interpretation, but remains consistent with the biblical story; it emphasizes the helplessness of the child and not the voluntary self-offering found in literary exegesis. Fourth, artistic interpretation expands the role of the ram. Whereas in the biblical story the ram appears to have been on Mount Moriah by chance, the artistic representation emphasizes the significance of the ram through its size and prominent position. Artistic interpretation offers its own insight into the development of the Akedah in Jewish thought. An examination of the literary interpretation on its own, although illustrative of the diversity of literary tradition, does not tell the whole story.

## Conclusion

The diversity of Jewish and Christian representations of the Sacrifice of Isaac is striking. For many, the biblical story has been viewed solely from a literary perspective, but I have shown that artistic representations are extremely important and should not be ignored. Indeed, artists who created images based on the biblical story should be viewed as exegetes in their own right for they have offered their own interpretations, some of which conflict with the better-known interpretations found in the writings of the church fathers or the rabbis.

An investigation of the biblical story from the perspective of the artist shows a number of significant similarities between the representations of Jewish and Christian artists. Indeed, a number of these show variations from the biblical text, such as the ram being tied to a tree (rather than caught by its horns in a bush). We should not be surprised to discover that Christian artistic interpretation sometimes follows the same pattern as Jewish (or vice versa). These similarities simply indicate a positive interaction between Jew and Christian and, as such, provide a good example of Jews and Christians working together in ancient times.

It is worth emphasizing the rich diversity of Jewish and Christian artistic interpretations of the Akedah. Some scholars and religious leaders have criticized these artistic representations, seeing in their diversity the possibility of danger and error. Jean D'Espagne, a seventeenth-century French Protestant theologian, was annoyed that in the contemporary Bible, 'Isaac is here painted on his knees before an altar and Abraham behind him holding a knife in his hand, which is lifted up to give the blow. But this picture is false and doth bely the holy History.'[37] Martin Luther also complained 'the picture commonly painted about Abraham about to kill his son is incorrect'.[38] In fact, from the very beginning the portrayal of the Akedah exhibits not errors but interpretations of the biblical text. Sometimes these interpretations mirror liturgical or literary developments. On other occasions, they are not found elsewhere.

Artistic interpretation is bound to the biblical text but has developed its own rules of interpretation. It must be examined as a form of biblical exegesis and is critical to any study of biblical interpretation. In the words of the church father Gregory of Nyssa (and this is valid for Jewish as well as Christian art), there are occasions when 'art clearly led the story'.[39] For this, students of biblical interpretation should be truly grateful.

---

37 J. D'Espagne, 1655, *Shibboleth: Or the Reformation of severall places in the Translation of the French and English Bible*, London, pp. 148–9.

38 Jaroslav Pelikan (ed.), 1964, *Luther's Works, vol. 4: Lectures on Genesis Chapters 21–25*, St Louis, MO: Concordia, p. 110.

39 Greg of Nys, On the Son of God.

# 9

# The Jewish People and Their Sacred Scriptures in the Christian Bible

## Introduction

After so many centuries of unhappy and traumatic relations between Christians and Jews, a new era has begun in the last couple of generations. Started by pioneers in the first half of the twentieth century, such as Claude Montefiore and James Parkes, the relationship received renewed and widespread attention as a consequence of the Shoah (Holocaust). This resulted in a general awareness of the immensity of the burden of guilt that the Church carried not only for its general silence, with some noble exceptions in 1933–45, but also because of the *Adversus-Iudaeos* tradition, which led to a 'teaching of contempt' towards Jews and Judaism, that the Church pursued for so many centuries.

As Jules Isaac showed immediately after the war, it was this that sowed the seeds of hatred and made it so easy for Hitler to use antisemitism as a political weapon. Cardinal Ratzinger, who wrote a warm foreword commending the document discussed below, shows awareness of this legacy, stating that 'the Biblical Commission could not ignore the contemporary context, where the shock of the Shoah has put the whole question [of the Scriptures] under a new light'.

The significance of *The Jewish People and their Sacred Scriptures in the Christian Bible (JPSSCB)* to Jewish–Christian relations is best understood in the context of earlier statements by the churches and meetings between Christians and Jews. There are a number of key moments in the second half of the twentieth century that illustrate Christian reassessment of Judaism. One need only mention the meeting at Seelisberg in 1947, which brought together Christians and Jews who issued a historically significant ten-point statement and agreed to found the International Council of Christians and Jews. Another important milestone was the creation of the World Council of Churches (WCC) in 1948 in Amsterdam and the growing ecumenical movement, which attempted to break down the barriers between the churches. Regular WCC meetings since then have contributed to the Christian reassessment of relations with Jews and Judaism.

In 1965, *Nostra Aetate* was published and in its wake came a rich growth in Catholic–Jewish dialogue. A key paragraph states:

> Since the spiritual patrimony common to Christians and Jews is thus so great, this sacred Synod wants to foster and recommend that mutual understanding and respect which is the fruit above all of biblical and theological studies as well as of fraternal dialogues.

According to Edward Flannery, *Nostra Aetate* 'terminated in a stroke a millennial teaching of contempt of Jews and Judaism and unequivocally asserted the Church's debt to its Jewish heritage'.[1] Most importantly of all, it ushered in a new era, fresh attitudes, a new language of discourse never previously heard in the Catholic Church concerning Jews. The concept of a dialogue now entered the relationship.

However, the success of the document was dependent upon 'things still to be worked out'. There were a number of questions left unanswered and, looking back over 40 years, what *Nostra Aetate* achieved was a series of possibilities that can be seen in such phrases as 'God holds the Jews most dear' and 'mutual understanding and respect'. These concerned issues such as preaching, Christian antisemitism and the interpretation of Scripture. For instance, *Nostra Aetate* stated that nothing was to be taught or

---

1 Edward Flannery, 1988, 'Seminaries, Classrooms, Pulpits, Streets: Where We Have to Go', in R. Brooks (ed.), *Unanswered Questions: Theological Views of Jewish–Catholic Relations*, Notre Dame, IN: University of Notre Dame Press, pp. 128–9.

preached that was 'out of harmony with the truth of the Gospel'.[2] The year 1965 was clearly still too soon to consider why texts in Matthew and John tended to excuse the disciples, but accuse more and more Jews by excluding more and more Romans. As I shall explore below, *JPSSCB* sets this question as one of a number of tasks in its exploration of the relationship between Scripture and the Jewish–Christian encounter. It aims to answer Cardinal Ratzinger, when he asks in the preface, 'has not the New Testament itself contributed to creating a hostility towards the Jewish people that provided a support for the ideology of those who wished to destroy Israel'?

Since 1965, both Protestant denominations and the Roman Catholic Church have issued significant statements on the Jewish–Christian relationship. The former include:

- The Rhineland Synod in 1980 (Evangelical Church in the Rhineland), entitled *Towards a Renewal of the Relationship of Christians and Jews*;
- The Lambeth Conference of 1988 (Anglican Communion), entitled *Jews, Christians, Muslims: The Way of Dialogue*;
- The Evangelical Lutheran Church in America in 1994, entitled *Declaration to the Jewish Community*;
- The Leuenberg Church Fellowship (consisting of the Reformation churches in Europe) in 2001, entitled *The Church and Israel*.

These statements demanded that Christianity abandon its historical religious animosity and misleading caricature of Judaism, which were admitted as wrong. As a result, Christianity began to shift from what was, for the most part, an inherent need to condemn Judaism, to a need to condemn Christian anti-Judaism.

The Roman Catholic Church has also produced a number of significant statements on Jews and Judaism since Vatican II. All

---

[2] Austin Flannery (ed.), 1981, *Vatican Council II: The Conciliar and Post Conciliar Documents*, Dublin: Dominican Publications, p. 741.

were issued by the Pontifical Commission for Religious Relations with the Jews and provide the basis for *JPSSCB*:

- 1974 *Guidelines and Suggestions for Implementing the Conciliar Declaration Nostra Aetate.*
- 1985 *Notes on the Correct Way to Present the Jews and Judaism in Preaching and Catechesis.*
- 1998 *We Remember: A Reflection on the Shoah.*[3]

This process has not led to a separation from all things Jewish, but in fact to a closer relationship with 'the elder brother'. Thus as far as a Christian contribution to antisemitism is concerned, the Protestant churches and the Roman Catholic Church instead of being part of the problem, have now become part of the solution. We have travelled a great distance from the time of my parents' generation, which felt so abandoned during the Holocaust and for long afterwards, when Jews wondered whether they would ever be accepted as part of humanity. It hardly seems conceivable that only one or two generations have passed since then.[4]

During this transformation in relations, it is possible to trace a gradual emergence of two themes with increasing clarity, both of which are becoming more and more significant in the Jewish–Christian encounter. Indeed, it is my view that they will remain central to the contemporary Christian encounter with Judaism. First, the documents point out that the history of Judaism did not end with the destruction of the Second Temple, but developed an ongoing innovative and living religious tradition. Second, they point out that Christians need to understand Judaism as a living

---

3 For the statements, see www.jcrelations.net

4 *We Remember* is somewhat different from *Nostra Aetate*, *Guidelines* and the *Notes*. While roundly condemning antisemitism, the Vatican had until then largely avoided the question of the Holocaust. In 1987, in the wake of controversy over the Pope's reception of Austrian President Kurt Waldheim, who had been an active Nazi, the Vatican promised to issue a document. *We Remember* stresses the evils of antisemitism, although it did not go as far as the French bishops who stated that 'it is important to admit the primary role played by the consistently repeated anti-Jewish stereotypes wrongly perpetuated by the Christians in the historical process that led to the Holocaust'.

faith and must strive to learn by what essential traits Jews define themselves in the light of their own religious experience.

For example, the 1985 *Notes on the Correct Way to Present the Jews and Judaism in Preaching and Catechesis* calls on preachers and catechists to 'assess it carefully in itself and with due awareness of the faith and religious life of the Jewish people as they are professed and practised still today'. This instruction is one of the criteria by which we need to judge the 2001 document – to what extent does *JPSSCB* show an appreciation of the modern Jewish understanding of Scripture? In other words, does Christianity appreciate Judaism on its own terms or does the old theology of *Adversus-Iudaeos* continue in more subtle ways?[5]

This means we need to explore the difference between Christian respect and reverence for Judaism and appropriation or replacement of Judaism. Is it possible – and perhaps we should also ask, is it desirable? – to expect Christians to integrate living Judaism to some extent into their identity? This desire, doubtless, lies behind the canonization of Edith Stein in 1999. As far as the Pope was concerned, her canonization made the suffering of Jews understandable to the majority of Catholics and teaches that an attack on Jews was an attack on the Church. One of the goals of the canonization was to develop a sense of communion with the Jewish people. However, a concern expressed by some Jews and Catholics represents the negative side of such integration – the appropriation of Jewish suffering by Christians.

It is clear from the above example that the modern Christian–Jewish encounter requires great patience. Yet in a very short space of time (the last 40 years), the Roman Catholic Church has produced a remarkable series of documents, which have not only repudiated its anti-Jewish theology but have reversed it. The Jewish

---

5 This is neatly illustrated by Yossi Klein ha Levi's remarkable portrait of an encounter with a Sister of the Beatitudes in Israel in *At the Entrance to the Garden of Eden*. The danger of the reassertion of the 'old theology', the sister informs the author, is illustrated when Christians simply say '"thank you, Jewish people, for giving us the Bible. Thank you for being the people of Jesus". But that's archaeology. Am I ready to encounter Judaism as it is or just for nostalgia?' *At the Entrance to the Garden of Eden*, 2002, New York: HarperCollins, p. 203.

people are no longer viewed as cursed but blessed. *JPSSCB* represents another key stage in the development of a new Christian understanding of Judaism.

*JPSSCB* represents current Roman Catholic teaching on the Jewish–Christian relationship in the context of biblical scholarship, and in the foreword states that it aims to 'advance the dialogue between Christians and Jews with clarity and in a spirit of mutual esteem and affection'. It is the first statement on Jewish–Christian relations issued by the Pontifical Biblical Commission. This is significant because it illustrates that consideration of the Christian–Jewish encounter extends beyond the Pontifical Commission for Religious Relations with the Jews. It is the concern of the Church as a whole.

The document is divided into three parts.

1. The first explains how the 'sacred Scriptures of the Jewish people are a fundamental part of the Christian Bible' and how the New Testament writings acknowledge that the Jewish Scriptures have a permanent value as divine revelation.
2. The second part examines key themes that link both the Jewish and Christian Scriptures.
3. The third addresses New Testament attitudes to Jews and Judaism.

## Sacred Scriptures of the Jewish People as a Fundamental Part of the Christian Bible

The first section tackles what the Pope has identified as the resurgence of Marcionism and emphasizes that the New Testament should not be viewed in opposition to the Old. Indeed, the Jewish Scriptures (generally used as an alternative to the term 'Old Testament') form an integral part of the Christian Bible (interestingly, at no point does the document refer to the Catholic Bible). In the second century CE, Marcion had argued, albeit unsuccessfully, that Christianity should reject the Jewish Scriptures (as well as most of the Gospels). The tension between the Scriptures is, therefore, as old as Christianity itself. The early Church insisted simultaneously on the continuity and the discontinuity of the relationship between the 'Old Testament' and the 'New Testament'. *Continuity* centred upon the claim that the God of the Hebrew Bible was the same as the God of Christ. *Discontinuity* derived from the belief that the Hebrew Bible pointed to a future saving event – to Christ. The use of terms such as 'continuity' and 'discontinuity' is also common in *JPSSCB*, but with one significant difference – neither term implies that Jews have lost their 'ownership' of their 'Sacred Scriptures'. Rather, Christianity and Judaism share a common heritage, 'the Sacred Scripture of Israel' (para. 10), which is no longer viewed as solely owned by the Church.

The ongoing Jewish 'right' to the Jewish Scriptures has significant implications for the present day and future Christian relations with Israel, for it rejects the claims of some Christians that Christianity has replaced Judaism as the New Israel. Acknowledgement of Jewish 'ownership' of the Scriptures marks another important step by the Roman Catholic Church in its abandoning of the 'teaching of contempt' and unease about its *Adversus-Iudaeos* heritage. The traditional teaching is based on the writings of the church fathers, as evidenced by Justin Martyr (d.160), who argued that the Church had taken over the Hebrew Scriptures from Judaism because only Christianity could offer the correct interpretation:

> Let all of us Gentiles come together and glorify God, because He has looked down upon us; let us glorify Him by the King of glory, by the Lord of hosts. For He hath taken pleasure even in the nations, and He receives the sacrifices more gladly from us than from you . . . I think that by these arguments I shall be able to persuade even those who are of slight intelligence. For the words have not been fitted together by me, nor adorned by human art, but they were sung by David, proclaimed as good news by Isaiah, preached by Zechariah, written down by Moses. You recognize them, Trypho? *They are laid up in your scriptures, or rather, not in yours but in ours, for we obey them, but you, when you read, do not understand their sense* [my italics].[6]

---
6 Dialogue with Trypho, 29.

Thus the Church has historically taught that the Jewish Scriptures did not belong to Jews, but had become the property of the Church and that Jewish interpretations were false as only Christianity offered the correct interpretations.[7] This view is no longer acceptable within the Roman Catholic Church. Even when *JPSSCB* uses the terms 'Old Testament' and 'New Testament' it emphasizes that the Church 'has no wish to suggest that the Jewish Scriptures are outdated or surpassed. On the contrary, it has always affirmed that Old Testament and the New Testament are inseparable' (para. 19). Misunderstanding these terms illustrates an ignorance – that the document aims to overcome – of the deep ties linking the New Testament to the Old, an ignorance that is based on the prejudice that Christians have nothing in common with Jews. Thus the document emphasizes 'the authority of the Jewish Bible as Divine revelation' (para. 1) so that the relationship between the two is not undermined. Again and again, it stresses the dependence of the New Testament upon the Old, regularly using the phrase 'the New Testament, in continuity with the Old' (e.g. paras 32 and 84 and elsewhere), and concludes that 'without the Old Testament, the New Testament would be an unintelligible book, a plant deprived of its roots and destined to dry up and wither'.

As a result, the document states, it is impossible to express the 'mystery of Christ without reference to the Jewish Scriptures' (para. 7). Jesus' human identity is determined on the basis of his bond with the people of Israel and with the Old Testament, as illustrated, for example, by his taking part in the synagogue and Jewish religious life. Significantly, the document calls for Christians to learn about Judaism and how it retained its vitality and continued to develop for over 2,000 years after the birth of Jesus. As far as Jewish interpretation of Scripture is concerned, it

---

7 Irenaeus, another second-century theologian, also focused on the relationship between the Hebrew Bible and the early Church. In Book 4 of *Against the Heresies*, he refutes the argument put forward by Marcion and other Gnostics that the Hebrew Scriptures and the New Testament were opposed to one another. His response to Marcion's criticisms became the basis for the standard patristic refutation of internal and external criticism and consists of treating difficult passages as *types* and *allegories* and claiming a unity of the Testaments.

radically calls for the use of Jewish commentaries by Christians (para. 22). This continues the emerging trend that the Church has identified a need for Christians to learn about Judaism as it developed in post-biblical times.

However, its courage in making a radical step is somewhat undermined by its failure to put this into practice. For example, *JPSSCB* commonly quotes from texts found at Qumran, which represent the Dead Sea Scroll community, in order to portray mainstream Jewish views, contemporaneous to Jesus. At best, it is questionable to state that 'the clearest expression of how Jesus' contemporaries interpreted the Scriptures are given in the Dead Sea Scrolls' (para. 1.D.1). Such an opinion may have been forthcoming, because the Pontifical Biblical Commission possesses more experts on the Dead Sea Scrolls than on rabbinic Judaism, but the lack of references to mainstream (rabbinic) Judaism indicates a serious weakness. The Dead Sea Scroll community did not at any time represent mainstream Judaism, and it would have been better to acknowledge that it represents a minority tradition within Judaism (closer to John the Baptist than Jesus). The demand – repeated in *JPSSCB* and commended in earlier Catholic documents – that a good understanding of Judaism is, according to the 1974 *Guidelines*, essential for the formation of Christian identity and 'a right relationship with Judaism', remains unfulfilled.

An example of this exaggerated concern with Qumran can be seen in the document's explanation of the Jewish understanding of covenant and its emphasis on the significance of the leader of the Dead Sea Scroll community, the Teacher of Righteousness, rather than on rabbinic explanations (para. 39). In fact, there is only one brief quotation from the rabbinic literature in the whole document (a brief mention of Hillel (para. 79)), which consists of over 100 pages of text and nearly as many pages of footnotes.

In its defence, one could argue that because the beginnings of rabbinic Judaism are shrouded in mystery and the earliest written texts are dated from the second century CE, the Pontifical Biblical Commission might have decided against making reference to the rabbinic writings. However, the strength of the oral tradition and the similarity between many of Jesus' statements and the words of the rabbis – the 'Golden Rule' being a famous example – demand that the document exhibit an awareness of the rabbinic contribution. In other words, the commendation to take Jewish commentaries seriously should have been implemented.

By failing to do so, *JPSSCB* inadvertently ignores contemporary scholarship, which is becoming increasingly aware of the interaction between Jewish and Christian biblical interpreters over the first few centuries.

This weakness is reinforced by the way the document tackles the Jewish understanding of Torah. For many hundreds of years Christians have identified Torah solely with 'Law' (as a result of its translation in the LXX as *nomos* and in the Vulgate as *lex*). The term 'Law' fails to depict the full meaning of the Hebrew word (the root of which means 'teaching'), which includes 'Law' – but much more besides. The document discusses the development and observance of Torah in Judaism and although it refers to post-biblical writings, limits itself to Baruch and Ben Sira and fails to mention the rabbinic understanding of Torah (para. 43).

One final example is worth mentioning – the surprising omission of the rabbinic context in the section that deals with prayer in the New Testament. In a discussion about the 'Our Father', the document simply notes that the formulas 'resemble Jewish prayer . . . but with an unparalleled sobriety' (para. 49). Even a brief mention of the 'Our Father' prayer in its Jewish context should refer to the rabbinic writings, since it has been shown that each line of the 'Our Father' prayer contains a parallel in the rabbinic literature. This most Jewish of prayers is an excellent example of how it is impossible to appreciate fully New Testament passages without their proper Jewish context.

## Key Themes in the New Testament and in the Jewish Scriptures

The second section examines key themes that link both Jewish and Christian Scriptures. It begins by explaining that the relationship between the Old and the New Testaments is based on reciprocity – on the one hand, the Old Testament has to be read in the light of the New; on the other, the Old needs to be read in the light of Jesus Christ. This approach causes difficulty because it can be overly dependent upon a typological or allegorical interpretation of Scripture. Neither *Nostra Aetate* nor the *Guidelines* commented on issues associated with typology, and the *Notes* simply highlighted the existence of a problem. The *Notes* (1985) explained that the Church had traditionally resolved the problem of the relation between the Old and New Testaments by means of typology, but admitted that this caused unease and was a sign of a problem unresolved. The *Notes* warned that 'we should be careful to avoid any transition from the Old to the New Testament which might seem merely a rupture' (para. 12).

*JPSSCB* tackles this problem squarely and is an important development in Roman Catholic teaching on interpretation of Scripture. It reiterates the point that 'the New Testament cannot be fully understood except in the light of the Old Testament' (para. 21), but acknowledges that links between the Old and the New were abused and that Scripture could be 'severed' from their context. As a result, 'interpretation became arbitrary' (para. 20). The document points to the dangers of a 'fundamental' approach to Scripture, stating that it 'would be wrong to consider the prophecies of the Old Testament as some kind of photographic anticipation of future events' (para. 21), particularly messianic prophecies. The emphasis on fulfilment of biblical prophecy can be seen not only in the writings of some Christians, but also of some fundamentalist Jews. For example, what was once viewed as an interpretation about the nature of the biblical word and promise has for some in the situation of Israel now become concretized in a contemporary event. *JPSSCB* refutes this approach to biblical interpretation.

The document suggests that one of the ways Catholics can overcome an unhealthy dependence upon typological interpretation is by increasing their knowledge of the rabbinic literature and the Jewish approaches to the Bible. This recommendation is based on a startling statement, that explores the value of Jewish approaches to Scripture:

Christians can and ought to admit that the Jewish reading of the Bible *is a possible one, in continuity with the Jewish Sacred Scriptures from the Second Temple Period* [my italics], a reading analogous to the Christian reading which developed in parallel fashion. Both readings are bound up with the vision of their respective faiths, of which the readings are the result and expression. Consequently, both are irreducible. On the practical level of exegesis, Christians can, nonetheless, learn much from Jewish exegesis practised for more than two thousand years, and, in fact, they have learned much in the course of history. For their part, it is to be hoped that Jews themselves can derive profit from Christian exegetical research (para. 22).

These words are both bold and significant. Catholics are now told that they should take into consideration rabbinic and contemporary Jewish interpretations of the Old Testament. They are also told that the Old Testament contains a divine revelation unrelated to the coming of Christ and Christianity. This was not only valid for the Hebrews at the time of its writing, but is still valid for contemporary Judaism. By stating that Jewish interpretation of Scripture is possible – I am told 'valid' is an appropriate understanding – the Pontifical Biblical Commission is applying the Pope's oft-repeated comment about the 'covenant remaining with the Jews' to the interpretation of the Jewish Scriptures. If the covenant remains with the Jewish people, alongside Christians, their interpretation of Scripture must, at the very least, remain 'possible'. Thus the document formally acknowledges themes that the Pope himself has long advocated.

Of course, the document does not deny the truth of the Christian interpretation of Scripture, but allows room for the validity of Jewish interpretation which, regardless of the lack of references to such Jewish interpretations mentioned above, is a major step forward in the Christian reconciliation with Judaism. It therefore contributes significantly to the creation of theological space required for a genuine interfaith encounter.

This section also devotes some time to the closely connected themes of covenant and election and discusses their place in both the Christian and Jewish Scriptures. Of all the New Testament passages considered, one of the most commonly cited is Romans 9–11, which (not coincidentally) has also been central to John Paul II's teaching about the Jewish–Christian relationship and the identity of the *verus Israel* (true people of Israel).

Once again we notice a significant development in *JPSSCB* in comparison with previous statements. *Nostra Aetate* presented the Church as the new people of God. The *Guidelines* avoided mention of supersessionism, although it warned against stereotypical descriptions of the Old Testament and Judaism as a religion of justice, fear and legalism in contrast to the New Testament and Christianity as a religion of compassion, mercy and love.[8] The *Notes* presented Jews as 'the people of the God of the Old Covenant, which has never been revoked' (para. 1). The new document moves the discussion on.

It begins by acknowledging a divergence of opinion about the identity of the 'children of God' – are they only Christians ('children of the promise' – Romans 9.6–8) or Christians alongside Jews because 'God has not cast off his people' (Romans 11.2)? Since 'the root is holy' (Romans 11.16), Paul is convinced that at the end, God, in his inscrutable wisdom, will graft all Israel back on to their own olive tree (Romans 11.24); 'all Israel will be saved' (Romans 11.26).

To the question of whether the election of Israel remains valid, the document explains that Paul gives two different answers: the first says that the branches (Jews) have been cut off because of their refusal to believe (Romans 11.17, 20), but 'a remnant remains, chosen by grace [Christians]' (Romans 11.5). The second response says that Jews who became 'enemies as regards the gospel' remain 'beloved as regards election, for the sake of the ancestors' (Romans 11.28) and Paul foresees that they will obtain mercy (Romans 11.27, 31). The Jews do not cease to be called to live by faith in the intimacy of God 'for the gifts and calling of God are irrevocable' (Romans 11.29; para. 36).

---

8 Cf. Claude G. Montefiore, 1910, *The Synoptic Gospels*, vol. 1, London: Macmillan, pp. 326–7.

The document concludes that 'the Church ... understands her own existence as a participation in the election of Israel and in a vocation that belongs, in the first place, to Israel, despite the fact that only a small number of Israelites accepted it' (para. 36). This passage serves to provide the theological space for present-day Judaism as we highlighted earlier, but how, might one ask, does the document deal with those New Testament texts that stand in opposition to this teaching? One thinks of the Epistle to the Hebrews in particular as an example of a New Testament book that argues for the replacement of the old Israel (Judaism) by the new Israel (Christianity). It is interesting to notice that *JPSSCB* does not tackle this directly, but summarizes the position of Hebrews in one short paragraph. It states that the author of Hebrews rejects the temple sacrifices of Second Temple Judaism and teaches that 'the covenant announced and prefigured in the Old Testament is fulfilled' (para. 42). It does not elaborate on what Hebrews means by 'fulfilled' ('replaced' is what Hebrews really means, which of course allows no room for Judaism theologically). In contrast, the document points out that Paul's comments in Romans 9–11 do allow for the theological space for Jews and Judaism. *JPSSCB* reduces the significance of Hebrews by giving precedence to Paul and states forthrightly that 'far from being a substitution for Israel, the Church is in solidarity with it' (para. 65).

Does this imply a two-covenant view of salvation, which would have the effect of undermining contemporary missionary activity towards Jews? Does it move away from the efforts of the earliest Church to convert Jews? The statement certainly raises questions about the way the Church understands Jews and salvation, demanding further reflection on the significance of the universality of Christ's redemptive action. To what extent does salvation of Jews depend primarily on their own covenant rather than on the universal work of Christ? This question remains unanswered for the moment and will perhaps be tackled by another document in the not too distant future. However, the very question sets a challenge (or a threat?) to evangelicals outside the Church and conservatives within it, who criticize the Church for abandoning evangelism and replacing it with dialogue, which, in their view, compromises Christianity itself. It should be noted that their position now stands outside the teaching of the Roman Catholic Church.

The result of the discussion on covenant and election is that the Church now teaches that although Jews do not recognize God's salvific plan in the Old Testament, they remain the people of God. This is part of God's mysterious plan of salvation, the final outcome of which is the salvation of all Israel, 'a very important doctrine which Christians should never forget' (para. 59).

The document acknowledges a special status of 'elder brother' for the Jewish people, thereby giving them a 'unique place among all other religions' (para. 36). At the end-time, however, the Church expects Jews to realize the truth of Christianity. Does such an eschatological expectation cause difficulty for Jewish–Christian relations? No, because Judaism also expects the *eschaton* to reveal the truth of its position. In other words, Jews have their own eschatological expectations. Both communities are convinced they possess the ultimate truth.

A striking passage that deals with eschatological expectations states that 'Jewish messianic expectation is not in vain'. Thus the Roman Catholic Church now teaches that Jews, alongside Christians, are commended for keeping alive the messianic expectation. The difference is that for Christians, 'the One who is to come will have the traits of the Jesus who has already come and is already present and active among us' (para. 21). What Christians believe to have been accomplished in Christ 'has yet to be accomplished in us and in the world'.

*Nostra Aetate* had not touched on the Jewish 'no' to Jesus while the *Guidelines* had called on Catholics to understand the difficulties for the 'Jewish soul' with its 'pure notion of divine transcendence when faced with the mystery of the incarnate word' (Section I). The *Notes* suggested that the Jewish 'no' was 'a sign to be interpreted within God's design' (para. 6), but the new document (*JPSSCB*) develops this much more fully. It shows that the Jewish Scriptures, with their associated Jewish interpretations, can make a contribution to the Christian understanding of the Scriptures when previously they had been a point of difference and argument. The acknowledgement of the legitimacy of a Jewish understanding of waiting for the Messiah is a good example because the document identifies Jewish expectations of the coming of the Messiah with the second coming of Jesus. Both Jews and Christians share this anticipation. 'Christians, like Jews, live in expectation.'

## The Portrait of Jews and Judaism in the New Testament

The third and final section of *JPSSCB* addresses New Testament attitudes to Jews and consists of a detailed survey of statements about Jews in Christian Scripture. It repeats the Second Vatican Council's condemnation of the view that the New Testament supports contempt and hostility towards Jews. Although the New Testament exhibits reproach towards Jews (which increases in virulence for those who actively oppose Christians), the document denies that the New Testament contains an attitude of contempt. 'Real anti-Jewish feeling, that is, an attitude of contempt, hostility and persecution of the Jews as Jews, is not found in any New Testament text and is incompatible with its teaching' (para. 87).

The document explains the polemic by an argument of detailed contextualization, pointing out that it is influenced by the later redactional context and that it is similar to the polemic found in the prophetic writings, as well as in apocalyptic literature. This makes its 'vigour . . . less astonishing'. The document explains that the polemic in the New Testament was also a response to

- the Jewish rejection of Jesus;
- arguments between Jews and Jewish Christians;
- harassment of Christians by Jews.

Most importantly, the document explains that the polemic was 'for the most part internal, between two groups both belonging to Jerusalem' (para. 70). Although this phrase is mentioned almost in passing, it seems to me that polemic directed towards those Jews who did not accept Jesus as Messiah by those Jews who did, provides the most obvious explanation for its existence in the New Testament. If only the fact that the New Testament records arguments between groups of Jews (sometimes bitter, sometimes less so) were more widely known, their harmful consequences might not have been so severe. The New Testament is not an account of arguments between Christians and Jews! This teaching needs to be widely taught in the Roman Catholic Church (and also within the Jewish community).

It is somewhat disappointing to note that *JPSSCB* failed to explore why Christian Scripture has been used to justify persecution of Jews. Why have the consequences of the New Testament polemic towards Jews proved so destructive? The contextualization of the polemic is a valuable tool in tackling the problem, but it would also have been valuable to tackle why the problem exists in the first place. Why have some Christians (and others) used the New Testament as a tool to disparage Jews? This brings us back to the challenge set by Cardinal Ratzinger when he stated that Jewish–Christian relations need to be considered in the light of the Holocaust. The document mentions the Shoah only once when it states that 'the horror in the wake of the extermination of the Jews (the Shoah) during the Second World War has led all the Churches to rethink their relationship with Judaism and, as a result, to reconsider their interpretation of the Jewish Bible, the Old Testament' (para. 22). Although no one would deny that Nazism was opposed to Christianity, it is well-known that Hitler often justified his antisemitism with reference to the Church and Christian attitudes towards Judaism.[9] The document fails to examine to what extent there is a relationship between the Shoah (and the history of Christian antisemitism) and the New Testament.

I am not suggesting that the New Testament is antisemitic – such a charge is false – but it has been *used* to justify antisemitism, and the Pontifical Biblical Commission missed an opportunity to

---

9 See the excellent summary in R. L. Rubenstein and J. K. Roth, 1987, *Approaches to Auschwitz*, London: SCM Press, pp. 199–228.

tackle the reasons for this abuse of Scripture. A study of the relationship between Jews, Christians and the Bible – for this is true also of the Old Testament as well as the New – should consider why it has been interpreted to promote hatred, discrimination or superiority of one group over another. It has been altogether too common to come across a biblical text used for the purpose of the subjugation of women to men, black to white, Jew to Christian. The document would have benefited from acknowledging that the traditional 'teaching of contempt' has fostered an abuse of the Sacred Scriptures.[10]

The document does of course tackle difficult texts in the New Testament, which it notes were provoked in a time of conflict. It explains that the situation has radically changed since then and that the polemic has no relevance to contemporary Jewish–Christian relations. 'The New Testament polemical texts, even those expressed in general terms, have to do with concrete historical contexts and are never meant to be applied to Jews of all times and places merely because they are Jews.'

Among the troublesome passages tackled include the Passion narratives, which are some of the most difficult texts in the New Testament because they exaggerate Jewish responsibility for the death of Jesus and downplay Roman responsibility. Consequently, they have been extremely harmful in Jewish–Christian relations. The document is troubling at this point, because it claims that the leadership of the Jewish people was intent on killing Jesus and destroying Christianity, whereas it is more likely that the Roman government and Pontius Pilate were particularly oppressive, not the Pharisaic leadership. The document might even have pointed out that in Passion narratives the one Jewish group that disappears from the accounts is the Pharisees. This fact, it seems to me, is highly significant not only for the biblical account but also for modern Jewish–Christian relations, since the Pharisees were the forerunners of rabbinic Judaism.

---

10 This is a problem shared by both Jews and Christians for there are Old Testament texts that are equally problematic – for example, Psalm 137.5.

## Conclusion

Overall, *JPSSCB* makes an important contribution to our understanding of the Sacred Scriptures and Jewish–Christian relations. It also contributes to an improved understanding of Judaism among Christians. The document does of course have a number of weaknesses, notably the lack of awareness of the debt that the New Testament owes to rabbinic Judaism, over-emphasizing the Dead Sea Scrolls and a reluctance to explain why biblical texts are open to abuse.

Nevertheless, its strengths far outweigh these weaknesses and it is to be commended. Those of us who have been touched by the angel of interfaith dialogue and who are presently engaged in the Jewish–Christian encounter, should take heart. Most noteworthy is the courageous call for the use of Jewish commentaries by Christians, since Jewish interpretation of Scripture is legitimate, and the challenging statement that Jewish messianic expectation is not in vain.

The document prepares the ground for future documents, which are likely to consider theological issues, possibly those concerning salvation. *JPSSCB* succeeds in advancing the dialogue between Christians and Jews and is another step towards the healing of the world (*tikkun olam*). It also clears much debris and, to adopt imagery from Isaiah 29.17, ploughs the land and plants the seeds so that in the future a fruitful field can develop. This future field will generate theological space for Jews and Christians, which is essential for today's encounter.

Appropriately, the document concludes with a quotation from a papal speech made in 1997. This illustrates the personal perspective of John Paul II, which is central to the message of *JPSSCB*. It also provides the basis for the future dialogue with Jews and Judaism:

> This people has been called and led by God, creator of heaven and earth. Their existence is not a mere natural or cultural happening... It is a supernatural one. This people continues in spite of everything to be the people of the covenant, and, despite human infidelity, the Lord is faithful to his covenant.

# 10

# Reasoning with Violent Scripture: With a Little Help from Job

> If you have seen evil, it was shown to you in order that you learn of your own guilt and repent; for what is shown to you is also within you. (Baal Shem Tov, 1698–1760)

This chapter will offer a variety of approaches to the interpretation of violent biblical texts, the most important of which finds its justification in a single verse from the Book of Job. This is valuable in a world where violence is often carried out in the name of religion, justified by a particular interpretation of one or more sacred texts. I will begin with a brief consideration of the traditional Jewish responses to violence in biblical, rabbinic and modern times. The survival of Judaism in the face of external attacks is not a new phenomenon, and I suggest that recognition among Jews today of the ideas put forward in the rabbinic writings may provide some help in developing an appropriate response in an increasingly violent world. In addition, the realization among Jews that there now exist partners in this exercise should strengthen our resolve to tackle these texts. Christianity, for so long an instigator of violence against and contempt for Judaism, has in recent years become a friend who has respect and admiration for Judaism. Awareness of this transformation in Christian attitudes towards Judaism may contribute to the development of a hermeneutical principle by which both Jews and Christians can read and interpret violent texts. I hope that some of these suggestions would also be of value to Muslims in their reasoning with the Qur'an.

## The Traditional Jewish View of Violence

Until recently, the traditional and most common Jewish response to violence was based on Jeremiah 29.4–7:

> Thus saith the LORD of hosts, the God of Israel, unto all the captivity, whom I have caused to be carried away captive from Jerusalem unto Babylon: Build ye houses, and dwell in them, and plant gardens, and eat the fruit of them; take ye wives, and beget sons and daughters; and take wives for your sons, and give your daughters to husbands, that they may bear sons and daughters; and multiply ye there, and be not diminished. And seek the peace of the city whither I have caused you to be carried away captive, and pray unto the LORD for it; for in the peace thereof shall ye have peace.

The yielding to outside power and acceptance of the violence that prevailed were strategies that ensured the survival of Judaism. By relinquishing a desire for sovereignty, Jews gained some autonomy in regulating their lives. Under the motto *dina d'malkhulta dina* ('the law of the land is the law'), the Jewish community based its existence on the law of the host society. 'A person must be at all times yielding like a reed', said the rabbis, 'and not unbending like a cedar.'[1] This approach ensured Jewish survival and enabled Judaism to develop and flourish in the face of violence until the rise of antisemitism in the nineteenth and twentieth centuries, when the passiveness of the rabbinic model, with its acceptance of pogroms, massacres and finally the Holocaust, offered no respite.

Arthur Waskow points to the 1880s as the time when Jews began to realize that they could no longer live by the rabbinic model, and desired to take control of their own destiny. Self-determination in the land of Israel became the goal. The Zionism of the left-wing *Palmach* as well as the right-wing *Irgun* produced a military model that aimed to protect Jews in the land of Israel by force. For the most part, the effort to secure and defend

---

[1] BT Ta'anit 20a.

territory on which to build a Jewish society allowed for compromise, partition and self-restraint. However, in the last few years a more aggressive response to violence has become noticeable, and the military decision-making process, which had been based on the use of military force sparingly and defensively, has now changed into the use of force liberally and belligerently – for conquest as well as for self-defence.[2]

There are many difficulties with this approach, one of which is that it is unlikely that a small people living in Israel can wage a long-term ethical military effort and at the same time develop a decent society. Not even the Soviet Union, a continental superstate, could shoulder this burden. It is not altogether clear that even the richest country in the history of the world, the United States, can for generations wage continuous war – even 'a war against terror' – and remain a decent society at home.

The chances that Israel can do so are very small. It may seem implausible at first, but if we turn to some of the more violent passages from Scripture and examine the rabbinic interpretations alongside them, we will find some surprisingly relevant and refreshing comments, which can provide guidance in developing a response to the issues raised by this problem.

## Reading the Bible

The centrepiece of the Jewish service is the reading of the Written Torah, the five books of Moses. Jews traditionally read each and every verse, including the more problematic verses. These include violent passages such as Deuteronomy 20, which deals with fighting a war and the ethics of warfare and begins with a remarkably democratic, enlightened and morally topical message:

> When thou goest forth to battle against thine enemies, and seest horses, and chariots, and a people more than thou, thou shalt not be afraid of them; for the Lord thy God is with thee, who

---

[2] Arthur Waskow, 2002, 'The Sword and the Plowshare as Tools of Tikkun Olam', *Tikkun*, vol. 17, pp. 42–9. Available at www.theshalomcenter.org/node/216.

brought thee up out of the land of Egypt. And it shall be, when ye draw nigh unto the battle, that the priest shall approach and speak unto the people, and shall say unto them: 'Hear, O Israel, ye draw nigh this day unto battle against your enemies; let not your heart faint; fear not, nor be alarmed, neither be ye affrighted at them; for the Lord your God is He that goeth with you, to fight for you against your enemies, to save you.' And the officers shall speak unto the people, saying: 'What man is there that hath built a new house, and hath not dedicated it? Let him go and return to his house, lest he die in the battle, and another man dedicate it. And what man is there that hath planted a vineyard, and hath not used the fruit thereof? Let him go and return unto his house, lest he die in the battle, and another man use the fruit thereof. And what man is there that hath betrothed a wife, and hath not taken her? Let him go and return unto his house, lest he die in the battle, and another man take her.' And the officers shall speak further unto the people, and they shall say: 'What man is there that is fearful and faint-hearted? Let him go and return unto his house, lest his brethren's heart melt as his heart.' And it shall be, when the officers have made an end of speaking unto the people, that captains of hosts shall be appointed at the head of the people.

The Bible proposes a volunteer army and suggests that many groups of people should not be expected to fight in a war, particularly those who

- recently moved into a new home;
- planted a vineyard but have not yet reaped its fruits;
- are shortly to be married;
- fear war.

The passage goes on to explain that the city to be attacked should first be offered terms for a peaceful surrender, but if it refuses, it should be besieged. Upon victory, its women and children should not be harmed. So far, so enlighteningly good, but verses 16–18 are especially problematic:

Howbeit of the cities of these peoples, that the Lord thy God giveth thee for an inheritance, thou shalt save alive nothing that breatheth, but thou shalt utterly destroy them: the Hittite, and the Amorite, the Canaanite, and the Perizzite, the Hivite, and the Jebusite; as the Lord thy God hath commanded thee; that they teach you not to do after all their abominations, which they have done unto their gods, and so ye sin against the Lord your God.

The Bible commands that the cities of the Hittites, Amorites, Canaanites, Peruzites, Hivites and Jebusites should be destroyed and that every man, woman and child (and animal) should be killed. Although these cities, from the perspective of Scripture, may symbolize the Nazis of their time, how should such verses be interpreted, particularly in today's violent world?

The rabbis decreed that military power should no longer be used. They did this by evading, nullifying, and otherwise interpreting away the genocidal commands against the Canaanites and other idolatrous people. Instead of extrapolating from these commands that it was right – even obligatory – to wipe out a people that rejected the one true God, the rabbis went in the opposite direction, ruling that the Canaanite example was null and void. Since the Canaanite peoples no longer existed – the rabbis explained that the Assyrians had scattered them as well as the ten lost tribes of Israel in 721 BCE – the rabbis ruled that the commands to use military action against the Canaanites were a dead letter.[3] If military action against the Canaanites was no longer necessary, then military action itself was no longer commanded.

The rabbis were creative in applying Torah to a new situation. They could have understood the six nations as symbols for ongoing dangers to be dealt with militarily, but chose instead to annul the genocidal meaning of the text and even rejected the command to execute a rebellious Israelite child or wipe out a rebellious Israelite city.[4] This was an ethical decision not to carry

---

3 Based on Mishnah Yadayim 4.4.
4 Mishnah Sanhedrin 8.1–4; BT Sanhedrin 71a.

out literally the command of Torah. One could argue that to a certain extent the rabbis were simply being pragmatic, given the power of the Roman and Byzantine empires; but these rulings also point to an ethical rejection of the use of violence. Indeed, the rabbis mostly rejected the violent punishments prescribed in Torah, indicating that a court that sentences even one person to death in 70 years is a court of murderers.[5]

Consequently, rabbinic Judaism constructed a non-violent way for the Jewish people to live in the world. Living as a vulnerable minority in a Christian (and Muslim) society, Jewish communities in the rabbinic period abandoned the hope of overcoming oppressors. Only within ourselves, said the rabbis, can Jews overcome evil. According to one tradition, when all Jews truly observe the Sabbath twice in a row, the Messiah will come and transform the world.[6] It is noteworthy that such a transformation will take place as a result of divine action rather than human interference. For almost 2,000 years, with few exceptions, Jews accepted their suffering passively. They experienced expulsions, pogroms and burnings, believing that they would live beyond such events. This survival technique is illustrated by the fact that even as the Jewish lights of Western Europe were extinguished one by one – expelled from England (1290), France (1306) and Spain (1492) – new Jewish centres were being established in Eastern Europe, Turkey and the Middle East.

It is unsurprising that over the centuries a mentality permeated the minds of most Jews – one that saw the Jewish community as still being utterly engulfed by enemies. The legacy of this mentality exists today and must be overcome. The need to develop friendships and build positive relations with like-minded faith communities is essential. This need is increased by the danger that a small people will suffer another catastrophe in the land of Israel. Judaism needs allies for this challenge. The mindset of isolation imbued both biblical and rabbinic Judaism. It developed in the effort to conquer Canaan against what was viewed as an ocean

---

5 Mishnah Makkot 1.10.
6 BT Shabbat 118b.

of idolaters and grew in the effort to survive the Roman Empire. This mindset was reinforced by inquisitions and pogroms and even by the gentler Muslim habit of treating Jews like tolerated pets. The Shoah and the continued threats to the State of Israel fuel it even further.

Whether Jews survived by military means in the ancient land of Israel, or lived a life of non-violence among other civilizations, both biblical and rabbinic Judaism reinforced the perception among Jews that they were on their own, that no one else shared their vision and that all outsiders were enemies. For centuries, this may well have reflected considerable truth. However, in the last 100 years, Jews have begun to discover that there are other communities in the world with which they can share a vision of a decent society. The transformation in Christian attitudes towards Judaism is one example. Indeed, a positive relationship between Judaism and Christianity is one of the few pieces of good news in media reports about religious encounters in today's violent world.

## Transformation in Christian Perceptions of Judaism

In the last 100 years, the need for Christianity to abandon its historical religious animosity towards and misleading caricature of Judaism has been overwhelming. These are now generally admitted as being wrong and their full and public rejection was required before the rebuilding of good relations with Judaism could begin. Thus what was required was a shift from what was, for the most part, an inherent need to condemn Judaism to a need to condemn Christian anti-Judaism. This transformation might have tempted some to follow a Marcionite approach and reject all things Jewish, but in fact led to a closer relationship with 'the elder brother'. In the words of German theologian Johannes Metz, 'Christian theology after Auschwitz must stress anew the Jewish dimension of Christian beliefs and must overcome the forced blocking-out of the Jewish heritage within Christianity.'[7] Social ethicist John Pawlikowski stated that, 'the Holocaust has made it immoral for Christians to maintain any Christology that is excessively triumphalistic or that finds the significance of the Christ Event in the displacement of the Jewish People from an ongoing covenantal relationship with God'.[8]

As far as reasoning with the Bible is concerned, this has led to the tackling of the traditional teaching of contempt of Judaism (known as *Adversus-Iudaeos*) in Christian interpretations of Scripture – a teaching that had become part of Christian identity. The extent to which this has been successfully completed is subject to some disagreement among scholars – critics both within and outside the Church believe that there is more to be done. However, the changes have been dramatic, and it is clear that many of the main divisive issues between Judaism and Christianity have been either eliminated or taken to the furthest point at which agreement is possible. The efforts of Catholics and Protestants towards respect of Judaism are reflected in documents that project attitudes unthinkable a few decades ago. Christian theology has been profoundly revised at the official level – all churches are committed to the fight against antisemitism and to teaching about the Jewishness of Christianity. This is illustrated by the recent document published by the Pontifical Biblical Commission entitled *The Jewish People and their Sacred Scriptures in the Christian Bible* (2001), which among other things called for Christians to read and learn about rabbinic interpretations of Scripture, and stated that the Jewish messianic expectation was not in vain.[9]

Few would deny that a massive change in attitude has taken place, and that for the most part Christianity, in the West at least, is no longer part of the problem of antisemitism but part of its solution. As far as Scripture is concerned, Christians are

---

7 Johannes-Baptist Metz, 1984, 'Facing the Jews: Christian Theology after Auschwitz', in Elisabeth Schüssler Fiorenza and David Tracy (eds), *The Holocaust as Interruption*, Concilium 175, Edinburgh: T & T Clark, p. 27.

8 John Pawlikowski, 1998, 'Christology after the Holocaust', *Encounter*, vol. 3, p. 346.

9 *The Jewish People and their Sacred Scriptures*, op. cit.

now taught that the Hebrew Bible is not simply a foil for the New Testament, possessing little authority in its own right. It was necessary for some kind of balance to be restored between the Hebrew Bible and the New Testament and reverence towards the *graphai* (Scriptures) as a whole has been reasserted in Christian biblical interpretation. Jewish biblical interpretation is valued and respected by Christians to an extent that would have caused disbelief just a couple of generations ago.

While Christian biblical scholarship has rejected its former negative stereotyping of Jews and Judaism, resulting in a revised approach to the teaching of biblical studies, some Jewish writers have focused more on how to read the Bible in light of the Shoah. In general, Jewish responses to the Shoah tend to fall into two categories, both of which have an impact upon the Jewish reading of the Bible. The first is represented by figures such as the philosopher Emil Fackenheim, the theologian Richard Rubenstein and the author Elie Wiesel. They have all argued that the Shoah has resulted in a 'rupture' in the relationship between Jews and God and a consequent Jewish distancing from Scripture.

Richard Rubenstein offered an 'atheistic' reaction in his 'death of God' theology. In *After Auschwitz* (1966), he stated that the Shoah had buried any possibility of continued belief in a covenantal God of history and that instead of interpreting the Bible in traditional terms, Jews should consider it simply in terms of an earthly existence. In his revised second edition of the same work (1992), Rubenstein offered a more mystical approach. What has not changed is his affirmation of a view of God quite different from the mainstream view of biblical and rabbinic Judaism and his rejection of the notion that Jews are in any sense a people either chosen or rejected by God.[10]

The second response is to view events between 1933 and 1945 as one would persecution and oppression during other periods of extreme Jewish suffering. This view is represented by Jewish

---

10 Richard Rubenstein, 1992, *After Auschwitz: History, Theology, and Contemporary Judaism*, 2nd edn., Baltimore: Johns Hopkins University Press, pp. 311–12.

scholars such as Jacob Neusner, Eliezer Berkovits, Eugene Borowitz and Michael Wyschogrod. The latter makes their position clear when he states that 'the voices of the prophets speak more loudly than did Hitler'.[11] According to this argument, traditional approaches to Scripture provide the means by which to come to terms with the Shoah.

It may be that a combination of the two approaches will best help us in our reasoning with Scripture, particularly violent Scripture in the light of the Holocaust. In other words, reasoners need to be aware that on the one hand a 'rupture' has taken place, the scale of which has not been experienced before; on the other, sacred texts provide us with the heritage to which we are bound in an attempt to make some kind of sense of this experience.

Emil Fackenheim calls for a struggle with the biblical text and, if need be, a fight against it. He accepts the biblical text as primary but views it as 'naked'; Jews are impelled to tackle the biblical text because they are also 'naked':

> After the Holocaust Jews cannot read, as they once did, of a God who sleeps and slumbers not; so enormous are the events of recent history ... that the Jewish Bible ... must be struggled with, if necessary fought against.[12]

Fackenheim examines a number of previous approaches to the Bible and rejects them all. For instance, Martin Buber had proposed that each generation in turn 'struggled' with the Bible. Before the Shoah, Buber stated that:

> [t]he generations are by no means ready to listen to what the book has to say, and to obey it; they are often vexed and defiant; nevertheless, the preoccupation with this book is part of their life, and they face it in a real world.[13]

---

11 Michael Wyschogrod, 1972, 'Faith and the Holocaust', *Judaism*, vol. 20, p. 294.
12 Emil Fackenheim, 1992, *The Jewish Bible after the Holocaust*, Manchester: Manchester University Press, pp. vii–viii.
13 Martin Buber, 1948, 'The Man of Today and the Jewish Bible', in *Israel and the World: Essays in a Time of Crisis*, New York: Schocken.

After the Shoah, Buber asked whether one could dare recommend to Holocaust survivors, 'thank ye the Lord for He is good, for His mercy endures for ever' (Psalm 111.1). Adopting the phrase 'eclipse of God' (*hester panim*) as a means of describing the Shoah, he suggested that just as the moon can appear to block out the sun, so God was eclipsed during the Holocaust.[14]

But for Fackenheim the focus lies not with a metaphorical eclipse of God but with a more tangible struggle by Holocaust survivors:

> If these [survivors] open the Jewish Bible they are more than 'vexed' and 'defiant': the Book fills them with outrage; yet, too, more than merely 'preoccupied' with it, they clutch it as if for survival. So new, so paradoxical a relation is coming into being between the Book, then and there, and the 'generation' here and now. This is because of two events both referred to by names of places. One is Auschwitz, the other, Jerusalem.[15]

## Exegetical Relativity

To a certain extent, struggling with the meaning of Scripture lies at the heart of traditional rabbinic exegesis. The rabbinic Bible, the *Mikraot Gedolot*, with its commentaries spanning the centuries ranged around the biblical text, is rightly regarded as a celebration of the enduring nature of the debate about meaning. The rabbinic willingness to see a multitude of different possible meanings, in marked contrast to the single 'authentic' meaning backed by clerical or scholarly authority, provides us with the means of handling difficult biblical texts.

This approach may be described as exegetical relativity and is put forward by the rabbis as follows:

> In the School of Rabbi Ishmael it is taught: 'See, My word is like fire, an oracle of the Eternal, and like a hammer that shatters a

---

14 Martin Buber, 1953, *The Eclipse of God: Studies in the Relation between Religion and Philosophy*, London: Gollancz.

15 Emil Fackenheim, 1992, *The Jewish Bible*, op. cit., pp. 16–17.

rock' (Jeremiah 23:29). Just as a hammer divides into several sparks so too every scriptural verse yields several meanings.[16]

This approach to biblical interpretation can also be found in classical Christian exegesis. Although less well known in the West, because it derives from the Syriac tradition, the following passage from the fourth-century church father Ephrem is significant for our study:

> The facets of God's word are more numerous than the facets of those who learn from it. God depicted His word with many beauties, so that each of those who learn from it can examine that aspect of it which he likes. And God had hidden within his word all sorts of treasures, so that each of us can be enriched by it from whatever aspect he meditates on. For God's word is the Tree of Life which proffers to you on all sides blessed fruits; it is like the Rock which was struck in the Wilderness, which became a spiritual drink for everyone on all sides: 'They ate the food of the Spirit and they drank the draft of the Spirit'.[17]

An acceptance of the legitimacy of a variety of different meanings, each of which claims validity, is therefore found at the heart of traditional Jewish and Christian exegesis. The existence of exegetical relativity means traditional interpretations of Scripture allow for a breadth and plurality of viewpoint. In this way, both the Jewish and Christian exegetical traditions provide a means by which to deal with texts that run contrary to what we regard as the fundamental values of our tradition, or which may be read as a licence for violence or bigotry. The application of exegetical relativity is dependent upon one criterion: that biblical interpretation should reject any interpretation that promotes hatred, discrimination or superiority of one group over another.

---

16 BT Sanhedrin 34a. Cf. Jonathan Magonet, 2003, *Talking to the Other*, London: I B Tauris.
17 Commentary on the Diatessaron I:18–19.

This approach is justified by a hermeneutical principle shared by both Christians and Jews: humanity should live by the commandments and not die by their observance.[18] This means that because of the Shoah, biblical texts need to be examined in the light of potential damage they may cause (or the real damage they have caused). The rabbis coined the term *Pikuah nefesh*, referring to the duty to preserve life as taking precedence over the commandment: simply put, when human life is at stake, the biblical text needs reinterpretation.

The recognition that the biblical text can have more than one meaning is significant for contemporary Jewish and Christian interpretation of Scripture in particular, and Jewish–Christian relations in general. It is no longer appropriate to search for the one and only correct meaning of a text, but rather it is essential to examine a number of different interpretations, each within its own context, each worthy of consideration in its own right. The existence of exegetical relativity may leave the interpreter with an uncomfortable tension owing to the presence of a number of interpretations arising out of a single biblical passage. The multitude of possible interpretations may be disconcerting to some, but their existence illustrates the variety of interpretations applicable to Scripture.

In the Book of Job, the biblical text itself contains an inherent ambiguity. Consider the following opposing translations of Job 13.15:

- Behold, he will slay me; I have no hope. (RSV)
- Though he slay me, yet will I trust in him. (KJV)

The reason for the difference between the RSV and KJV is the result of a variation in the read and spoken versions. The Masoretic vocalization (spoken reading) indicates that Job has hope, while the consonantal text (written text) offers the view that Job has no hope. The Mishnah acknowledges the ambiguous meaning of the

---

18 For example, compare Mark 2.27 with MdRI on Exodus 31.12 or BT Sanhedrin 74a.

biblical text and has recognized that both translations are possible, 'the matter is undecided – do I trust in Him or not trust?'[19] The contradiction is meaningful as it expresses the tension of one who is torn between hope and doubt: the very tension that inhabits our mind, when we read the Bible today. According to André Neher, 'Job pronounces two words which signify *simultaneously* hope and hopelessness . . . I hope in Him, he shouts, but also do not hope in him.'[20]

Using this verse from Job as a hermeneutical springboard results in neither an easy nor a comfortable reading of Scripture, for it leaves the reader with unresolved tension and contradiction. Nevertheless, the two opposed readings of Job do offer a realistic approach to the text. Job's hope and – at the same time – lack of hope provide an insight into the divine–human relationship by demonstrating human failing in the encounter with God. This is particularly helpful for those who, like Fackenheim, struggle with the meaning of the Bible in the light of the Shoah. The principle of ambiguity derived from reasoning with this verse from Job can be equally applied to reasoning with violent texts in general. Awareness of the prevalence of ambiguity in Scripture can be liberating for Christians and Jews because it indicates that the plain, obvious and literal interpretation is not the final meaning of the text. In other words, more than one interpretation is not only acceptable but also to be expected.

In addition, by applying the principle of *kal v'homer* (from minor to major), the reasoner notices that the tension that arises from the interpretation of this one verse illustrates the tension that exists within the Jewish–Christian encounter as a whole: like the Bible and its interpretations, the Jewish–Christian relationship is full of ambiguity, demanding more than one approach, just as texts and stories shared by Judaism and Christianity demand more than one interpretation. Exegetical relativity, which is ultimately rooted in the sort of ambiguity that we found in Job 13.15,

---

19 Mishnah Sotah 5.5.
20 André Neher, 1970, *L'Exil de la paraole: du silence biblique au silence d'Auschwitz*, Paris: Editions du Seuil, p. 215.

suggests that biblical exegetes should approach the text not only with a hermeneutic of suspicion, but also with the newly found hermeneutic of ambiguity.

## Techniques for Handling Difficult Texts

This chapter has shown that although both Judaism and Christianity share difficult texts, each has within its own history of biblical interpretation the means to handle such texts. However, some polemical texts are particular to the Church. How should such texts be integrated?

The most important method is to *contextualize* them. This means to consider the implications of the fact that the mission and ministry of Jesus can only be understood in the context of first-century Palestinian Judaism. Not only is it essential to emphasize that the concerns of Jesus and his followers are Jewish concerns, as we mentioned above, but that Christianity in part shares the Jewish Scriptures and that the Jewish way of worship heavily influenced Christian modes of worship.

In addition, it is essential to read the text in the light of:

- Modern statements about the Christian relationship to Jews and Judaism such as the various Vatican statements, the Anglican Lambeth Conference 1988 Document entitled *Jews, Christians, Muslims: The Way of Dialogue*, and so on. For example, Pope John Paul II's famous comment in 1980, 'the people of the Old Covenant, never revoked by God' might be cited alongside Matthew 23. A comparison of post-Second World War statements would be worthwhile in the interpretation of such passages.
- The close relationship between Jesus and the Pharisees. For example, it was a Pharisee who warned Jesus about the intention of Herod (Luke 13.1); Jesus taught and associated with Pharisees; many of Jesus' teachings are paralleled in the rabbinic writings.

- More positive biblical passages. For example, one might compare negative interpretations associated with verses such as 'No one comes to the Father except through Me' (John 14.6) or 'nor is there salvation in any other, for there is no other name under heaven given among men by which we must be saved' (Acts 4.12) with passages such as 'Other sheep I have which are not of this fold' (John 10.16).
- Its abuse by later Christian interpretation, most noticeable in the *Adversus-Iudaeos* tradition. The dangers of abuse, such as the harmful consequences of Matthew 25.27, should be highlighted.

## Conclusion

Abraham Joshua Heschel tells the story of a band of inexperienced mountain climbers. Without guides, they struck recklessly into the wilderness. Suddenly a rocky ledge gave way beneath their feet, and they were tumbled headlong into a dismal pit. In the darkness of the pit, they recovered from their shock, only to find themselves set upon by a swarm of angry snakes. Every crevice became alive with fanged, hissing things. For each snake the desperate men slew, ten more seemed to lash out in its place. Strangely enough, one man seemed to stand aside from the fight. When the indignant voices of his struggling companions reproached him for not fighting, he called back: If we remain here, we shall be dead before the snakes. I am searching for a way of escape from the pit for all of us.[21]

Heschel points out that the killing of snakes will provide security for a brief moment, but not for ever. The killing of snakes is an inadequate response in reasoning with the Bible – especially in struggling with violent texts shared by our religious traditions. Moreover, a successful re-reading of the texts is more likely to be

---

21  Delivered in March 1938 at a Quaker conference in Frankfurt-am-Main, Germany. See Edward Kaplan, 1996, *Holiness in Words: Abraham Joshua Heschel's Poetics of Piety*, Albany: State University of New York Press, pp. 145–51.

achieved through partnership than isolation. Jews and Christians share many of the same texts as well as some of the same textual difficulties that these texts raise. At the same time, they have similar tools within their exegetical traditions by which to tackle these problems. The interpretation of one verse from the Book of Job has demonstrated the role that a hermeneutic of ambiguity can play, and thus the significance of exegetical relativity in reasoning with Scripture. Further, the way in which these hermeneutical principles have been at work in Jewish–Christian relations may provide a lesson of how we can learn from, and help, each other.

# PART 3

# Jews, Christians and Muslims

# 11

# A Jewish Approach to Dialogue with Christians and Muslims

## A Jewish Theology of Dialogue

The basis for a Jewish theology of dialogue can be found in Leviticus 19.33–34:

> When a stranger lives with you in your land, do not ill-treat him. The stranger who lives with you shall be treated like a native-born. Love him as yourself for you were strangers in the land of Egypt. I am the Lord your God.

Chief Rabbi Jonathan Sacks often mentions that the importance of *loving the stranger* is emphasized by the fact it is commanded on 36 separate occasions in the Pentateuch. Understanding the Other is dependent upon embracing the dignity of difference – in other words, there must exist a willingness to understand difference in order to get to know the Other.

Such a quest is never easy because it is not merely about the Other, nor where the Other differs from us. Rather, it consists of a direct meeting of two people and involves a reciprocal exposing of the full religious consciousness of the one with the Other. This meeting is dialogue, which speaks to the Other with a full respect of what the Other is and has to say. It is never less than personal because dialogue begins with the individual.

The biblical prophets were experts in a personal encounter, and Isaiah powerfully commends Israel to enter into a personal relationship with God stating, 'come now let us reason together'

(Isaiah 1.18). Consequently, dialogue entails a respect that takes the Other as seriously as one demands to be taken oneself – an immensely difficult exercise.

The Jewish pioneer of modern dialogue was Martin Buber, who greatly influenced Jewish–Christian dialogue and whose approach is equally applicable to the Abrahamic encounter. He explains how the covenant between God and the Jewish people remains unrevoked, but allows for the existence of covenants between God and other peoples. Since Vatican II, the Roman Catholic Church has adopted Buber's thought; for example, Pope John Paul II during his pilgrimage to the Holy Land in the year 2000 described Jewish–Christian dialogue as 'the meeting between the people of God of the Old Covenant, never revoked by God (cf. Romans 11.29), and that of the New Covenant'. Likewise, Archbishop Gregorios, a wonderful Patron and guide, wrote to me in 2006 about the 'indissoluble ties that bind Judaism and Christianity'.

Buber created his famous I–Thou formula and maintained that a personal relationship with God is only truly personal when there is not only awe and respect on the human side, but when we are not overcome and overwhelmed in our relationship with God. This has implications for the human encounter – it means that two people must meet as two valid centres of interest. Thus one should approach the Other with respect and restraint so that the validity of the Other's centre is in no sense belittled.

Further, not only is the essential being of the Other respected, but the world of 'faith' is also treated as valid and genuine; not an 'it' to be carelessly set aside, but a distinctive value of belief. An I–Thou relationship is a meeting not of religions, but of religious people. Note the emphasis on the individual.

Emmanuel Levinas, a more recent Jewish contributor to the dialogue, was greatly influenced by Buber. He argued in *Time and the Other* (1990) that the relationship with the Other is not an idyllic relationship of communion, or a sympathy through which we put ourselves in the Other's place; the Other resembles us, but is exterior to us. For Levinas, the face of the Other necessitates an ethical commitment. According to Levinas, when people look at each other, they see not only two faces but also the faces of other people, the face of humanity.

Consequently, the relationship is less 'I–thou' and more 'we–thou', entailing an ethical commitment to and responsibility for the other person of faith. The responsibility for the other is linked to the human approach to the Divine, for 'there can be no "knowledge" of God separated from the relationship with human beings. The Other is the very focus of metaphysical truth and is indispensable for my relation with God. He does not play the role of a mediator. The Other is not the incarnation of God, but precisely by His face, in which he is disincarnated, is the manifestation of the height in which God is revealed.'[1]

## Jewish–Christian–Muslim Dialogue Today

Dialogue, as defined above, between Christians and Jews has been taking place for at least 100 years but, on the other hand, dialogue with Muslims is a much more recent and fragile phenomenon.

It is all too easy to relate to others in a casual way with a lack of concentration on the reality and good of the Other. The basis for Jewish–Christian–Muslim dialogue is that each faith must be understood on its own terms. An example is Franz Rosenzweig's comment about the saying of Jesus in the Gospel of John (6.14) that 'No one can reach the Father except through Me'. Rosenzweig does not get round this saying by condemnation; indeed, he asserts that it is true, particularly when one remembers the millions who have been led to God through Jesus Christ. However, he continues, 'The situation is quite different for one who does not have to reach the Father because he is already with him. Shall I become converted, I who have been chosen?'[2] In a few sentences Rosenzweig introduces us to the crucial question of dialogue: can Christians (and Muslims) view Judaism as a valid religion – and vice versa?

---

1 Emmanuel Levinas, 1969, *Totality and Infinity: An Essay on Exteriority*, trans. Alphonse Lingis, Pittsburgh: Duquesne University Press, p. 78.

2 Franz Rosenzweig, 1976, *Gesammelte Schriften*, I, The Hague: Martinus Nijhoff, pp. 132ff.

From the Jewish perspective, Jews need to ponder the purpose behind the creation of Christianity and Islam. Does Jesus the Jew have any significance for Jews? What is the meaning that two billion followers of the Jew Jesus read in the Jewish Bible? As for Islam, what is the significance of 1.6 billion Muslims sharing many of the same customs as Jews (such as dietary laws) and adhering to a strict monotheism?

For Christians, there needs to be a profound reflection on the survival of the Jewish people and of the vitality of Judaism over nearly 2,000 years. The question of the validity of Judaism challenges some of the proclamations of Christian triumphalism. Questions such as whether Christianity can differentiate itself from Judaism without asserting itself as either opposed to Judaism or simply as the fulfilment of Judaism need to be considered.

For Muslims, particularly in the West, the interfaith encounter with Christians and Jews is a far more recent development. Developing a respectful and engaging relationship with Jews and Christians is more important now than ever. To what extent can Muslims understand the significance to Jews of the State of Israel or, in the words of HRH Prince Hassan of Jordan, can they internalize the meaning of the Holocaust?

## Jewish–Christian Dialogue

Before dialogue could really begin with Judaism, Christianity needed to shift from what was, for the most part, an inherent need to condemn Judaism to a need to condemn Christian anti-Judaism. This process led not to a separation from all things Jewish but, in fact, to a closer relationship with 'the elder brother'.

The dramatic reawakening among Christians to the Jewish origins of Christianity began in the first half of the twentieth century. Figures such as Travers Herford and George Foot Moore shed light on the vitality of Judaism in the first few centuries of the Common Era, overcoming misconceptions and prejudices of the majority of their contemporaries such as Emil Schürer and Julius Wellhausen. The latter argued inaccurately that rabbinic Judaism was a form of barren legalism, which was simply rejected by Jesus and replaced by Christianity. In their view, rabbinic Judaism represented a decaying religion. Thankfully, Herford and Foot Moore pointed out the errors and preconceptions of their German colleagues and expressed a hitherto unheard-of appreciation of rabbinic Judaism. They taught a new generation of scholars that the Judaism that was contemporaneous with Jesus and the early church not only showed vibrancy and vigour, but also had a positive influence on Jesus and on the development of the early Church.

Scholars in the second half of the twentieth century and during the first decade of the twenty-first have continued to improve our understanding of this period, highlighting the close relationship between Jesus and his fellow Jews, especially the Pharisees. The ramifications are manifold. We are now taught that Jesus, his family and his followers were Jewish. The Jewish background to Christianity is now stressed. The rediscovery of the Jewishness of the origins of Christianity has led to a greater awareness of the creative Jewish context. It is now appreciated more than ever before that Jesus was a faithful Jew.

This development has also had significance for Jews. In the early twentieth century, European Jewish scholars – such as Franz Rosenzweig, Martin Buber and Claude Montefiore – began a move towards a positive reassessment of Christianity and reminded Jews that Jesus was a fellow Jew (their 'great brother', as Martin Buber described him). This process continues today.

The impact of these changes extends beyond university lecture rooms and has begun to influence the curriculum in seminaries and in other educational institutions. For example, the Woolf Institute has developed innovative multi-disciplinary curricula, which are being implemented at undergraduate and postgraduate levels. It is also worth mentioning the International Council of Christians and Jews, established in 1947, which serves as an umbrella organization of 38 national Jewish–Christian dialogue bodies representing 32 different countries. As a result, the study and teaching of Jewish–Christian relations has begun to be transformed.

In the last 25 years, increasing interest is also being shown in rabbinic Judaism. There is a need for greater collaboration between Jewish and Christian biblical scholars, and my own work on the Akedah, Genesis 22, has shown the interaction between Jewish and Christian commentators, particularly that the Greek and Syriac church fathers were much closer than previously argued. An encounter with living and faithful Judaism can be profoundly enriching for Christian self-understanding.

On the Jewish side, there is a new interest in Christianity. In September 2000, a statement entitled *Dabru Emet* ('Speak Truth') was published. Prepared by four Jewish theologians, it was signed by over 250 international Jewish leaders and scholars, which gave it an unusual amount of authority. It consists of a cross-denominational Jewish statement on relations with Christianity and asserts that:

> Jews and Christians worship the same God. Before the rise of Christianity, Jews were the only worshippers of the God of Israel. But Christians also worship the God of Abraham, Isaac, and Jacob; creator of heaven and earth. While Christian worship is not a viable religious choice for Jews, as Jewish theologians we rejoice that, through Christianity, hundreds of millions of people have entered into relationship with the God of Israel.

*Dabru Emet* attempts to understand Christianity in Jewish terms and overcomes the natural temptation of accusation. This involves the difficult process of overcoming pain, and at times the triumphalism of pain. We Jews have gone through a period of accusation, of blaming Christianity for centuries of persecution and misunderstanding. There has been a Christian response to this in the form of revision of catechisms, of religious texts, and certain theological concepts. Yet there is much to be done. The memory of contempt, visible in Western culture up to our days, visible in the popular understanding of Jews and Judaism, requires ongoing educational programmes to erase the damage of past centuries, to cure a collective unconscious of images and feelings of anti-Judaism. Christian scholars have only just started to think through the consequence for Christian theology of the ongoing covenantal reality of Judaism.

Jews, for their part, have to overcome 2,000 years of memories, of images of persecutions, of resentment and hatred. While tackling the teaching of contempt is bearing meaningful results for many Christians, some Jews still struggle with overcoming the images of Christian anti-Judaism. They are transmitted through the collective unconscious of the people, from one generation to the other, and experienced in many ways in present life.

The transformation of relations between Christians and Jews has had an impact well beyond the bilateral dialogue. Accordingly it serves as a paradigm of reconciliation and an inspiration for Jews and Christians in dialogue with Islam. Jews and Christians are called (as the Children of Abraham) to be a blessing for humankind. In order to be so, we must first be a blessing to one another.

## Jewish–Muslim Dialogue

Because Jews and Muslims share the experience of being minority religious communities in Europe, they have parallel experiences and needs. Yet the dialogue is overshadowed by the failure of both communities to address the impact of the Middle East conflict on their own communities.

Understanding what lies behind this failure is key to the future success of Jewish–Muslim dialogue. The Arab–Israeli conflict is one of the main factors. For most Jews, the creation of the State of Israel is an ancient promise fulfilled – the ingathering of exiles and the creation of a vibrant nation state, guaranteeing physical and spiritual security. Yet for many Muslims, the permanent existence of a Jewish State in the Middle East is a religious and political anomaly. The *Nakba*, 'the Disaster', for many Muslims, is *Yom Ha'atzma'ut*, 'the Day of Independence', for most Jews,[3] and

---

3 The *Nakba* ('Disaster' or 'Catastrophe') refers both to the approximately 800,000 Palestinian refugees from the 1947–8 war as well as the war itself, from the Palestinian perspective. The establishment of the Jewish State of Israel is marked by most Jews as a celebration of *Yom Ha'atzma'ut* ('the Day of Independence'), and similarly the war is called *Milkhemet Ha'atzma'ut* ('War of Independence'). These terms illustrate diametrically opposed understandings of the same historical events.

it is no longer uncommon to come across the view that Islamic rule must be returned to the land of Israel.

As well as Israel, a major division between Judaism and Islam is the view that Islam fulfils both Judaism and Christianity. The question of supersessionism is a well-known subject for discussion in Jewish–Christian dialogue, but needs also to be addressed in Jewish–Muslim dialogue.

As important as these factors are, the most significant failing in the dialogue is ignorance. The lack of knowledge among Jews and Muslims provides a seedbed for prejudice. This makes the creation of the Centre for the Study of Muslim–Jewish Relations in 2006 welcome for enhancing mutual understanding and promoting understanding, wisdom and brotherhood between the Jewish and Muslim communities, in the land that is holy to both of them, and around the world. It is also welcome due to increasing antisemitism and Islamophobia, as well as anti-Christian prejudice. This means that when we come across prejudice and ignorance, whether it be within the Jewish, Christian or Muslim communities, we should not be afraid to condemn it.

However, we also need to recognize that because Jewish–Muslim dialogue lies so far behind Jewish–Christian dialogue, it is essential to be prepared for conflicting views. An authentic encounter must allow for sharp differences, especially since the modern dialogue is young and vulnerable. We return to the example of Israel. Jews view its creation as an act of national liberation following nearly 2,000 years of powerlessness and homelessness. As already noted, Muslims term the same events 'The Disaster', a time when an Islamic society was uprooted and became a minority in a land that was once *dar al-Islam*. Most Jews do not separate Zionism from its deep religious roots within Judaism. However, many Muslims make a distinction between Zionism and Judaism, failing to recognize that Zionism is an integral component of Judaism and not a 'racist' ideology.

Yet Jews and Muslims share a rich vocabulary because of the similarities between Hebrew and Arabic, and the fact that the entire medieval Jewish philosophy was developed within an Islamic milieu, which contributed both to concepts and to the Hebrew language itself. Jews provided the translations of Arabic texts that made their way into Latin via Hebrew. Medieval Hebrew religious and secular poetry is a direct consequence of exposure to Arabic models.

But even more significant is the fact that Judaism in its classical form, like Islam, is based on law, a law that comprehends every aspect of private and public life. Thus religion and politics belong together as inseparable parts of a total world view or, as it is commonly expressed, 'Judaism (and in this sense Islam) is not a "religion" but a "way of life".' Thus the approach to day-to-day issues and concerns, from food laws to marriage and divorce, is similar in both traditions, as are the legal methodologies used to address such matters.

How should Jews and Muslims progress the dialogue practically? A foundation of mutual trust and respect is best built step by step – for example, organizing reciprocal visits to synagogues and mosques, developing joint strategies on issues such as discrimination, as well as supporting each other's attempt to maintain a distinctive religious identity in a society that promotes conformity to the majority culture.

If the challenges faced by Muslim–Jewish dialogue seem daunting, consider the significant advances in Christian–Jewish relations in the last 100 years. Surely one of the few pieces of good news in today's encounter between religions, Christian–Jewish dialogue arose despite profound theological differences and many centuries of alienation and distrust. However, the fact that Jews and Christians have built mutual respect and understanding does not, of course, mean that this model can be wholly applied to Islamic–Jewish relations with the same positive results. Jews and Muslims today carry memories and issues far different from the historical baggage brought to encounters with Christians.

## Conclusion

We must move towards an encounter that will take us on the journey from disdain to recognition, and when we will see the Other as a creature of God and part of God's special design for humanity:

a respectful relationship that is called dialogue. In this regard, Judaism stands in many ways in a kind of middle ground between Islam and Christianity, shedding light on each, and thereby revealing its own dependence and uniqueness. From such a perspective Judaism is ideally placed to act as an intermediary in the difficult dialogue that is so essential today between Christianity and Islam, between the West and East.

Tragically, today, the Middle East conflict makes such a role or task virtually impossible, yet there remains hope that while in the past we have defined ourselves in contradistinction and in opposition to one another, today we have to define ourselves instead by our relationship to one another.

# 12

# The Sacrifice of Abraham's Son in Judaism and Islam

## Introduction

As a Jewish scholar trained in the study of Jewish–Christian relations, it is noticeable that the encounter between Jews and Muslims shares many similarities, particularly in the interpretation of Scripture. Yet although much has been undertaken to examine the Jewish influence on the development of Christian biblical interpretation and (to a lesser extent) vice versa, the encounter between Jews and Muslims on the basis of scriptural interpretation is relatively under-researched.

You might ask: What is the relevance of this discussion? The answer is that the possible existence of a two-way encounter provides a context to interfaith dialogue today and sets the scene for a conversation between religions.

I am particularly interested in the story of the near sacrifice of Abraham's son because it is central not only to understanding Jewish (and Christian) identity, but is also important for Muslims. The willingness of someone to give up his own life for a greater cause is not unknown to religion. The three Abrahamic faiths, Judaism, Christianity and Islam, all extol self-sacrifice, the virtue of which stands at the heart of each. This is illustrated by this most famous story – the Binding of Isaac (Genesis 22 is known in Christianity as the Sacrifice of Isaac) – and a similar account is found in the Qur'an. For Muslims, the festival of *Eid al-Adha* commemorates Ibrahim's willingness to sacrifice his son at Allah's command.

For all three faiths, the focus of the story is normally understood as Abraham's relationship with God and how his faith in, and commitment to, God was demonstrated by his willingness to sacrifice his long-awaited son at God's command.

## Genesis 22.1–14

v. 1 And after these things God tested Abraham, and said to him, 'Abraham!' And he said, 'Here am I.' v. 2 He said, 'Take your son, your only son Isaac, whom you love, and go to the land of Moriah, and offer him there as a burnt offering upon one of the mountains which I shall tell you.' v. 3 So Abraham rose early in the morning, saddled his ass and took two of his young men with him, and his son Isaac; and he cut the wood for the burnt offering, and arose and went to the place of which God had told him. v. 4 On the third day Abraham lifted up his eyes and saw the place afar off. v. 5 Then Abraham said to his young men, 'Stay here with the ass; I and the lad will go yonder, and worship, and come again to you.' v. 6 And Abraham took the wood of the burnt offering, and laid it on Isaac his son; and he took in his hand the fire and the knife. So they went both of them together. v. 7 And Isaac said to his father Abraham, 'My father!' And he said, 'Here I am, my son.' He said, 'Behold, the fire and the wood; but where is the lamb for a burnt offering?' v. 8 Abraham said, 'God will provide himself the lamb for a burnt offering, my son.' So they went both of them together. v. 9 When they came to the place which God had told him, Abraham built an altar there, and laid the wood in order, and bound Isaac his son, and laid him upon the altar, upon the wood. v. 10 Then Abraham put forth his hand, and took the knife to slay his son. v. 11 But the angel of the Lord called to him from heaven, and said, 'Abraham, Abraham!' And he said, 'Here am I.' v. 12 He said, 'Do not lay your hand upon the lad, or do anything to him; for now I know that you fear God, seeing that you have not withheld your son, your only son from me.' v. 13 And Abraham lifted up his eyes and looked, and behold, behind him was a ram, caught in the thicket by his horns; and Abraham went and took the ram, and offered it up as a burnt offering instead of his son. v. 14 So Abraham called the name of that place The Lord will provide; as it is said to this day, 'On the mount of the Lord it shall be provided.'

As a piece of writing, the biblical account has everything. It has tension and drama, with enough action for a five-act play. Yet it is compressed into 14 verses. It is packed with energy and dynamism. It is a paradigm of Aristotle's catharsis, arousing both terror and pity. It deals with the biggest themes and touches the deepest emotions – and it seems to have a happy ending.

It has everything bar one aspect – an immediately apparent, morally acceptable and topically relevant message. How could Abraham reconcile the bizarre demand by God to sacrifice his son against the divine promise that he would be the ancestor of a people who would spread throughout the world?

## Sura 37.99–113

99. He [Abraham] said: 'I will go to my Lord! He will surely guide me!' 100. 'O my Lord! Grant me a righteous (son)!' 101. So We gave him the good news of a forbearing son. 102. Then, when (the son) reached (the age of) (serious) work with him, he said: 'O my son! I have seen in a vision that I offer thee in sacrifice: now see what is thy view!' (The son) said: 'O my father! Do as thou art commanded: thou will find me, if Allah so wills, one of the steadfast!' 103. So when they had both submitted (to Allah), and he had laid him prostrate on his forehead (for sacrifice), 104. We called out to him 'O Abraham! 105. 'Thou hast already fulfilled the vision!' – thus indeed do We reward those who do right. 106. For this was a clear trial – 107. And We ransomed him with a momentous sacrifice: 108. And We left for him among generations (to come) in later times: 109. 'Peace and salutation to Abraham!' 110. Thus indeed do We reward

those who do right. 111. For he was one of Our believing Servants. 112. And We gave him the good news of Isaac – a prophet, – one of the Righteous. 113. We blessed him and Isaac: but of their progeny are (some) that do right, and (some) that obviously do wrong, to themselves.

The Qur'anic passage is noteworthy for its terse style, and like the biblical account it has been subject to numerous interpretations. One of the major differences when we read the account in the Qur'an is that the son is not identified and that it is not possible to determine conclusively which son is intended. Muslim exegetes were interested in many aspects of this story, but none more so than the son's identity. Both sons are identified in the Qur'an as prophets and Isaac (17 times) is mentioned more times than Ishmael (12 times), but Ishmael is identified with the important act of building the Ka'ba (2.127), and it is interesting that in the following Sura, the name Ishmael is mentioned before Isaac.

## Sura 2.78–79

Say: We believe in God, and that which has been sent down on us and sent down on Abraham and Ishmael, Isaac and Jacob, and the tribes, and that which was given to Moses and Jesus and the Prophets and their Lord; we make no division between any of them and to Him we surrender.

In the Qur'an, the son's immediate response is a willingness to accept his fate, and both Abraham and his son were ready to suffer in accord with God's command, and they both submitted their wills to Allah. Abraham is prevented from fulfilling the sacrifice since his inner intention already fulfilled God's command. This is reminiscent of the Christian portrayal of the account in the New Testament in the Epistle to the Hebrews.

## Hebrews 11.17–19

v. 17 By faith Abraham, when he was tested, offered up Isaac, and he who had received the promises was ready to offer up his only son, v. 18 of whom it was said, 'through Isaac shall your descendants be named' [Gen. 21.12, 19] He considered that God was able to raise men even from the dead; hence, figuratively speaking, he did receive him back.

My concern in this chapter is not to draw attention to the extent to which Jews and Muslims (and Christians) share the same scriptural account of the story, but to explore some of the interpretations of the story, which shed light on commonality as well as difference. In my view, Jewish and Muslim interpretations of the story can shed light on Muslim–Jewish relations because both Jews and Muslims, like Christians, lived – and continue to live – in a scripturally orientated culture.

We will notice a number of similarities between Jewish and Muslim approaches to Scripture, which include an insistence on the harmony of Scripture and an emphasis on the unity of the text. Consequently, the interpretations of Jewish and Muslim commentators would have been understandable to adherents of both religions, suggesting the possibility of encounter on the basis of scriptural interpretation. Nowhere is an encounter more apparent than in approaches to the story of the attempted sacrifice of Abraham's son. Indeed, I would suggest that neither Jewish nor Muslim interpretations could be understood properly without reference to the other.

This is significant because the Muslim–Jewish encounter today demonstrates much ignorance and misunderstanding, which conceals a history of relations between Muslims and Jews that was, for many hundreds of years, fruitful and tolerant, particularly when compared with Jewish–Christian relations in medieval Christendom, which was characterized by suspicion, prejudice and (primarily) Christian violence against Jews.

Before we consider two examples of Jewish and Muslim interpretations, a brief word is necessary about their approaches to Scripture. For Muslims, the most reliable Qur'anic commentary is contained in the Qur'an itself, and commentary (*tafsir*) begins on this principle. Like the rabbinic hermeneutical principle, 'Scripture explains Scripture', for Muslim commentators the ways in which one verse (*ayat*) clarifies another is regarded as being the most significant form of commentary. A second form of Qur'anic commentary is how the Prophet interpreted the Qur'an, which is recorded in the hadith. The word *tafsir* is derived from the root 'fassara' – to explain, to expound. It means 'explanation' or 'interpretation' and similarly refers to explanation and interpretation of the scriptural text.

*Tafsir* is similar to midrash, a Hebrew term for asking, searching, inquiring and interpreting. In their interpretations of Scripture, the rabbis produced anthologies and homilies, including both lore and law, which were later written in the form of a commentary on a particular book of the Bible.

## Which Son?

As already pointed out, the Qur'an does not make clear the identity of the son. The biblical account, however, is clear, and Jewish interpreters expound on the significance of Isaac being chosen, as the following passages demonstrate. The two passages below are found in early midrash – Genesis Rabbah is a fifth-century CE Palestinian text, and the Fragmentary Targum possibly originates slightly earlier.

### *Genesis Rabbah 39.9 and 55.7*

> God said to Abraham: 'Please take your son.' Abraham said: 'I have two sons, which one?' God: 'Your only son.' Abraham: 'The one is the only son of his mother and the other is the only son of his mother.' God: 'Whom you love.' Abraham: 'I love this one and I love that one.' God: 'Isaac.'

## Fragmentary Targum[1] Genesis 22.10

Abraham stretched out his hand and took the knife to kill Isaac, his son. Isaac answered and said to Abraham his father: Bind my hands properly that I may not struggle in the time of my pain and disturb you and render your offering unfit and be cast into the pit of destruction in the world to come. The eyes of Abraham were turned to the eyes of Isaac, but the eyes of Isaac were turned to the angels of heaven. Isaac saw them but Abraham did not see them. In that hour the angels of heaven went out and said to each other: Let us go and see the only two just men in the world. The one slays, and the other is being slain. The slayer does not hesitate, and the one being slain stretches out his neck.

Muslim commentators are divided. It seems that the earlier commentators tended towards identifying Isaac as the son chosen for sacrifice, but from the medieval period onwards Ishmael was commonly identified as the son. For example, Muhammad ibn Jarir al-Tabari (838–923), one of the earliest Persian historians and exegetes of the Qur'an, wrote *Tarikh al-Tabari* (*History of the Prophets and Kings*) and *Tafsir al-Tabari*. He identified Abraham's son as Isaac. A few centuries later, Ismail ibn Kathîr (1301–73), an Islamic scholar from Syria, produced the famous commentary on the Qur'an that is called *Tafsir ibn Kathir*, which is one of the most widely used explanations of the Qur'an today. He argued in favour of Ishmael and is representative of later tradition, which remains mainstream understanding today.

## Al-Tabari

As for the above-mentioned proof from the Qur'an that it really was Isaac, it is God's word which informs us about the prayer

---

[1] The Targum is a Jewish translation of the Hebrew Bible into Aramaic, dating from late antiquity (first to eighth centuries CE). Targums, however, are not literal translations, but allow for interpretation.

of His friend Abraham when he left his people to migrate to Syria with Sarah. Abraham prayed, 'I am going to my Lord who will guide me. My Lord! Grant me a righteous child.' This was before he knew Hagar, who was to be the mother of Ishmael. After mentioning this prayer, God goes on to describe the prayer and mentions that he foretold to Abraham that he would have a gentle son. God also mentions Abraham's vision of himself sacrificing that son when he was old enough to walk with him. The Book does not mention any tidings of a male child given to Abraham except in the instance where it refers to Isaac, in which God said, 'And his wife, standing by laughed when we gave her tidings of Isaac, and after Isaac, Jacob', and 'Then he became fearful of them'. They said. 'Fear not!' and gave him tidings of a wise son.[2]

## Ibn Kathîr

On 'So We gave him the good news of a forbearing son':

> And this son is Ishmael for he is the first son whose good news was brought to Abraham. He is older than Isaac according to Muslims and *ahl al-Kitâb* (i.e. the People of the Book) too. It is even said in their Scripture that Ishmael was born when Abraham was 86 years old and Isaac was born when Abraham was 99. In their Scripture as well, God is said to have ordered Abraham to sacrifice his only son and in another version his firstborn . . . we never say 'only son' except to a person who hasn't got but one son. Moreover, the firstborn has got a special place [in the heart of his father] that is not given to the following children and the order to sacrifice him is therefore a greater test. Some knowledgeable people were inclined to say that the sacrificed was Isaac. This was reported from some people of *the salaf* (i.e. people of the previous generations) and it was even reported

---

2 Al-Tabari, 1987, *The History of al-Tabari, Vol II, Prophets and Patriarchs*, trans. William M. Brenner, Albany, NY: State University of New York Press, p. 89.

from some Companions but [this opinion] does not have any bearings from the Book (i.e. the Qur'an) nor from the Sunnah.³

Although I have only provided two examples, Reuven Firestone, in his excellent study,⁴ examines a wide selection of writings from a range of other commentators that demonstrate this divergence of opinion. He suggests that the argument often rested on the commentator's view of the location of the sacrifice. If the sacrifice took place in Syria, then Isaac was identified; if it took place in Mecca, then it was Ishmael.

## Satan

Another topic of mutual interest was the involvement of Satan, who was portrayed as meeting Sarah, Abraham and Isaac.

### Genesis Rabbah 56.4

> Samael went to the Patriarch Abraham and upbraided him saying, 'what means this, old man! Hast thou lost thy wits? Thou goest to slay a son granted to thee at the age of a hundred!' 'Even this I do,' replied he. 'And if He sets thee an even greater test, canst thou stand it?' said he, as it is written, *If a thing be put to thee as a trial, wilt thou be wearied (Job 4.2)?* 'Even more than this', he replied. 'Tomorrow He will say to thee, "Thou art a murderer and art guilty."' 'Still I am content', he rejoined. Seeing that he could achieve nought with him, he approached Isaac and said: 'Son of an unhappy mother! He goes to slay thee!' 'I accept my fate', he replied. 'If so', said he, 'shall all those fine tunics which thy mother made be a legacy for Ishmael?'

---

3 See Mishael M. Caspi and Sascha B. Cohen, 1995, *The Binding (Aqedah) and its Transformations in Judaism and Islam*, Lampeter, Wales: Edward Mellen Press, pp. 96–122.

4 Reuven Firestone, 1989, 'Abraham's Son: Qur'an 37:99–113', *Journal of Semitic Studies*, vol. 34, pp. 95–132.

## Tanhuma Va-yera 23

> Satan visited Sarah in the guise of Isaac. When she saw him she asked, 'What did your father do to you, my son?' He replied, 'My father led me over mountains and through valleys until we finally reached the top of a certain mountain. There he erected an altar, arranged the firewood, bound me upon the altar, took a knife to slaughter me. If the Holy One, Blessed be He, had not called out, "Lay not your hand upon the lad" I would have been slaughtered.' He had hardly completed relating what had transpired when she fainted and died, as it is written 'And Abraham came to mourn for Sarah'. From where did he come? From Moriah.

Neither the biblical nor the Qur'anic accounts mention the role of Sarah or Satan, yet Jewish and Muslim commentators include both the fallen angel (sometimes called Mastemah in the rabbinic writings) and Isaac's mother in their interpretations. Perhaps the purpose of including Satan was to remove God from being viewed as the instigator of the test, and consequently to minimize the possibility of God being criticized for initiating the trial; another reason for this may have been to have increased the severity of the test on Abraham, Isaac/Ishmael and Sarah as well as the drama of the sacrifice. Each was equal to the challenge and each provides a model for Jews and Muslims to follow, particularly in times of hardship.

As for Sarah, it is interesting to mention that Syriac Christian commentators – who may well have known both Jewish and Muslim interpretations – also mention Sarah in their interpretations, although the mainstream position is that Abraham did not inform her of the impending sacrifice. However, there is a strand of Christian exegesis represented by Romanos and Pseudo-Ephrem Graecus which suggests that Abraham did tell Sarah about the sacrifice. A published fourth-century Greek Bodmer Poem also describes how Abraham tells Sarah that 'the Immortal God wishes that I should bring noble Isaac',[5] and Sarah responds

---

5 Fourth-century Greek Bodmer Poem.

positively, advising Isaac to 'take courage'. Romanos, a sixth-century Christian poet (probably of Jewish origin), describes how Sarah asked Abraham why God gave them a child if he wanted to take him back? In reply, Abraham told Sarah not to blemish the sacrifice with her tears and that they were merely returning to God what was his. Eventually Sarah accepted the necessity of the sacrifice and told Isaac to go with his father.[6]

A number of early Muslim commentators mentioned this interpretation, including Ka'b al Akhbar (d.655–6), a Jewish convert to Islam who is likely to have translated Jewish midrash for *tafsir* literature. It is also discussed by Ahmad ibn Muhammad al-Thalabi (d.1036) and by Muhammad ibn Abd al-Kisai (d.805), who wrote *Tales of the Prophets* (*Qisas Al-Anbiya*).

In these accounts, Satan appears as a man known to Abraham. He first goes to Sarah and asks where Abraham and Isaac went. She replies that they went 'to do an errand' or to 'gather firewood'. Satan informs Sarah that Abraham actually intended to sacrifice Isaac and Sarah responds that Abraham would never do that, or that he is even more compassionate to the boy than she is, but asks why he would ever wish to sacrifice him. Satan answers that Abraham claimed God commanded that of him. Sarah replies: 'If God commanded that of him, then he should do it!' (According to al-Kisai, she curses Satan and throws him out.) Satan then appears to Isaac and receives the same replies. Finally, he goes to Abraham, who says (according to the interpretation of Ka'b al-Akhbar) 'by God, if my Lord commanded that of me, I would do it!'

## Conclusion

Although we have only looked at a small number of interpretations, I would suggest there existed an exegetical relationship between Jewish and Muslim commentators, suggesting a close

---

6 M. Moskhos, 1974, 'Romanos' Hymn on the Sacrifice of Abraham: A Discussion of the Sources and a Translation', *Byzantion*, vol. 44, pp. 310–28.

encounter between the faiths. The exegetical encounter on the basis of a shared story – even though there are significant differences in the scriptural texts – implies a relationship based on familiarity.

The interpretations collected above do not simply demonstrate parallel thinking but rather shared interpretations, which indicate not only a common approach to the sacred text but that these interpretations were viewed with mutual interest and value. Such was the closeness of the interpreters that their interpretations moved between and among Jews and Muslims.

The existence of exegetical encounters has implications for the study of Abrahamic relations. Scholars of Jewish biblical interpretation, for instance, must take seriously *tafsir* (and, of course, patristic interpretations as argued earlier in this book). Muslim (and Christian) scholars should also be aware of Jewish biblical interpretation. In order to understand properly Jewish or Muslim exegesis, it is essential to understand each other's interpretations and the influence of one upon the other.

# 13

# Changing Landscapes: Jewish–Christian–Muslim Relations Today

In their contemporary encounter with Muslims, Jews and Christians have much to discuss. Theologically, it is commonly argued that Islam is more similar to Judaism than Christianity since both have problems with Christian Trinitarian theology, stress religious law and the centrality of monotheism and have no priesthood. The 2008 Muslim Letter to the Jewish Community, *Call to Dialogue*,[1] initiated by Muslim scholars at the Centre for the Study of Muslim–Jewish Relations in Cambridge, is an example of a contemporary attempt to demonstrate the commonality between these two faiths. However, the rise of modern political Zionism, the creation of the State of Israel and the Israeli–Palestinian conflict have become major sources of tension between Jews and Muslims, not just in the Middle East but throughout the world.

There are also important similarities between Islam and Christianity – both have a strong sense of mission to people of other religions, and Jesus is revered by Muslims as a prophet. The 2007 letter from Muslim scholars to the Christian world, *A Common Word*,[2] outlines the similarities between the two faiths.

---

1 *An Open Letter: A Call to Peace, Dialogue and Understanding between Muslims and Jews*, 2008, at www.woolf.cam.ac.uk/cmjr/assets/pdf/letter.pdf

2 *An Open Letter and Call from Muslim Religious Leaders to His Holiness Pope Benedict XVI*, 2007, at www.acommonword.com/lib/downloads/CW-Total-Final-v-12g-Eng-9-10-07.pdf

Tensions also exist, demonstrated by outbursts of violence between Muslims and Christians in Africa (e.g. Nigeria's *sharia* riots in 2006 and again in 2008, in which hundreds of Muslims and Christians died) and the fall-out from Pope Benedict XVI's controversial Regensburg address (2006),[3] in which he was accused of fermenting anti-Muslim feeling. Anti-Christian violence followed in parts of the Muslim world.

Similarities and dissimilarities could provide the substance for fruitful and respectful debates. There are problems with this scenario, however, partly because the three faiths, particularly Islam, have difficulty with their fundamentalists. For example, Islam's Wahabi sect, which has a following among many Muslims, including among diaspora communities in the West, seeks to return to an idealized form of certain early Islamic values, and strongly condemns many other forms of Islam, as well as other religions.

Christian and Jewish fundamentalism also exists and is growing (alongside similar movements in Hinduism and other world religions). Jewish fundamentalists generally focus on issues related to the land and State of Israel and many take hardline political positions. In recent years, they have emerged as a significant political and religious force within Israel as well as in the diaspora. *Haredi* fundamentalists not only affirm the literal truth of the Bible, but seek to impose many biblical and Talmudic laws and ordinances upon the State of Israel. Some, both within and outside Israel, have joined with Christian fundamentalists in calling for the building of a Third Temple in Jerusalem. While largely secluded from mainstream society, following a tightly regulated lifestyle, their ultra-orthodox beliefs and moral understanding of the world have similarities to those of some evangelical communities. Christian allies of Jewish fundamentalists believe the creation of the Jewish State in 1948 and the yet-to-be-built Third Temple are theological prerequisites for the second coming of Jesus. Some

---

3 *Faith, Reason and the University: Memories and Reflections*, Pope Benedict XVI's Address to the University of Regensburg (12 September 2006), at www.vatican.va/holy_father/benedict_xvi/speeches/2006/september/documents/hf_ben-xvi_spe_20060912_university-regensburg_en.html

of these same fundamentalists also actively seek the conversion of Jews to Christianity.

Both Jewish and Christian fundamentalists reject modern scriptural criticism, particularly the documentary theory of biblical scholarship, the Darwinian concept of human evolution, and are profoundly opposed to abortion and euthanasia. Christian and Jewish fundamentalist leaders have sometimes worked together, advocating a broad public policy agenda that opposes the strict separation of Church and state and 'secular humanism', a pejorative term used to describe opponents of fundamentalism. Often, fundamentalists have a special loathing of co-religionists whose views do not fit their own: for example, the al-Qaeda movements has (have) been quite as prepared to kill other Muslims as it has Jews and Christians, Americans and British, and other perceived enemies.

Zionism and the creation of the State of Israel in 1948 has been a cause of controversy not only between Jews and Christians, but also with Muslims. For Jews, the establishment of the State of Israel in the wake of the Shoah was considered a miracle. However, for the Arab Palestinians, the vast majority of whom are Muslim, this marks the beginning of their *Nakba*, 'the Catastrophe', in which approximately two-thirds of their population became refugees and lost control and ownership over the majority of the land they inhabited prior to the War of Independence. In addition to the political conflict between Israelis and Palestinians, Israel occupies the third holiest Muslim site, the al-Aqsa Mosque, located on the Haram al-Sharif, known to Jews as the Temple Mount, in the Old City of Jerusalem. These holy places are at the centre of both religious ideology and rhetoric as well as the focus of much global attention (and contention). Their symbolic value to Christians, Muslims and Jews worldwide cannot be overestimated. I will return to the subject of Israel later.

The positive developments in Jewish–Christian relations, in the last 50 years in particular, are viewed with distrust by some Muslims, who regard it as an attempt to marginalize and disempower them. The recent creation of interfaith structures, which include Muslims alongside Jews and Christians (such as the Three Faiths Forum and International Council of Christians and Jews), may help to change this negative point of view. At the same time, more positive contemporary Muslim relations with Jews and Christians are also dependent upon intra-Islamic discussions that would admit more internal diversity, and articulate and apply more generous attitudes towards other religions than the noisiest ones that emanate from some parts of Islam.

For Christians, intra-faith conversation and relations (ecumenism) is also a recent movement, beginning in the early twentieth century but only really gaining momentum after 1948, the year the World Council of Churches (WCC) was founded. Originally the ecumenical Christian movement paid significant attention to Jews only as the objects of mission, but two factors caused a profound change of heart. First, the Swiss theologian Karl Barth (1886–1968) insisted that Jews were *verus Israel*, the true Israel, and that it was appropriate to speak of 'the Church *and* Israel'.[4] Then in 1965 *Nostra Aetate* affirmed 'the sacred spiritual bond linking the people of the new covenant with Abraham's stock'.[5] The Faith and Order Commission of the WCC expressed its conviction in the same year that the Jewish people still had theological significance of their own for the Church, and in 1982 *Ecumenical Considerations on Jewish–Christian Dialogue* was published. It argued that the Jewish people were full partners in dialogue: 'The spirit of dialogue is to be fully present to one another in full openness and human vulnerability.'[6] Yet mission to the Jewish people was not repudiated, which reflected the many different views held by WCC member churches.

For Jews, intra-Jewish conversations about Christianity have been much more limited, and Claude Montefiore's call for a Jewish

---

4  See Karl Barth, 1957, *Church Dogmatics*, II.2, ed. and trans. G. W. Bromley and Thomas F. Torrance, Edinburgh: T & T Clark.

5  *Nostra Aetate: Declaration on the Relationship of the Church to Non-Christian Religions*, Second Vatican Council (28 October 1965), at www.vatican.va/archive/hist_councils/ii_vatican_council/documents/vat-ii_decl_19651028_nostra-aetate_en.html

6  *Ecumenical Considerations on Jewish–Christian Dialogue*, 1982, World Council of Churches, at www.oikoumene.org/resources/documents/wcc-programmes/interreligious-dialogue-and-cooperation/interreligious-trust-and-respect/ecumenical-considerations-on-jewish-christian-dialogue.html

theology of Christianity in 1923 has yet to be fully realized. Even *Dabru Emet* ('Speak Truth'), the cross-denominational Jewish statement on Christians and Christianity published in 2000, begins the process of reflecting on the place of Christianity in contemporary Jewish thought. *Dabru Emet* stresses that it is time for Jews to reflect on what Judaism may now say about Christianity, and asserts eight points: Jews and Christians worship the same God; Jews and Christians seek authority from the same book (the Bible); Christians can respect the claim of the Jewish people upon the land of Israel; Jews and Christians accept the moral principles of Torah; Nazism was not a Christian phenomenon; the humanly irreconcilable differences between Jews and Christians will not be settled until God redeems the world; a new relationship between Jews and Christians will not weaken Jewish practice; and Jews and Christians must work together for justice and peace.[7]

Contemporary Muslim communities are also grappling with the place of Judaism and Christianity in Islamic thought. In one sense, Islam's relationship can be dealt with under the familiar theme of supersessionism, since Muslims believe that Islam was the final religion revealed by God through the Prophet Muhammad (*c*.570–632). Islam sees itself as perfecting the two monotheistic religions and the Qur'an calls both Jews and Christians *ahl al-Kitâb* (People of the Book). One consequence of Islamic supersessionism on Jewish–Christian relations is that it provides Christians with an insight into the difficulties raised by traditional Christian supersessionism of Judaism and what is sometimes called replacement theology.

More Muslims are playing an important role in the wider interfaith community, building on the pioneering work of leading figures such as Prince Hassan of Jordan and the American-based Pakistani academic, Akbar Ahmed, both of whom have devoted their lives to the interfaith endeavour. There are signs that they are no longer alone, as demonstrated by the action of King Abdullah of Saudi Arabia, the Custodian of the Two Holy Places, who opened a World Conference on Dialogue in 2008 and called

---

7 *Dabru Emet*, op. cit.

for dialogue between Muslims and non-Muslims, in the face of criticism from some senior clerics in Saudi Arabia. Yet it is too early to predict what results these events will have.

Despite the challenge to search for a common language and potential symbiosis, there are major doctrinal and psychological barriers to a trialogue with the three monotheistic religions and collective memories prevent uninhibited dialogue: for example, Jews think of Christianity in terms of suffering and persecution; while Muslims have not forgotten the Crusades, and see in Western aspirations for world hegemony the old Crusader mentality in a new guise. All three religions have wide experience in polemics and apologetics, but interfaith dialogue remains limited to a minority.

## Abraham

Abraham is often regarded as a symbol of hope in the Jewish–Christian–Muslim encounter and acclaimed as a spiritual mentor and guide. For example, Karl-Josef Kuschel calls for 'an Abrahamic ecumenism', in which Jews, Christians and Muslims work together in mutual respect and for the common good.[8] The first decade of the twenty-first century has witnessed a number of interfaith initiatives adopting the term 'Abrahamic' in their title. Since Judaism, Christianity and Islam all trace their spiritual ancestry to Abraham, viewing him as a paradigm of the human–divine relationship, there is an attempt to depict him as a figure who can help reconcile three related but divided religions (the 'Abrahamic faiths').

While Abraham is certainly an important figure to the three faiths, it is just as possible that his significance to each can be interpreted as undermining his importance to the others because they have not interpreted him appropriately. For example, for Jews the Bible's descriptions of Abraham's encounters with God are viewed most commonly in terms of God's promises concerning

---

8 Karl-Josef Kuschel, 1999, 'Children of Abraham: On the Necessity of an Abrahamic Ecumene between Jews, Christians, and Muslims', *Convergence*, vol. 10, pp. 34–40.

continuity of family and inheritance of the land of Israel. Jewish claims to be the inheritors of the land of Israel through the promises of Abraham have been, and remain, a source of controversy between Jews, Christians and Muslims.

The New Testament reveals both continuities and discontinuities with the patriarch. Jesus descends from the seed of Abraham, but ancestry from Abraham is not sufficient to avoid divine wrath. Narratives of the early Church reinforce the division between those who believe in the Christ and are spiritual, and Jews who adhere to the Torah. The Qur'an describes Abraham as the *hanif*, the God-seeker par excellence. Muslims revere Abraham as a holy figure, and trace their lineage back to his son Ishmael. Muslim traditions elaborate the biblical narratives, understanding, for example, the object of Abraham's sacrifice narrated in Genesis 22 to be Ishmael rather than Isaac. For Jews and Christians, the child of the promise is Isaac: it is through Isaac that Abraham becomes the father of the people of Israel and of the nations.

The Qur'an designates Islam as 'the religious community of Abraham' (*millat Ibrahim*) and portrays Muhammad as a follower of the monotheistic faith of Abraham (16.123). But who does Abraham belong to? According to a common translation, the Qur'an affirms that:

> Abraham was not a Jew nor yet a Christian; but he was true in Faith, and bowed his will to Allah's (Which is Islam), and he joined not gods with Allah. Without doubt, among men, the nearest of kin to Abraham, are those who follow him, as are also this Messenger and those who believe: And Allah is the Protector of those who have faith. (3.67f.)[9]

The translator's interpretative gloss, 'which is Islam', shows how Abraham has become a Muslim possession, the father of those who truly submit in faith to God, and do not associate other gods

---

9 Sura 3. 'The Family of 'Imran, The House of 'Imran', at www.islamicity.com/quaran/3.htm

with him; namely, Muslims. Note the difference from a more recent translation of the Qur'an published by Oxford University Press:

> Abraham was neither a Jew nor a Christian. He was upright and devoted to God, never an idolater, and the people who are closest to him are those who truly follow his ways, this Prophet and [true] believers – God is close to [true] believers.[10]

Nevertheless, some Jews, Christians and Muslims seek reconciliation of these differences by appealing to the fact that each tradition hearkens back to the biblical Abraham. The resolution of their theological and communal differences will depend upon how carefully they negotiate the virtues of Abraham that belong to all three traditions and appreciate the particular claims made by each of them. Clearly, Abraham can be a model of faith for the three, but the point at issue is whether each one of these religions can allow him to be a model for members of the other two (or, conceivably, for members of one of them but not the other). Even if Abraham is not as promising a figure as many assume or press him to be, the long history of suspicion and bloodshed between Jews, Christians and Muslims surely motivates them to search for common ground.

## Memory and Identity

Unlike national identities, religious identities are sacred to those who hold them and their key events have usually occurred much further in the past than most national events. For example, Muslims find contemporary meaning in the *hijra*, the emigration from Mecca to Medina of Muhammad and his followers in 622 CE. Likewise, Jews view the exodus from Egypt as of contemporary significance, as Christians view the death and resurrection of Jesus.

Let's take Passover as an example. For Jews, Passover is connected to the historical commemoration of the exodus from Egypt, and the Torah commands the Israelites to recall this event

---

10 M. A. S. Abdel Haleem, 2004, *The Qur'an*, Oxford: Oxford University Press.

(Deuteronomy 16.2, 6–7). Deuteronomy 16.3 refers to unleavened bread as 'the bread of affliction', remembering the Egyptian oppression. Christians for their part associate the festival with the death of Jesus. The eucharistic liturgy during the Easter season includes the words: 'Christ our Passover is sacrificed for us. Therefore let us keep the feast.' These words derive from Paul's first letter to the Corinthians (5.7–8), where he compares clearing out the bad elements of their lives with getting rid of the old yeast or leaven.

For Jews, Christians and Muslims, the inheritance of the past is important to their religious identity and their encounter, but so too is the continuing relevance of this past. Learning from the past does not require us to live there – but there are some believers who wish to restore the past, by force if necessary, and others who wish to forget:

> Thus says the LORD, who makes a way in the sea, a path in the mighty waters, who brings forth chariot and horse, army and warrior; they lie down, they cannot rise, they are extinguished, quenched like a wick: 'Remember not the former things, nor consider the things of old. Behold, I am doing a new thing; now it springs forth, do you not perceive it?' (Isaiah 43.16–18.)

So spoke Isaiah, prophet of the exile to his people, encouraging the Israelites to believe that there was the hope that they would return to the land of Israel. Strikingly, the prophet speaks in terms of forgetting the past, for the sake of the future. To what extent we should forget the past clearly has an impact on memory and on identity.

There are those religious believers who are not prepared to forget about the past, just as there are those who prefer to forget. For the latter, the baggage of the past makes no sense. They hold, for example, that the search for simple certainties is mistaken and unethical and that theological and ideological questions, such as seeking truth, serve to (at best) confuse and (at worst) abuse memory and identity. Of course, it may well be that their view is correct, but it does not necessarily follow that passing over the past is a constructive way to form memory and identity.

Commemorations of past events help preserve a sense of historical continuity, identity and even social integration. Collective memory contains a strong conservative force furnishing a community with a sense of historical continuity. However, a preoccupation (some might call it obsession) with the past may be harmful. The memory of a founding event that is recollected and re-enacted may become a danger if it results in a negative identity and self-understanding, especially if it becomes the only or primary lens through which reality and the changing world is viewed.

For example, the legacy of being a victim has left an enduring mark on the Jewish psyche and impacts on the Jewish encounter with Christians and Muslims. A history of being surrounded by oppressive nations has become a feature of Jewish memory and identity, leading to a sense of victimization. Taking to heart the Bible's command to the Children of Israel to remember (*zachor*), because 'you were slaves in the land of Egypt', Jews are reminded to remember the suffering of Israel in Egypt; the Torah also reminds them to remember the violence committed against the Israelites by the surrounding nations.

A modern example of a focus upon victimization is the 614th commandment proposed by Emil Fackenheim, in his reflection on the Holocaust.[11] One dangerous consequence of demanding Jewish continuity so as not to give Hitler a posthumous victory is that Jewish identity can easily became Shoah-centred, as can relations between Jews and Christians. The Holocaust reinforced a mentality in the Jewish world that Jews are a small minority and that the Jewish people, even Jews in Israel, are surrounded by hostile non-Jews. Consequently, a young Jew will easily construct a negative Jewish identity which, without the positive side of Judaism, will not be of value to be handed down over the generations. A young Christian will come away with an exclusive picture of the Jew as victim, without an awareness of the positive aspects of Jewish culture. If the Jew disappears from the historical horizons from the death of Jesus in 33 CE and only reappears

---

11 Emil Fackenheim, 1994, *To Mend the World: Foundations of Post-Holocaust Jewish Thought*, 2nd edn, Bloomington, IN: Indiana University Press, p. xix.

again when Hitler came to power in 1933, not only will a negative identity be formed, but Jewish–Christian relations will also be based on a victim–perpetrator relationship.

Like Jews, Muslims also tend to view the outside world as a threat, which may lead to a preoccupation with a memory of suffering. Akbar Ahmed's recent studies of the views of Muslims in the twenty-first century[12] lists numerous examples of Muslims feeling 'under attack by the West and modernity', which are viewed as a 'Judeo-Christian' creation. While carrying out research, Ahmed asked Muslims across the Muslim world: 'What do you think is the number one problem in the world today?' He expected the answer: 'Israel, Iraq and Afghanistan'. However, to Muslims in Damascus, in Karachi and London, the number one problem was the perception that Islam was deliberately being distorted in the West; that Islam was under attack.

Attitudes within the Muslim community in the United Kingdom had begun to harden in the late 1980s, when the controversy around Salman Rushdie's novel *The Satanic Verses*[13] erupted, and Muslims saw themselves depicted as little more than an angry community of book-burners. Often the target of racism and discrimination, they resented the negative depiction of Islam in the media. The 1990s marked the coming of age of a new generation who were marginalized and alienated from mainstream society not only in the United Kingdom, but also in the rest of Europe. Many Muslims were convinced that however integrated and Westernized they were, their 'Muslimness' would still exclude them from being accepted as part of Western society.

## *Memoria Futuri* – Memory for the Future

One way to disarm an obsession with the past is to adopt a critical approach to it in order not to become victims of an ideological 'vindication' of the past that is nostalgic, dogmatic and sometimes

---

[12] Akbar Ahmed, 2007, *Journey into Islam*, Washington, DC: Brookings Institution Press; Akbar Ahmed, 2010, *Journey into America*, Washington, DC: Brookings Institution Press.

[13] Salman Rushdie, 1988, *The Satanic Verses*, London: Viking Penguin.

irrational. If the past is approached critically, it can reveal new interpretations and understandings of the world that can be liberating and constructive.

For example, although reflection on and reaction to the Shoah are essential for an understanding of Jewish–Christian relations, positive relations cannot be built solely on responses to antisemitism and Christian feelings of guilt. Certainly, the past must be remembered and memories have to find a way to be reconciled so that horrors are not forgotten, otherwise, as George Santayana stated, 'Those who cannot remember the past are condemned to repeat it.'[14] However, no healthy and enduring relationship between people is built on guilt. If recent Christian soul-searching in the aftermath of the destruction of European Jewry leads to a new approach and a revision of traditional anti-Jewish teaching, so much the better. However, the future relationship cannot be built on the foundations of guilt. The sense of guilt is transient and does not pass to the next generation; moreover, it is unstable, inherently prone to sudden and drastic reversal. So it is necessary for Jews and Christians to negotiate a better stance towards a compromised past in order to look forward to a more hopeful future. Indeed, redeeming a compromised past offers grounds for hope in Jewish–Christian relations, but also in relations with Muslims and other faith communities.

Walter Kasper, previous President of the Pontifical Commission for Religious Relations with the Jews, has called for a renewed *memoria futuri* and for Jews and Christians to reflect on the more positive aspects of memory. Religious remembrance, he argued, is not an act of nostalgia, but empowers in the present. For example, in their liturgy, Jews and Christians remember not only what God has done for them in the past, but remember that God's people continue to have a role today.

Christianity has recognized that past practices about, and traditional views of, Jews are wholly unacceptable and have worked to

---

14 George Santayana, 1905, *The Life of Reason*, 1, New York: Charles Scribner's Sons, p. 284.

create a new relationship. The tackling of Christian triumphalism and the *Adversus-Iudaeos* tradition illustrates a shift from what was, for the most part, an inherent need to condemn Judaism to a need to condemn Christian anti-Judaism. It has also led to a closer relationship with 'the elder brother' and not, as some feared, to the undermining of Christian teaching. The rediscovery of a positive relationship with Judaism facilitates a positive formation of Christian identity and memory.

For Jews, *memoria futuri* may help them view diaspora life not primarily in negative terms (as an anti-Jewish environment and exemplifying a continuous history of oppression), but in positive terms (as a fruitful environment facilitating vigorous Jewish existence and dynamic development). Traditionally, diaspora was equated with *golah*, 'exile', implying that life outside of Israel is a life of exile (an undesirable situation). However, diaspora is a Greek word meaning 'dispersion' (a voluntary situation desirable to the individual), which can be a positive experience for the Jewish people living among the nations of the world, leading to constructive interaction.

As a minority, Jews have thrived, having lived in a diaspora community since at least the fall of the First Temple in the sixth century BCE. After 70 CE, Jews had to create a sense of religious identity without the possession of Jerusalem or the Temple and, arguably, rabbinic Judaism survived and flourished precisely because it had not been so attached to the rites of the Temple as the Sadducees.

Thriving in a diaspora means that communities are affected by change in the wider society. This leads to a change in an individual's identity or the now more common notion of hybrid identity, when one's identity is constituted by a multiplicity of different identities – cultural, religious, ethnic, linguistic, national – that were once considered distinct.

This is a relatively new development in Europe, but has a longer history and is more common in the United States. An example of hybrid identity is an American-born citizen of Israeli origins. With the increased communication and ease of travel today, many

American citizens of Israeli origin can participate in the cultural and religious world of Israel while simultaneously participating in the cultural and linguistic world of the United States. If asked about one's identity, this person would most probably reply with a hyphenated response such as 'American–Israeli'. Pushed further, one might discover even deeper layers of identity in an answer, such as 'American–Israeli–Sefardi'.

A consequence of hybrid identities is that people regularly cross boundaries that divide insider from outsider, thus blurring identity boundaries that were previously more clearly defined. In the process, change occurs – and because people have to readjust and redefine who they are, their identities can become fragile. It is no easy task to redefine one's identity, which can easily lead to prejudice as a defensive mechanism. The reaction against rapidly shifting boundaries of identity, especially when one or more identity is 'perceived' to be under threat, inevitably leads to an over-rootedness in one's identity and a subsequent decrease in a desire to engage in dialogue with the 'Others'.

One example of the changing historical situation can be seen in changes in immigrant areas. For example, in East London, a highly populated immigrant area, the Brick Lane Jamme Masjid (mosque) presently serves local Bangladeshi Muslims. It was originally built in 1743 as a French Protestant church, turned into a Methodist chapel in 1819, converted into the Spitalfields Great Synagogue in 1898, and finally became the Brick Lane Jamme Masjid in 1976. When the Jewish community decided to sell the building, they wanted it to continue being a house of worship. Therefore they sold the building to the Bengali Muslim community for a low price, thus ensuring that the synagogue would become a mosque. As a relic of the interfaith and communal past, there remains a sign in Hebrew commemorating some of its former Jewish community members.

Another change affecting relations can be seen in the growth of secularism, a challenge that can bring Jews, Christians and Muslims together. The secular challenge has led some to call for a 'common mission' and for religious leaders to see one another as allies opposing religious indifference, which is understood as a greater threat than religious differences. This may lessen the sense of rivalry that characterized past relations and pave the way for joint approaches on issues of common interest, both at national leadership level and in local areas. This can be illustrated by Jewish, Christian and other faith communities demonstrating together in the jubilee year (2000) against poverty and for the relief of Third World debt. This led to further joint interfaith action, such as the 200,000 people who travelled to Edinburgh during a meeting of the G8 leaders in 2005 to support the Make Poverty History campaign.

On the other hand, practitioners of interfaith dialogue are apt to overlook the fact that some of their colleagues in this enterprise are attached to their religion not because of faith in God, but for community reasons, or because they like its artistic and aesthetic values. For example, a number of Christians go to church because of its liturgical and musical excellence or for cultural or other reasons. Likewise, many Jews are secular, but retain their identity as Jews in terms of culture. Secular Jews may have a rather tenuous connection with Judaism, but are as likely to be involved in interreligious conversation as observant Jews. Indeed, proponents of dialogue may be convinced of its ability to bring together and reconcile members of antagonistic religious faiths, but lack any great degree of personal faith themselves. The assumption that a strong, personal faith is at the heart of religion is often a Protestant Christian emphasis. Equally, however, outsiders often assume that Christians possess – or at least declare – such a faith when many in fact do not.

## Israel

Nowhere is the subject of peace and understanding – or perhaps, more realistically, violence and misunderstanding – more evident than in the Middle East, and more discussed than in the tea rooms and coffee parlours of Jerusalem and Tel Aviv, as well as Ramallah and Bethlehem.

## JEWS, CHRISTIANS AND MUSLIMS IN ENCOUNTER

The 2008–09 war in Gaza is a reminder of what seems to be an intractable conflict between Israel and the Palestinians. A story is told about an Israeli and a Palestinian leader meeting with God and asking whether there will ever be peace in the Middle East in their lifetime. 'Of course there will be peace'. God told them. They looked relieved. 'However,' God continued, 'not in my lifetime.' Some 120 years after the beginning of modern Zionism, a peaceful solution seems some distance away.

For Jews, the centrality of the land of the Bible, as well as the survival of over a third of world Jewry, is at stake. The creation of the State of Israel is an ancient promise fulfilled – the ingathering of exiles and the creation of a vibrant nation state, guaranteeing physical and spiritual security. Christians, for their part, not only disagree as to the place of Israel in Christian theology, but many understandably feel particular concern for Arab Christians who live in Israel and in the future state of Palestine. For many Muslims, the permanent existence of a Jewish State in the Middle East is a religious and political anomaly. It is not an uncommon view that Islamic rule must be returned to the land of Israel.

Israel is controversial because it cannot be viewed simply as a geographical and political entity whose emergence is like the establishment of any new state. Political, social, cultural and religious concerns all affect its place in the Jewish–Christian–Muslim relationship. Dialogue between Jews, Christians and Muslims is sometimes mistakenly transformed into an Israeli–Palestinian or Israeli–Arab conversation, with national identity emphasized far more than religious difference.

For Jews, the will to survive in the diaspora generated messianic hopes of redemption, which occasionally led to a high level of anticipation and the extraordinary claims of self-appointed messiahs such as Bar Kokhba and Shabbetai Zvi. One of the common features of these times of messianic fervour was that the Promised Land became a symbol of redress for all the wrongs that Jews had suffered. Thus modern Zionism became in part the fusion of messianic fervour and the longing for Zion. Jews took their destiny into their own hands and stopped waiting for a divine solution to their predicament. This was a dramatic break from the diaspora strategy of survival, which advocated endurance of the status quo as part of the covenant with God. For many Jews, the Jewish State offered the best hope not only for survival in response to the breakdown in Europe in the late nineteenth and early twentieth centuries, but also for religious and cultural fulfilment.

Martin Buber explained the Jewish historical attachment to the land of Israel in a letter to Mahatma Gandhi, written in response to Gandhi's November 1938 declaration, which was critical of Zionist aspirations. Gandhi had recommended that Jews remain in Germany and pursue *satyagraha* ('holding on to truth', which was the basis for his non-violent resistance to British rule) even unto death. Buber forcefully rejected this argument and explained the connection between the Jewish people and the land as follows:

> You say, Mahatma Gandhi, that a sanction is 'sought in the Bible' to support the cry for a national home, which 'does not make much appeal to you'. No, this is not so. We do not open the Bible and seek sanction there. The opposite is true: the promises of return, of reestablishment, which have nourished the yearning hope of hundreds of generations, give those of today an elementary stimulus, recognized by few in its full meaning but effective also in the lives of many who do not believe in the message of the Bible.[15]

Jews may view the creation of the State of Israel as an act of national liberation following nearly 2,000 years of powerlessness and homelessness. Yet many Muslims term the same events 'The Disaster', a time when an Islamic society was uprooted and became a minority in a land that was once *dar al-Islam*. Relations between Muslims and Jews are overshadowed by the failure of both communities to address the impact of the Middle East conflict on their own communities.

How ironic that both Muslims and Jews feel vulnerable and under attack! They share the experience of being minority commu-

---

15 Nahum N. Glatzer and Paul Mendes-Flohr (eds), 1991, *The Letters of Martin Buber*, New York: Schocken, pp. 479–80.

nities in Europe and the United States and have parallel experiences and needs. Xenophobia and prejudice know no boundaries.

Roman Catholicism's attitude towards Zionism changed greatly in the course of the twentieth century. In 1904, Pope Pius X (1903–14) rejected Herzl's plea for support, unequivocally stating that 'The Jews have not recognized our Lord, therefore we cannot recognize the Jewish people.'[16] However, Vatican II and the 1965 document *Nostra Aetate*, while not explicitly mentioning Israel, began the process that eventually led to the Vatican's signing of the Fundamental Agreement with the State of Israel on 30 December 1993, and then exchanging ambassadors in May 1994. Increasing awareness among Roman Catholics of the place of Israel became much more noticeable during the papacy of John Paul II, demonstrated by the Pontiff's pilgrimage to Israel in 2000, and the everlasting image of his visit to the Western Wall. Following Jewish tradition, the Pope placed a written prayer in a crevice of the Western Wall. The short typed prayer with an official seal read:

> God of our fathers, you chose Abraham and his descendants to bring your Name to the Nations. We are deeply saddened by the behaviour of those who in the course of history have caused these children of yours to suffer, and asking your forgiveness we wish to commit ourselves to genuine brotherhood with the people of the Covenant.[17]

Nevertheless, even though there have been great changes in Christian teaching on Judaism, a resurgence of anti-Israeli attitudes, particularly in Europe, has taken place in the last few years, and the feeling remains that while the Church has for a long time been grappling with issues related to Christian antisemitism, attitudes towards the land and State of Israel continue, from the

---

16 Marvin Lowenthal (ed.), 1956, *The Diaries of Theodor Herzl*, New York: Dial Press, pp. 429–30.

17 'Prayer of the Holy Father at the Western Wall', John Paul II's Pilgrimage to the Holy Land (26 March 2000), at www.vatican.va/holy_father/john_paul_ii/travels/documents/hf_jp-ii_spe_20000326_jerusalem-prayer_en.html

theological perspective, to be more difficult to tackle. Simply put, it has been easier for Christians to condemn antisemitism as a misunderstanding of Christian teaching than to come to terms with the re-establishment of the Jewish State. As a result, the subject of Israel has probably caused as much disagreement and division within the Church as any other topic in Jewish–Christian dialogue. Alice Eckardt is one of a number of scholars who points out the contrast between Christian willingness to tackle antisemitism and the Shoah and Christian reticence on the subject of Israel.[18]

There are also dangers when those who, in the name of dialogue, move from a position of commitment to the well-being of Israel, to one of almost 'Israel can do no wrong'. This is not conducive to dialogue for it is not an honest and sober conversation firmly related to present realities. For example, although evangelical Christian Zionists strongly support Israel and especially the Settler Movement, their agenda is dominated by an eschatological timetable. Their hope, as they freely admit, is that the Jewish return to Zion will be followed by a second coming and the acceptance of Jesus by the entire Jewish people. David Flusser, the eminent Israeli scholar of first-century Judaism, once told the following story, based on his encounter with a group of evangelical Christians visiting Israel:

> 'Why should we quarrel?' I asked, 'You believe in the coming of the Messiah – so do we. So let us both work for it and pray for it. Only, when he arrives, allow me to ask him one question first, "Excuse me, sir, but is this your first visit to Jerusalem?"'[19]

There is another danger to mention: what happened 100 years ago to Jews outside of Israel is considered by some as historically remote compared to biblical events, which are viewed as almost contemporary. The present becomes transformed into biblical language and geography, which leads to the danger of giving

---

18  Alice L. Eckardt, 1992, 'The Place of the Jewish State in Christian–Jewish Relations', *European Judaism*, vol. 251, p. 4.

19  Edward Kessler, 1999, *Jewish–Christian Relations: The Next Generation*, Cambridge: CJCR Press, p. 5.

metaphysical meaning to geographical places. The fundamentalist Jew in Israel interprets the ownership of the land of Israel in terms of a divine gift. This creates the great danger of bestowing divine importance on Israel, and the vocation of the Jew becomes a dedication to the existence and the restoration of the cosmic state. Thus the return to the land of Israel is a fulfilment of the divine promise and reflects a return to the original fullness. However, the biblical promises do not define the same borders, and by choosing the widest ones the fundamentalist abuses the idea of the promise, which is related to the land.

So where do we go from here? Much of Israel's history has been about winning wars in the face of great hostility. Israeli Jews are aware, however, that a successful future may depend on an even harder task: winning the peace.

Israel has won great military victories, none greater than the Six Day War in 1967, when the State of Israel appeared to be in a hopeless situation. The Israeli army heroically defended their country against apparently overwhelming odds. However, the qualities that win wars are not necessarily the same qualities that win the peace. For one thing, winning wars often results in a tendency to glorify military prowess, leading to an unhealthy self-reliance and self-belief, bordering on arrogance. For another, war inevitably engenders enmity and hatred, neither of which provides a foundation upon which peace can be built. Palestinians living in the West Bank since 1967 have, for the most part, only experienced Israeli occupation and power. It is surely little wonder that the attitudes of many are so negative towards Israel.

Israelis are surely right to recognize that their country must remain armed while there is the danger of renewed aggression from neighbours or regional superpowers. Iran's threat to 'remove Israel from the map of the world' serves to reinforce this outlook. Israelis are possibly right to hold on to territorial gains until wide-ranging peace is agreed; but in the end there will be no security for Israel until mutual grievance is replaced by mutual trust. To win the peace, Israel needs not only to make territorial concessions, as it did by returning Sinai to Egypt (1979) and by leaving Gaza (2005). It must also strive to build bridges of understanding and friendship, between ordinary Israelis and Palestinians in particular and Arabs in general.

For over half a century Israel has passed one military test after another. Until fairly recently, Arab states did not want peace with Israel. They rejected the partition plan of 1947 and for many years denied the right of a Jewish State to exist at all. Some still do, and the rhetoric and actions of Hamas are sober reminders of those days. However, the historic visit of Sadat to Israel in 1977 and the warm welcome he received from the Israeli public made it clear that peace is a realistic possibility. Since then, there have been sporadic outbursts of peace evidenced by the signing of peace treaties with Jordan and the Palestinian Liberation Organization.

There is no doubt that there are Arabs, whatever may have been their past record, who genuinely desire peace. There are others, of course, who still seek the destruction of the Jewish State. Yet in the face of this ongoing hostility, Israelis need to remember the courage of leaders like Anwar Sadat who, like Yitzhak Rabin, lost his life at the hands of a fellow countryman because of his desire for peace.

If there is a desire for peace on both sides, the first condition of its attainment has been achieved. There is, however, a second condition, which has been severely tested in recent decades. Winning the peace requires compromise and concessions on all sides. This is not a call for pacifism. As William Ralph Inge said, 'It is useless for the sheep to pass resolutions in favour of vegetarianism while the wolf remains of a different opinion.'[20]

At the root of the problem is a clash between two peoples laying claim to the same land. This is neatly illustrated by the following apocryphal story told to me in the Arab market in Jerusalem some years ago:

There were two brothers. Each owned half a field, but each wanted the half he did not have and neither would give up his half. They called in a rabbi known for his wisdom. He lay down with his ear to the ground under a tree in the field and appeared

---

20 William Ralph Inge, 1919, *Outspoken Essays*, First Series, London: Longmans, Green & Co.

to fall asleep. After a time the brothers grew impatient, complaining that the rabbi was wasting their time. But he told them that he had been listening to the ground. It had told him that neither of them owned the ground. It owned them. And one day, he said, they would be inside it.

The conflict will not be resolved in the long term by military means, but only by political compromise and territorial concession. To an outsider it seems obvious what ought to happen – limited autonomy must evolve into independence and eventually into a federation of states, initially consisting of Israel, Palestine and Jordan, leading perhaps to an economic community of Middle Eastern States.

At some points in the future, morality and expediency will coincide and Israelis and Palestinians will have the opportunity to bring peace to the region. It is in Israel's self-interest to make peace, as the vast of majority of Jews recognize. The State of Israel survived and flourished because it was able to withstand decades of attacks. It won the military battles. Its future survival now also depends on winning the peace.

The debate about the place of Israel will continue in the future for God-knows how long. Unless we intend to carry on talking at each other during and beyond our lifetimes – as in the story I told earlier – we need to change our course: listening to each other's views with generosity would be a good place to start.

# Postlude

## MARTIN FORWARD

I've read these chapters with a mixture of nostalgia and joy. Working with Ed to set up the Centre for the Study of Jewish–Christian Relations was the finest time of my professional life, and it was made more special by the close rapport that grew up between us. I reference this personal dimension not simply to indulge myself, but out of the conviction that if good friendship can be the result of such interfaith collegiality, then this is surely a splendid reason to encourage more collaborations between Abraham's children.

Ever since the Centre was founded in 1998, it has pursued the vision of improving and deepening relations between Jews and Christians through the medium of education. If our world is to survive and flourish, then Jews, Christians and Muslims need to renew their present and future relationships by choosing prudently from their shared past. As they attempt this *mitzvah* ('commandment' or 'good deed'), they need knowledge to understand why their communities of faith so often mistrust one another, and wisdom to know how to overcome this baleful legacy. Dr Kessler has been at the forefront of teaching us things about our shared and separate histories that encourage us to promote the common good.

It would be impertinent and pointless of me to attempt any kind of survey of these chapters, since he writes so clearly and persuasively. Instead, I'll use them to ask, in a somewhat impressionistic way, where Jewish–Christian relations stood in 1998 when Dr Kessler began his pioneering work in Cambridge; where we are now, especially given the added dimension of Islam in the Woolf Institute; and where we are heading. If, for the most part, I contribute a Christian perspective, it's because we've moved a long way since my undergraduate days at Cambridge University, when I learnt both Judaism and Islam from Christians or secularists, and few people, me included, could see the irony and the inappropriateness in a (just about) post-imperial world of learning about other great religions without any input from their practitioners. If we're to speak about the 'Other', we should do so dialogically (trialogically?) and only in a spirit that we hope would be shown by the Other talking about us.

We began the dialogical task with Jewish–Christian relations, and with, as Dr Kessler describes them, the problematic legacy of 'two immense' events: the Shoah; and the creation of the State of Israel. Moreover, certain flash points threatened to dissipate any goodwill between Jews and Christians. For example, the question of whether Pope Pius XII was, in fact, Hitler's Pope (John Cornwell's eponymous book that focused on the issues at stake was first published in 1999), simmered at the surface of Catholic–Jewish relations, endangering the friendliness built up by the papacies of John XXIII and John Paul II. Behind these significant but ephemeral and potentially solvable disputes lay the much more important issue of whether Christian theology was intrinsically and irredeemably antisemitic. If so, what could be done about it?

In fact, quite a lot had been done by Christians, starting with the Roman Catholic reforms of the Second Vatican Council, which themselves inspired Protestant and even some Orthodox Christian statements about relations with Jews, through the World Council of Churches (WCC) and individual denominations. These statements made some positive assessments of Jewish faith and practice, and sometimes even began a tentative reappraisal of Christian teaching. The Roman Catholic Church, for example, looked again at its claim to be the only vehicle of salvation, and some Protestant churches, for the most part very cautiously, sniffed around the issue of Christian supersessionism of God's covenant with the Jewish people. From a contemporary perspective, much of this was far too hesitant and also expressed in terms *de haut en bas*, but a significant start had been made by Christians to overcome wicked practice and even bad beliefs.

POSTLUDE

Back in 1998, there was some disappointment in Christian circles that, by and large, Jewish religious organizations hadn't responded more positively to these Christian *aggiornamenti* of faith and action. I suppose that most Jews felt that this was an internal Christian issue and were not inclined, given previous historical experiences, to get involved in discussions with Christians, especially over issues freighted with such loaded baggage from the past. Furthermore, on the topic of Israel, which galvanized many Jews, pro-Palestinian Christians must often have seemed antisemitic to many Jews, with their frequently partial and partisan understanding of the issues at stake, and with a shameful failure to acknowledge the profound Christian involvement in the sufferings of the Jewish people. Dr Kessler was one of a relatively small number of Jewish academics who encouraged a friendly, non-partisan dialogue between Jewish and Christian scholars and leaders. Given the appalling Christian treatment of Jews in the past, Christians can only be grateful that Dr Kessler and other Jewish scholars and leaders have taken the risk of believing that many contemporary Christians are genuinely interested in overcoming the legacy of the past so that together Jews and Christians can help mend the world.

Indeed, the years since have seen a greater willingness of some Jewish leaders to recognize and respond positively to the attempts of Christians to redeem the past, as evidenced in the 2000 document *Dabru Emet*. Now that these Christian acts of self-examination aren't invariably ignored or regarded with suspicion, it's become possible for both Jews and Christians to disagree amicably and respectfully with each other, even about centrally important matters of religious conviction.

With apologies to St Paul, the deeds of the first generation of post-Holocaust Christian scholars who attempted to overcome Christianity's long history of contempt for the Jewish people must surely be accounted to them as righteousness, and certainly arose out of a conviction that faith must be good faith, not bad faith. Even so, many (though by no means all) Christian scholars who were then at the forefront of seeking a new and positive dialogue with Jews seem to have been ready to trade away key Christian beliefs, especially about the traditional meanings of Jesus, if that's what it took to amend the past and establish good relations with Jews. For example, some argued *in nuce* that the concept of Jesus' messiahship separates Jews from Christians, that much modern German biblical scholarship contends that Jesus never claimed to be the Messiah, and therefore Jews and Christians can agree that Jesus wasn't the Messiah. This is unconvincing for a number of reasons. At their best, great religions are conservative institutions, in the sense that they conserve things of value from the past to fashion our lives by. While it's true that they also conserve things that need to be reappraised or even abandoned, simply to toss out centrally important beliefs or practices for the sake of good relations is hardly likely to impress Jews for whom tradition is greatly important. It's also likely to puzzle or even offend large swathes of the Christian community who treasure things that aren't even being negotiated away, but simply disposed of. In fact, some of these Christian attempts at radical surgery upon the body of Christian teachings would have been better attempted in conversation with Jewish partners.

Indeed, since Jews and Christians share the common text of the Hebrew Bible or Old Testament, joint engagements with it and its issues surely provide an obvious focus for dialogue between Jews and Christians. Although Dr Kessler has written eloquently about the legacies of both the Shoah and the creation of the State of Israel for Jews and Christians, he also warns us that good relations between them can't be built on Christian guilt about the long history of contempt that made Christians complicit in many terrible anti-Jewish atrocities, or upon Jewish indignation with that history or with Christian anti-Zionism. Many of his chapters in this book are discerning engagements with Scripture, where Jews and Christians have much to learn from each other.

There hasn't been enough joint engagement with the Bible, but there has been some. One of Dr Kessler's significant contributions as a biblical scholar has been to show us that Jewish and Christian scholars have long influenced each other, as, for example, in the writings of rabbis and church fathers about the story of the Binding of Isaac. There has also been a small, now growing, number of Jewish scholars who have examined the New Testament in, for the most part, a friendly manner. As an example, Dr Kessler writes of assessments of Jesus by Jewish scholars that take seriously his Jewish faith and historical context. Initially, this work was ignored by many Christian biblical scholars. In fact, my generation of Christian specialists in the Bible was in thrall to the learned German tradition that in retrospect seems philosophical more than historical, making Jesus into a forerunner of German idealism. It was also often instinctively antisemitic: many of its writers talked of 'Late Judaism' (*Spätjudentum*) as though Judaism came to an end after the Second Temple period, or should have. This is particularly disgraceful, since many of these writers lived through the horrors of the Second World War, but seemed to have learnt nothing of importance from barbaric acts towards Jews. As a young man, I thought these German assessments of Jesus formed probably the last word on christological matters. With age comes at least a little wisdom, and now they seem an interesting blind alley: over-sceptical as history, and beside the point – and mostly wrong – in their cautious evaluation of Jesus as a critical outsider to his own religious heritage. Whatever the disagreements between Jews and Christians about the historical Jesus, which are always going to be many and ultimately incompatible, Christians are far more likely to understand Jesus within the context of first-century Judaism than as a forerunner of Hegel. This being so, they have much to learn from Jewish scholars of that period.

A major reason why Jewish scholars have ignored the New Testament has been that it isn't Scripture for them as the Old Testament is for Christians. Another reason is that Christians have interpreted some New Testament passages to justify their vilification of Jews, to the point where the New Testament can plausibly be viewed as intrinsically antisemitic, a charge that Dr Kessler graciously denies. But if you hold this position, why then deal with a poisonous document? To be sure, Christian interpretations of, for example, Matthew 27.25 have caused immense suffering to Jews. Nothing can justify or explain away the vile uses to which such a verse has been put. But Dr Kessler points out that Jews also have their own passages of Scripture that justify suffering or violence, which, being part of the Hebrew Bible, Christians also share. His suggestion that, in order to begin to understand them, we contextualize them provides one way of beginning to come to terms with them that can help both communities of faith to appreciate their significance. This potential for mutual reflection on scriptural passages offers a much more profitable way to deal with Scripture than many Christians showed, even just a few years ago.

This tradition of mutuality ought surely to be recovered and built upon. Indeed, Dr Kessler shows us how, in his Jewish re-evaluation of Mary, the mother of Jesus. Clearly, as we read Chapter 6, we've made a long journey from the pioneering, understandably somewhat cautious work of, for example, Joseph Klausner, and even from the enthralling, though occasionally polemical, work of someone like Geza Vermes. Instead, we find a respectful, humorous, very Jewish reading of Scripture that will not entirely convince Christians, but offers insights into and wisdom about New Testament texts. Actually, Protestant Christians like me are often unable to see the point of Catholic and Orthodox interpretations of Mary, and are sometimes even a little embarrassed by them. So it's both amusing – but also rather telling – that a Protestant Christian may get more from a Jewish reading of Mary than from many Catholic and Orthodox ones.

Dr Kessler points out that Roman Catholic Christians are now encouraged to recognize the insights of the rabbis and contemporary Jewish scholars into the interpretation of the Old Testament. This could be an interesting pointer to the future of Christian biblical studies. If Christians were really to take the rabbinic approaches to the Bible seriously, to the point of emulating them, they might find themselves liberated – not just from a Eurocentric approach to the text, but into a more credible and reasonable attitude towards the authority of the Bible. In the United States, where I now live, the Bible is regarded by many Christians as an inerrant guide to just about anything. That's the theory. In practice, this stance makes Christian faith seem irrational and an enemy of scientific exploration; and, of course, it misses major aspects of the religious life entirely, since such fundamentalist readings of the Bible often justify immoral, self-serving and exclusive opinions and deeds. In our post-imperial world, some African, Asian and

## POSTLUDE

South American Christians have begun to develop strategies to contextualize the Bible so as to live faithfully and find it, as the writer of 2 Timothy puts it, a 'God-breathed' and 'useful' guide to contemporary faith and practice. It's surely also possible and very desirable for Christians to take seriously some strategies of the rabbis to understand Scripture. Indeed, given the many centuries of Jewish engagement with the biblical text, it would be foolish to ignore the well-honed processes by which Jews come to carve meaning out of Scripture, as well as those meanings themselves. The rabbis took the divine origin of the Bible very seriously indeed, but argued with each other about the meaning of texts, sometimes humorously, sometimes testily, sometimes reading passages for their obvious meaning – and sometimes allowing themselves considerable dramatic licence. Compared with Jewish ways of reading Scripture, which, whatever the aims of individual rabbis, leave readers of their writings with very many different attempts to establish the relevance and meaning of biblical passages, many Christian exegetes seem to be trying to find the single, truthful meaning of any given passage. The major problem with such a Christian approach is that the results are often divisive, or else trivial or even nonsense. In reality, any meaningful scriptural insight is found in a dialogue with others about the text, and with the text itself. Jews understand that much better than Christians do. Christians have much to learn.

Now that a Centre for the Study of Muslim–Jewish Relations has become part of the Woolf Institute, the third part of the Abrahamic family of faiths has been included in Dr Kessler's observations. I find it particularly interesting that the emphasis is upon Muslim–Jewish relations. In many ways, as Dr Kessler points out, Judaism and Islam are much closer to each other than to Christianity, because of their strict monotheism and the importance to them both of religious law. It's also true that, until recent years, the history of their shared relationships was, for the most part, much more amicable than the interactions either of them had with Christianity. That amity was destroyed by the creation of Israel, as Dr Kessler records. Still, Islam is a religion of the Book, so it's possible for Jews, Christians and Muslims to profit from reading

Scripture together, as in the shared story of the Binding of Isaac. The fact that Muslims have a different text in the Qur'an, rather than a common text differently interpreted, adds a certain extra frisson to the encounter. With very rare exception, Muslims have regarded their sacred text as, quite literally, God's word, to the point that some Muslim scholars have been wary of the science of *tafsir*, or scriptural interpretation, lest it intrude humanness into the meaning of the divine word. Not all of them, though, as proved by Dr Kessler's reference to the discussion of Muslim exegetes about whether the son whom Abraham was willing to sacrifice was Isaac or Ishmael. Ishmael became the favoured option and nowadays most Muslims aren't even aware that there was any discussion about it. But there was.

In fact, Islam isn't the monolithic religion it's often made out to be, not only by many uninformed Europeans and Americans, but also by a minority of shrill Muslim advocates of violence and of a rigid sectarian understanding of their own tiny room within the House of Islam. Some of my most treasured memories are of the tolerant, mystic-imbued Muslims of India who looked after me all those years ago when I lived in Hyderabad. It takes all sorts to make a religion, and dialogue can help uncover not only difficult issues that need some resolution, but also different internal interpretations that can sometimes be more inclusive than the generally accepted ones.

Take the Muslim form of supersessionism as an example. Muslims believe Islam to be the last and final religion but, for the most part, where they form a majority, permit a limited toleration of other monotheistic faiths. In practice, Muslims have sometimes been intolerant even of other peoples of the Book, but contrariwise they have sometimes extended toleration even towards Hindus and other people of faith that cannot easily be described as monotheistic – or even theistic at all.

Moreover, the strong mystical traditions in Islam, which have never been eradicated because they are so integral a part of the religion, often accept but at the same time subvert so-called orthodox teaching, and display a surprising generosity towards others, because to mystics the heart is at least as important as the mind in living religion. It may be that, in dialogue or trialogue, Jews and Christians will have things to teach Muslims based on their experience of dealing with Christian supersessionism, and equally the case that some of these Muslim expressions of religion of the heart can remind dialogue partners of similar instances of openheartedness towards the 'Other' in Judaism and Christianity.

Dialogue is rarely well done by those who underestimate the difficulties attending it. Dr Kessler's characteristic realism compels him to name some of the obstacles that lie in the path of Muslim dialogue with Jews and Christians: the problem of Israel; the aftermath of Pope Benedict XVI's ill-advised speech at Regensburg; pervasive European and North American Islamophobia matched by anti-Americanism and hatred of the United States, allies among many Muslims; the fallout of two wars in Iraq and Afghanistan. We can add other things, such as the reverberations of the Arab Spring, which have produced rising expectations for political and economic change among many Muslims of the region (who, though, form only a small number of the world's Muslims, whose major population areas lie in Indonesia and South Asia).

Nevertheless, the Woolf Institute provides the opportunity for genuine dialogue between the Abrahamic faiths. And just as the renewal of beliefs and practices of Orthodox Christians has taken place in the diaspora rather than Russia and other Orthodox-majority countries, so it's likely to be true that the regeneration of Islam is likely to take place in Muslim minority countries where Muslims are free to act and believe as they will, and are also freed from a long-established but somewhat problematic conviction that Muslims should form a majority in areas where they live. This issue of Islam's revival is a delicate one, especially when raised by a Christian Englishman living in a post-imperial world. Still, Islam is the last of the Abrahamic faiths to resist the claims of modernity and postmodernity, and though some Muslims are proud of this, it raises more problems than it solves for Muslims. To many sympathetic as well as hostile outsiders, Muslims seem to have a naïve and unhistorical understanding of their own past. Increasingly, difficult questions are being asked by academics about the origins of Islam, which bring into dispute the traditional

Muslim accounts of the life of the Prophet Muhammad and of the early Arab conquests. Organizations like the Woolf Institute provide a congenial place for Muslims to discuss such matters with members of religions who've already faced up to similar serious issues.

As to the future of Jewish–Christian relations, there have been hiccups to remind us that not all is smooth progress as, for example, when the papal nuncio to Israel threatened to boycott a Yad Vashem Holocaust Memorial ceremony on the eve of Yom HaShoah in 2007, because of, as he wrote, 'the way Pius XII is represented at Yad Vashem'. Dr Kessler refers to this interruption in the progress of good relations between Jews and Catholics, and there have been other glitches in Jewish–Christian relations. Even so, on the whole things seem transformed for the better since 1998, when the Woolf Institute was set up, initially under the name of the Centre for the Study of Jewish – Christian Relations. There's been progress in such areas as: increasing Christian recognition of God's abiding faithfulness to his covenant with his Jewish people; a growing Jewish recognition of Christian attempts to overcome the teaching of the past so as to build a better future between Jews and Christians; and imaginative and collaborative studies of not only the common shared tradition between Jews and Christians, but also of the other's tradition by individual scholars. All this is mirrored in Dr Kessler's chapters in this book.

If I can be greedy and look forward to future writings by Dr Kessler, I wonder whether the Woolf Institute might provide a hospitable setting for reflection upon questions asked by the New Atheists. Much of their work strikes me as discourteous, uninformed and trivial, as do some religious responses to it. The Abrahamic faiths can surely not only look inwards to heal self-inflicted wounds, but also outwards to offer views of the world that have often benefited from the intellectual, ethical and hospitable traditions of Jews, Christians and Muslims. That's a comment offered in hope, but is tempered by gratitude for the riches we've already received.

# Further Reading

Akbar Ahmed, 2007, *Journey into Islam*, Washington, DC: Brookings Institution Press.
Akbar Ahmed, 2010, *Journey into America*, Washington, DC: Brookings Institution Press.
Naim Ateek, 1989, *Justice and Only Justice: A Palestinian Theology of Liberation*, Maryknoll, NY: Orbis Books.
M. Barnes, 2002, *Theology and the Dialogue of Religions*, Cambridge: Cambridge University Press.
M. Barnes, 2005, *Presence and Engagement*, London: Church House Publishing.
Gregory Baum, 1976, *Christian Theology after Auschwitz*, London: Council of Christians and Jews.
Zygmunt Bauman, 1991, *Modernity and the Holocaust*, Cambridge: Polity Press.
Eliezer Berkovits, 1973, *Faith after the Holocaust*, New York: Ktav.
Reimund Bieringer *et al.*, 2001, *Anti-Judaism and the Fourth Gospel*, Louisville, KY: Westminster John Knox Press.
R. Boase (ed.), 2005, *Islam and Global Dialogue: Religious Pluralism and the Pursuit of Peace*, Aldershot: Ashgate.
Daniel Boyarin, 1997, *A Radical Jew: Paul and the Politics of Identity*, Berkeley, CA: University of California Press.
Daniel Boyarin, 2004, *Border Lines: The Partition of Judaeo-Christianity*, Philadelphia: University of Philadelphia Press.
Mary C. Boys, 2000, *Has God Only One Blessing? Judaism as a Source of Christian Self-Understanding*, New York: Paulist Press.
Marcus Braybrooke, 2000, *Christian–Jewish Relations: The Next Steps*, London: SCM Press.
Allan, Brockway *et al.*, 1988, *The Theology of the Churches and the Jewish People: Statements by the World Council of Churches and its Member Churches*, Geneva: World Council of Churches.

Roger Brooks and John J. Collins (eds), 1990, *Hebrew Bible or Old Testament? Studying the Bible in Judaism and Christianity*, Notre Dame, IN: University of Notre Dame Press.
Walter Brueggemann, 1977, *The Land*, Philadelphia: Fortress Press.
Martin Buber, 1958, *I and Thou*, 2nd edn, New York: Charles Scribner's Sons.
David Burrell, 2011, *Towards a Jewish–Christian–Muslim Theology*, Oxford: Wiley-Blackwell.
John Cornwell, 1999, *Hitler's Pope: The Secret History of Pius XII*, London: Viking.
Philip A. Cunningham et al., 2011, *Christ Jesus and the Jewish People Today: New Explorations of Theological Interrelationships*, Grand Rapids, MI: Eerdmans.
C. Disbrey, 2004, *Listening to People of Other Faiths*, Oxford: Bible Reading Fellowship.
C. W. Dugmore, 1944, *The Influence of the Synagogue upon the Divine Office*, Oxford: Clarendon Press.
J. D. G. Dunn, 1992, *The Partings of the Ways between Christianity and Judaism, and their Significance for the Character of Christianity*, London: SCM Press.
A. Roy Eckardt and Alice L., 1970, *Encounter with Israel: A Challenge to Conscience*, New York: Association Press.
A. Roy Eckardt and Alice L., 1988, *Long Night's Journey into Day: A Revised Retrospective on the Holocaust*, Detroit, MI: Wayne State University Press, and London: Pergamon Press.
Marc H. Ellis, 1997, *Unholy Alliance: Religion and Atrocity in Our Time*, London: SCM Press.
E. L. Fackenheim, 1988, *The Jewish Bible after the Holocaust*, Manchester: Manchester University Press.
E. L. Fackenheim, 1994, *To Mend the World: Foundations of Post-Holocaust Jewish Thought*, Bloomington, IN: Indiana University Press.
R. Firestone, 2008, *Who Are the Real Chosen People? The Meaning of Chosenness in Judaism, Christianity and Islam*, Woodstock, VT: Skylight Paths.
Edward H. Flannery, 1965, 1985, *The Anguish of the Jews: Twenty-Three Centuries of Anti-Semitism*, New York: Macmillan.
David Flusser, 2001, *Jesus*, Jerusalem: Magnes Press (first published in English in 1969).
Paula Fredriksen, 2000, *Jesus of Nazareth, King of the Jews: A Jewish Life and the Emergence of Christianity*, London: Macmillan.
H. P. Fry (ed.), 1996, *Christian–Jewish Dialogue: A Reader*, Exeter: University of Exeter.

## FURTHER READING

Tikva Frymer-Kensky *et al.* (eds), 2000, *Christianity in Jewish Terms*, Boulder, CO: Westview Press.
Marc Gopin, 2002, *Holy War, Holy Peace: How Religion Can Bring Peace to the Middle East*, New York: Oxford University Press.
I. Greenberg, 2004, *For the Sake of Heaven and Earth: The New Encounter between Judaism and Christianity*, Philadelphia: Jewish Publication Society.
Yossi Klein Halevi, 2001, *At the Entrance to the Garden of Eden*, New York: HarperCollins.
Richard Harries, 2003, *After the Evil: Christianity and Judaism in the Shadow of the Holocaust*, Oxford: Oxford University Press.
Abraham Joshua Heschel, 1976, *God in Search of Man: A Philosophy of Judaism*, New York: Noonday Press.
Michael Hilton, 1994, *The Christian Effect on Jewish Life*, London: SCM Press.
M. Hirshman, 1996, *A Rivalry of Genius*, New York: SUNY Press.
David E. Holwerda, 1995, *Jesus and Israel: One Covenant or Two?*, Grand Rapids, MI: William B. Eerdmans.
Jules Isaac, 1964, *The Teaching of Contempt: The Christian Roots of Anti-Semitism*, New York: Holt, Rinehart & Winston, Inc.
Louis Jacobs, 2000, *A Tree of Life: Diversity, Flexibility, and Creativity in Jewish Law*, 2nd edn, London: The Littman Library of Jewish Civilization.
J. Katz, 1973, *Out of the Ghetto*, Cambridge, MA: Harvard University Press.
Edward Kessler, 2004, *Bound by the Bible: Jews, Christians and the Sacrifice of Isaac*, Cambridge: Cambridge University Press.
E. Kessler and M. Wright (eds), 2004, *Themes in Jewish–Christian Relations*, Cambridge: Orchard Academic.
Wlliam Klassen, 1996, *Judas, Betrayer or Friend of Jesus?*, Minneapolis: Fortress Press.
L. Klenicki (ed.), 1991, *Toward a Theological Encounter: Jewish Understandings of Christianity*, Mahwah, NJ: Paulist Press.
Melody D. Knowles, Esther Menn, John T. Pawlikowski and Timothy J. Sandoval (eds), 2007, *Contesting Texts: Jews and Christians in Conversation about the Bible*, Minneapolis: Fortress Press.
Stanislaw Krajewski, 2005, *Poland and the Jews*, Krakow: Austeria.
B. Krondorfer, 1995, *Remembrance and Reconciliation: Encounters between Young Jews and Germans*, New Haven: Yale University Press.
James L. Kugel, 1997, *The Bible as It Was*, Cambridge and London: Belknap, Harvard University Press.
Karl-Joseph Kuschel, 1995, *Abraham: Sign of Hope for Jews, Christians, and Muslims*, New York: Continuum.

P. Lapide and J. Moltmann, 1981, *Jewish Monotheism and Christian Trinitarian Doctrine*, trans. Leonard Swidler, Philadelphia: Fortress Press.

P. Lapide and K. Rahner, 1987, *Encountering Jesus–Encountering Judaism*, New York: Crossroad.

Goran Larsson, 1998, *Bound for Freedom: The Book of Exodus in Jewish and Christian Traditions*, Peabody, MA: Hendrickson.

Jon D. Levenson, 2012, 1993, *Inheriting Abraham: The Legacy of the Patriarch in Judaism, Christianity, and Islam*, Princeton: Princeton University Press.

Jon D. Levenson, *The Death and Resurrection of the Beloved Son: The Transformation of Child Sacrifice in Judaism and Christianity*, New Haven: Yale University Press.

Emmanuel Levinas, 1998, *Entre Nous: On Thinking-of-the-Other*, trans. from the French by Michael B. Smith and Barbara Harshav, New York: Columbia University Press.

Amy-Jill Levine, 2006, *The Misunderstood Jew: The Church and the Scandal of the Jewish Jesus*, San Francisco: HarperSanFrancisco.

Amy-Jill Levine and Marc Z. Brettler (eds), 2011, *The Jewish Annotated New Testament*, Oxford: Oxford University Press.

J. Lieu, 1996, *Image and Reality: The Jews and the World of Christianity in the Second Century*, Edinburgh: T & T Clark.

Ora Limor and Guy G. Stroumsa, 1996, *Contra Iudaeos: Ancient and Medieval Polemics between Christians and Jews*, Texts and Studies in Medieval and Early Modern Judaism 10, Tübingen: Mohr.

Deborah Lipstadt, 1993, *Denying the Holocaust: The Growing Assault on Truth and Memory*, New York: The Free Press.

F. H. Littell, 1986, *The Crucifixion of the Jews: The Failure of Christians to Understand the Jewish Experience*, Macon, GA: Mercer University Press.

Marcia Sachs Littell and Sharon Weissman Gutman (eds), 1996, *Liturgies on the Holocaust: An Interfaith Anthology*, Valley Forge, PA: Trinity Press International.

Jonathan Magonet, 2003, *Talking to the Other: A Jewish Interfaith Dialogue with Christians and Muslims*, London: I B Tauris.

J. Moltmann, 1974, *The Crucified God: The Cross of Christ as the Foundation and Criticism of Christian Theology*, London: SCM Press.

Stephen Motyer, 1997, *Your Father the Devil: A New Approach to John and 'the Jews'*, Milton Keynes: Paternoster Press.

M. J. Mulder and H. Sysling (eds), 1988, *Mikra: Text, Translation, Reading, and Interpretation of The Hebrew Bible in Ancient Judaism and Early Christianity*, Philadelphia: Fortress Press.

Franz Mussner, 1984, *Tractate on the Jews: The Significance of Judaism for Christian Faith*, Philadelphia: Fortress Press.

# FURTHER READING

D. Novak, 1983, *The Image of the Non-Jew in Judaism: A Constructive Study of the Noahide Laws*, New York: Edwin Mellen Press.

George C. Papademetriou, 1990, *Essays on Orthodox Christian–Jewish Relations*, Bristol, IN: Wyndham Hall Press.

James W. Parkes, 1934, reprint 1974, *Conflict of the Church and Synagogue*, New York: Hermon Press.

John Pawlikowski, 1982, *Christ in Light of the Christian–Jewish Dialogue*, Eugene, OR: Wipf & Stock.

John Pawlikowski, 1989, *Jesus and the Theology of Israel*, Collegeville, MN: Liturgical Press.

F. E. Peters, 1990, *Judaism, Christianity, Islam: The Classical Texts and their Interpretation*, Princeton: Princeton University Press.

F. E. Peters, 2004, *The Children of Abraham*, Princeton: Princeton University Press.

Jacob Petuchowski and Michael Brocke, 1978, *The Lord's Prayer and Jewish Liturgy*, New York: Seabury Press.

Didier Pollefeyt, 1997, *Jews and Christians: Rivals or Partners for the Kingdom of God*, Grand Rapids, MI: Eerdmans.

Alan Race, 1982, *Christians and Religious Pluralism: Patterns in the Christian Theology of Religions*, New York: Orbis Books.

Adele Reinhartz, 2001, *Befriending the Beloved Disciple: A Jewish Reading of the Gospel of John*, New York and London: Continuum.

Ellis Rivkin, 1984, *What Crucified Jesus?*, London: SCM Press.

Franz Rosenzweig, 1985, *The Star of Redemption*, trans. William Hallo, Notre Dame, IN: University of Notre Dame Press.

John K. Roth (ed.), 1999, *Ethics after the Holocaust: Perspectives, Critique, and Responses*, St Paul, MN: Paragon House.

Richard L. Rubenstein, 1992, *After Auschwitz: History, Theology, and Contemporary Judaism*, 2nd edn, Baltimore: Johns Hopkins University Press.

Richard Rubenstein, 1972, *My Brother Paul*, New York: Harper.

Miri Rubin, 1999, *Gentile Tales: The Narrative Assault on Late Medieval Jews*, London and New Haven: Yale University Press.

Miri Rubin, 2009, *Mother of God: A History of the Virgin Mary*, Yale: Yale University Press.

Rosemary Radford Ruether, 1974 and 1975, *Faith and Fratricide: The Theological Roots of Anti-Semitism*, New York: Seabury Press.

Jonathan Sacks, 2002, *The Dignity of Difference: How to Avoid the Clash of Civilisations*, London: Continuum.

E. P. Sanders, 1985, *Jesus and Judaism*, London: SCM Press.

E. P. Sanders, 1977, *Paul and Palestinian Judaism*, London: SCM Press.

David Sandmel, Rosann M. Catalano and Christopher M. Leighton, 2001, *Irreconcilable Differences?*, Boulder, CO: Westview Press.

J. F. A. Sawyer, 1996, *The Fifth Gospel: Isaiah in the History of Christianity*, Cambridge: Cambridge University Press.

Peter Schäfer, 2007, *Jesus in the Talmud*, Princeton: Princeton University Press.

Heinz Schreckenberg, 1996, *The Jews in Christian Art: An Illustrated History*, New York: Continuum.

Alan Segal, 1990, *Paul the Convert*, New Haven: Yale University Press.

David Sim, 1998, *The Gospel of Matthew and Christian Judaism: The History and Social Setting of the Matthean Community*, Edinburgh: T & T Clark.

Michael A. Signer (ed.), 2001, *Memory and History in Christianity and Judaism*, Notre Dame, IN: University of Notre Dame Press.

David Sim, 1998, *The Gospel of Matthew and Christian Judaism: The History and Social Setting of the Matthean Community*, Edinburgh: T & T Clark.

M. Simon, 1986, *Verus Israel: A Study of the Relations between Christians and Jews in the Roman Empire* (AD 135–425), The Littman Library of Jewish Civilization, Oxford: Oxford University Press.

R. Kendall Soulen, 1996, *The God of Israel and Christian Theology*, Minneapolis: Fortress Press.

Kevin P. Spicer (ed.), 2007, *Antisemitism, Christian Ambivalence and the Holocaust*, Bloomington, IN: Indiana University Press.

Shalom Spiegel, 1967, *The Last Trial: On the Legends and Lore of the Command to Abraham to Offer Isaac as a Sacrifice: The Akedah*, New York: Schocken.

Helen Spurling and Emmanouela Grypeou, 2009, *The Exegetical Encounter between Jews and Christians in Late Antiquity*, Jewish and Christian Perspectives, Leiden and Boston: Brill.

Günter Stemberger, 1995, *Jewish Contemporaries of Jesus: Pharisees, Sadducees, Essenes*, Minneapolis: Fortress Press.

Günter Stemberger, 2000, *Jews and Christians in the Holy Land: Palestine in the Fourth Century*, Edinburgh: T & T Clark.

Krister Stendahl, 1976, *Paul among Jews and Christians*, Philadelphia: Fortress Press.

Krister Stendahl, 1996, *A Final Account*, Philadelphia: Fortress Press.

Geza Vermes, 2000, *The Changing Faces of Jesus*, New York: Viking.

Geza Vermes, 1973, *Jesus the Jew*, London: SCM Press.

Katharina von Kellenbach, 1994, *Anti-Judaism in Feminist Christian Writings*, Atlanta: Scholars Press.

P. Weller (ed.), 2007, *Religions in the UK: Directory, 2007–10*, Derby: University of Derby in association with the Multi-Faith Centre.

Robert L. Wilken, 1983, *John Chrysostom and the Jews: Rhetoric and Reality in the Late Fourth Century*, Berkeley, CA: University of California Press.

Clark M. Williamson, 1993, *A Guest in the House of Israel*, Louisville, KY: Westminster John Knox.

Clark M. Williamson and Ronald J. Allen, 1989, *Interpreting Difficult Texts: Anti-Judaism and Christian Preaching*, London: SCM Press.

T. Winter et al., 2005, *Abraham's Children: Jews, Christians and Muslims in Conversation*, London: T & T Clark.

Michael Wyschogrod, 2004, *Abraham's Promise: Judaism and Jewish–Christian Relations*, ed. and intro. R. Kendall Soulen, Grand Rapids, MI: Eerdmans.

John Howard Yoder, 2002, *The Jewish–Christian Schism Revisited*, London: SCM Press.

## *Recommended Internet Resources*

- www.pluralism.org/
- www.interfaith.org.uk
- www.bbc.co.uk/religion
- www.bc.edu/research/cjl.html
- www.world-faiths.com
- www.iaw.org.uk
- www.islamic-foundation.org.uk
- www.irr.org.uk
- www.jcrelations.net
- www.worldfaiths.org

# Acknowledgements

### Chapter 1

'Jewish–Christian Relations: The Next Generation' (Hugo Gryn Memorial Lecture), *Themes in Jewish–Christian Relations*, vol. 1, 1998, pp. 1–16.

### Chapter 2

'Jewish–Christian Relations in the Global Society: What the Institutional Documents Have and Have Not Been Telling Us', in E. Kessler, J. Pawlikowski and J. Banki (eds), 2002, *Jews and Christians in Conversation*, Cambridge: Orchard Academic, pp. 53–74.

### Chapter 3

Land and Memory, Woolf Institute 10th Anniversary Conference, September 2008.

### Chapter 4

'Contemporary Questions about Covenant(s) and Conversion: A Public Dialogue', Lecture at St Joseph's University, PA, 2007.

### Chapter 5

'"Whom do men say that I am?" (Matthew 16.13)', Lecture to Cambridge Theological Federation, 2007.

ACKNOWLEDGEMENTS

## Chapter 6

'Mary – The Jewish Mother', *Irish Theological Quarterly*, vol. 76, 2011, pp. 211–23.

## Chapter 7

'Bound by the Bible: Jews, Christians and the Binding of Isaac', in E. B. Korn and J. T. Pawlikowski (eds), 2005, *Two Faiths, One Covenant? Jewish and Christian Identity in the Presence of the Other*, Lanham, MD: Sheed & Ward, pp. 11–28.

## Chapter 8

'The Sacrifice of Isaac (the Akedah) in Christian and Jewish Tradition: Artistic Representations', in M. O'Kane (ed.), 2002, *Borders, Boundaries and the Bible*, JSOTSS, 313, London: Sheffield Academic Press, pp. 74–98.

## Chapter 9

'The Jewish People and Their Sacred Scriptures in the Christian Bible', *Scripture Bulletin*, vol. 33, 2003, pp. 29–45.

## Chapter 10

'Reasoning with Violent Scripture: With a Little Help from Job', *Scriptural Reasoning*, vol. 4, 2004.

## Chapter 11

'A Jewish Approach to Dialogue with Christians and Muslims', 2008 Hellenic Lecture, London.

## Chapter 12

'The Sacrifice of Abraham's Son in Judaism and Islam', in E. Kessler and A. Hoti (eds), *Themes in Muslim–Jewish Relations*, Cambridge: CMJR, pp. 17–23.

## Chapter 13

'Changing Landscapes: Jewish–Christian–Muslim Relations Today', *Melilah*, vol. 3, 2010, pp. 1–23.

# Index of Biblical References

**Genesis**
Chapter 22    xviii–xix, 128, 131, 140–141, 196, 201–202, 219
22.1–2    112–121
22.3    121
22.6–8    120–130
22.13    136
Fragmentary Targum    207
23.5    118
24.67    145
49.10    81

**Exodus**
Chapter 2    143
3.4–5    120
3.5    149
12.13    141
13.12; 25    127
20.34    131

**Leviticus**
19.33–34    xxi, 191

**Deuteronomy**
16.2; 6–7    220
16.3    220
Chapter 20    173
20.16–18    xx

**Joshua**
5.15    149

**1 Samuel**
Chapter 16    143

**2 Samuel**
7.14    83

**1 Kings**
Chapter 17    143

**Isaiah**
1.18    192
29.17    18, 170
42.6    72
43.16–18    221

**Jeremiah**
23.29    182
29.4–7    172
31.31–34    61

**Ezekiel**
Chapter 37    143

| | | | |
|---|---|---|---|
| Zechariah | | 27.25 | 91, 239 |
| 9.9 | 83 | 28.19 | 69 |
| Chapter 14 | 144 | | |
| 14.1–4 | 83 | | |
| 14.16 | 53 | Mark | 82 |
| | | 7.27 | 69 |
| | | 12.18–27 | 79 |
| Psalms | | 14.61–62 | 82 |
| 2.7 | 83 | | |
| 89.35 | 113 | | |
| 110.4 | 117–120 | Luke | 79, 82, 90, 99, 108 |
| 111.1 | 181 | 2.22–23 | 93 |
| 118.22–23 | 81 | 13.1 | 85, 185 |
| | | 22.67–68 | 82 |
| | | 24.53 | 97 |
| Job | 171, 183, 187 | | |
| 4.2 | 209 | | |
| 13.15 | 183–184 | John | 24, 56, 154 |
| | | 4.25–26 | 82 |
| | | 6.4 | 193 |
| Proverbs | | 8.44 | 91 |
| 25.6 | 118 | 10.16 | 85, 186 |
| | | 14.6 | 85, 186 |
| | | 19.17–21 | 125 |
| Daniel | | | |
| 7.13 | 83 | | |
| | | Acts of the Apostles | |
| | | 1.14 | 97 |
| 1 Chronicles | | 4.11 | 81 |
| 21.15 | 127 | 4.12 | 85, 186 |
| | | 5.17 | 80 |
| | | 5.36–37 | 81 |
| 2 Chronicles | | Chapter 10 | 44 |
| 3.11 | 142 | 23.7–8 | 80 |
| | | 28.28 | 69 |
| Matthew | 24, 33, 82–83, 99, 154 | | |
| | | Romans | 67 |
| 10.6 | 69 | Chapters 9—11 | xvi, 11, 66, 68, 164–165 |
| 16.13 | 79 | | |
| Chapter 23 | 185 | 9.6–8 | 164 |
| 25.27 | 186 | 11.2 | 164 |
| 26.63–64 | 82 | 11.5 | 164 |

## INDEX OF BIBLICAL REFERENCE

| | | | |
|---|---|---|---|
| 11.16 | 164 | **1 Thessalonians** | |
| 11.17; 20 | 164 | 1.1 | 82 |
| 11.17–24 | 69 | 2.14–16 | 91 |
| 11.24 | 164 | | |
| 11.26 | 164 | | |
| 11.27; 31 | 164 | **2 Timothy** | 241 |
| 11.28 | 164 | | |
| 11.28–29 | 59 | | |
| 11.29 | 31, 68, 164, 192 | **Hebrews** | 119, 163, 165, 204 |
| | | 11.17–19 | 205–206 |
| **Ephesians** | | | |
| 2.12 | 64 | | |

# Index of Names and Subjects

*A Common Word* 213
Aaron, brother of Moses 100, 119, 140
Abdullah, King of Saudi Arabia 217
Abraham, biblical patriarch xviii, xxii, 13–14, 47, 67, 80, 111–121, 123–130, 135, 137–141, 145–147, 149–151, 201–211, 218–220, 230, 235, 242
Abrahamic Faiths xxii–xxiii, 58, 197, 241, 243-244
*Adversus-Iudaeos* Tradition 20–22, 24–25, 30, 70, 93, 101, 106–107, 152, 156, 158, 178, 186
Ahmed, Akbar x, 217, 223
Alexandria Declaration 58
Alexej II 26
Al-Akhbar, Ka'b 211
Al-Kisai, Muhammad ibn Abdallah 211
Al-Tabari, Muhammad ibn Jarir 207–208
Al-Thalabi, Ahmad ibn Muhammad 211
Amichai, Yehuda 130
Anglican Church 16, 52
  Lambeth Conference
    1948 21
    1988 24–25, 35–36, 74, 154, 185
    2008 60

Anglican Communion *see* Anglican Church
Anglican–Roman Catholic International Commission 95
Anselm, Archbishop of Canterbury 107
Anti-Judaism *see* Antisemitism
Antisemitism xiii–xiv, 26, 39, 49, 172, 198
  and Nazism 3, 168
  Christian xviii, xxii, 19, 20–21, 25, 28–29, 33, 47, 56, 69, 91, 93, 101, 153–155, 168, 177, 194, 196–197, 225, 230
  Christian attitudes to 8, 20, 23, 25–30, 33, 35, 38, 43, 94, 153, 155, 177–178, 194, 224–225, 230–231
Arab–Israeli Conflict xiv, xxii, 42, 197, 200, 213, 215, 227, 229, 234
  Peace Process vii, 21–22
'Arab Spring' 243
Arafat, Yasser 58
Archbishop of Canterbury 51
Assyrians 175
Ateek, Naim 51, 54
Augustine 134
Auschwitz
  Carmelite Convent at 8
  Theological reaction 26, 177, 179, 181

# INDEX OF NAMES AND SUBJECTS

Baal Shem Tov 171
Balfour, Lord Arthur James 53
Bar Kokhba, Simon 46, 228
Barak, Ehud 58
Barth, Karl 216
Basil of Seleucia 136
Beit Alpha 146–147
Ben Bag Bag, Rabbi xviii
Benedict XVI 94, 214, 243
  Good Friday Prayer Controversy 71
*Berith see* Covenant
*Bereshit Rabbah* 14, 124–125, 206, 209
Berkovits, Eliezer 129, 180
Bible xvi, xviii, 12, 46, 110, 124, 151, 169, 206, 214, 217–218, 222, 229, 238–241
  Artistic representations of 133
  Christian (*see also* New Testament) xix, 60, 65, 85, 95, 152–170
  Coptic 146
  Jewish (*see also* Old Testament, Tanach) xxi, 33, 97, 157–159, 168, 179–181, 184, 238–239
  *Mikraot Gedolot* (Rabbinic Edition) 181
  Jewish interpretation of 54, 89, 162–163, 179
  Land of *see* Land of Israel
  Violence in 170–187
Borowitz, Eugene 180
Boyarin, Daniel 66
Boys, Mary 66
Brick Lane Jamme Masjid 226
British Mandate of Palestine 51
Buber, Martin vii–ix, 32, 89, 180–181, 192, 195, 229
Bultmann, Rudolf 83
Byzantine Empire 48, 176
  Art of 140, 144

*Call to Dialogue* 213
Camus, Albert 27
Catholic Academy of Theology in Warsaw 8
Celsus 102
Centre for the Study of Jewish–Christian Relations *see* Woolf Institute
Chaucer, Geoffrey 106
Chief Rabbis of Israel 51
Christian–Muslim relations 24–25, 36, 74
Christianity
  Arab Christians 53–54, 228
  Conversion of Jews to xv, 15, 33–36, 59–75, 72, 106, 215
  in ancient Palestine 47
  Influence upon Judaism xvi, 12–15, 128
  Jewish origins of xvii, 11, 30–38, 74, 93, 97, 101, 109, 111, 158, 178, 185, 194–195
  Jewish attitudes towards 86–92, 98, 102, 104–107, 119, 124–125, 196, 216–218
  Mission xv, 30–37, 38, 62, 69–75, 90, 165, 213, 216
  Orthodox Christianity xxi, 15, 26, 57, 240, 243
  Relations with Judaism xiv, 9–10, 94, 236
  Proselytism 34, 36, 72, 74
Christology 53, 62, 70, 83, 98, 136, 138, 140–141, 178, 239
Church fathers 15, 102, 132–133, 135, 142, 158, 196
  and Rabbis xviii–xix, 13, 112–130, 150, 238
Covenant, biblical concept xv–xvi, xx, 16, 30–31, 46, 48, 52, 59–75, 80, 95–96, 110–111, 113, 117, 129, 160, 163, 165–166,

170, 178–179, 192, 196, 228, 230, 236, 244
New Covenant 61, 63, 192, 216
Old Covenant xvi, 61, 68, 113, 164, 185, 192
Constantine 47, 134
Cornwell, John 236
Council of Elvira 132
Council of Ephesus 102
Crusades xxii, 47–48, 108, 218
Cunningham, Philip x, xv, 61–62
Cyril of Alexandria 121, 123, 125

*Dabru Emet* vii, 29, 32–33, 35, 39, 124, 196, 216–217, 237
Daniel, biblical figure 133, 139
David, King of Israel 46, 83, 113, 143, 158
Dead Sea Scrolls 81, 160, 170
D'Espagne, Jean 151
Diaspora, Jewish 48, 214, 225, 228
  Perceptions of xxiii, 46
  Relations with the State of Israel xiv, 7
Diaspora, Muslim xxiii, 214
Diaspora, Orthodox Christian 243
*Dominus Iesus* 35, 70
Drakulic, Slavenka 40
Dulles, Avery 119
Dura-Europos
  Chapel 133,
  Synagogue 142–146, 147, 149

Eckardt, Alice 231
*Ecumenical Considerations on Jewish–Christian Dialogue* 216
Egeria 108, 140
*Eid al-Adha* xxii, 201
Elijah the Prophet 143
Emden, Jacob 63
Enlightenment 63, 129
Ephrem 137, 139, 182
Essenes 79, 90, 95–96

Esther, biblical figure 143
Eucharist xviii, 105, 112, 136, 140–141, 221
Evangelical Christians 37, 65, 74–75, 165, 214, 231
Evangelical Church of the Rhineland 30, 154
Evangelical Lutheran Church in America 154
Exodus from Egypt 80, 100, 139, 220
Ezekiel the Prophet 143–144, 149

Fackenheim, Emil xiii, 4, 179–181, 184, 222
Firestone, Reuven 209
First Temple 225
First World War 6, 130
Flannery, Edward 23, 153
Flusser, David 56, 86, 89–90, 92, 231
Foot Moore, George 31, 194–195
Franco, Antonio 51

Gamaliel the Elder 81
Gamaliel II 132
Gandhi, Mahatma 229
Gavin, Frank 20
Geiger, Abraham 86–87
*Genesis Rabbah* see *Bereshit Rabbah*
Globalization 19, 39–41
Gnostics 90
Goodenough, Erwin Ramsdell 144
Green, Arthur 98
Gregorios of Thyateira and Great Britain 192
Gregory of Nyssa 114–116, 121, 133, 141, 151
Gryn, Hugo xiii, 10, 17
*Guidelines and Suggestions for Implementing the Conciliar Declaration Nostra Aetate* 37, 155, 160, 162, 164, 166

# INDEX OF NAMES AND SUBJECTS

Hadrian 46
Ha-Levi, Judah 48, 107
Hannah, mother of Samuel 95
Hanina ben Dosa 90
Hartman, David 64
Hasmonean Dynasty 132
Hassan, Prince of Jordan x, 194, 217
Hegel, Georg Wilhelm, Friedrich 239
Helena, mother of Emperor Constantine 47
Herford, Travers 194–195
Herod Agrippa 185
Herzl, Theodor 49–50, 230
Heschel, Abraham Joshua 186
Heschel, Susannah 86
Hess, Moses 48
Hillel 86–87, 101, 160
Hitler, Adolf xiii, 3–4, 70, 152, 168, 180, 222
Holocaust *see* Shoah
Holwerda, David 65–66
Holy Land *see* Land of Israel
Hooker, Roger 75
Hussar, Bruno 58

Ibn Kathir, Ismail 207–209
Ibrahim *see* Abraham
Inge, William Ralph 233
International Christian Embassy in Jerusalem (ICEJ) 53
International Council of Christians and Jews 153, 195, 215
Intifada 57
Isaac, Jules 3, 84, 152
Isaac, biblical patriarch ix, 99
  Binding xviii, 13–14, 110–151, 196, 201–212, 219, 238, 242
  Artistic representations 131–151
  Christological interpretations 14, 118, 122–124, 127, 134–136, 142

  in Islamic tradition 201–212
  Parallels with the Eucharist xviii, 111–112, 136, 140–141
*Akedah see* Binding of Isaac
Sacrifice *see* Binding
Isaiah the Prophet 158, 191, 221
Ishmael, son of Abraham ix, 145, 204, 207–210, 219, 242
Islam xxi–xxii, 7, 43–44, 64, 107, 145, 194, 198–200, 213, 217–219, 223, 228–29, 235–236, 241–242
  Discussion within 216
  Encounter with Judaism and Christianity xxi, 197, 200
  in the Western world 223
  Militant forms of 57, 214
Israel
  Land of xv, 5, 42, 46–50, 56–57, 172, 176, 198, 214, 217–219, 221, 228–232
  People xx, 11, 13, 21, 25, 29, 31, 35, 37, 51–52, 60–69, 73, 81, 83, 87, 89, 91, 95, 97, 100–101, 104, 108, 111, 113, 126, 129–130, 141, 142, 154, 158–159, 164–166, 172, 174, 191, 194, 196, 216, 219–222
  Christian mission to 30–37
  New Israel *see* Verus Israel
  Ten lost tribes 175
  *Verus Israel* 59, 66–68, 164–165, 216
  State of xiii–xv, 5–7, 15, 23, 42–43, 50–58, 94, 162, 173, 177, 198, 214–215, 222–223, 225, 227–234, 237, 243–244
  Creation xiii, xx, 3, 5, 54, 68, 197, 213, 215, 228–229, 236, 238, 241
  *Nakba see* 'The Disaster'
  'The Disaster' 197, 215
  War of Independence

261

Hostility towards 22, 42, 51–52, 154, 230
Recognition by the Vatican 5–6, 50

Jacob, biblical patriarch ix, 139, 196, 204, 208
Janner, Greville 10
Jerome 112
Jerusalem xv, 42, 45–48, 50, 53, 55, 58, 80, 83, 90, 93–94, 100–101, 109, 140, 144, 146, 167, 172, 181, 214–215, 225, 227, 231, 233
Jesus xvi, xviii, 13–14, 16, 30–32, 34, 44, 47, 60–61, 64–67, 69, 79, 82–84, 99–101, 105, 107–108, 117, 134, 136, 159–160, 162, 166, 169, 185, 193, 195, 219–222, 237–240    as a Jew xvii, xxi, 11, 32, 65, 84–85, 87, 89–97, 101, 109, 111, 195
Crucifixion 13–14, 88, 104, 109, 122–123, 125, 134, 136
in Islam 204, 213
Jewish attitudes towards xvii, 33, 52, 63, 66–67, 70–71, 79, 86–92, 102, 104, 108, 166–168, 194
'Jews for Jesus' 37, 74, 79
*Toledot Yeshu* 105
Relation with the Pharisees 31, 79–81, 86, 96, 185, 195
Second Coming of 53, 167, 214, 231
*Jewish-Christian Guidelines for the Anglican Communion* 24, 154, 185
Jewish–Christian relations xiii–xvi, xix, xxi, 3–12, 15, 17–19, 23, 30, 32, 39–42, 56, 59, 62, 70–71, 84, 86–87, 94, 110–112, 129–130, 152, 154 155, 157, 164, 166, 168–170, 183–184, 187, 192–195, 198, 201, 205, 213, 215–218, 222, 224, 228, 231, 235–236, 244
in 'New Europe' 7–11
*Jews, Christians, Muslims: The Way of Dialogue* see *Jewish-Christian Guidelines for the Anglican Communion*
Job, biblical figure 171, 182–184
John XXIII 23, 236
John Chrysostom 45, 115, 121, 144
John Moschus 105
John Paul II vii, xvi, 27–28, 31, 50, 55, 68–69, 71, 94, 113, 164, 170, 185, 192, 230, 236
John the Baptist 160
Jonah the Prophet 133
Josephus Flavius 79–81, 84, 95–96, 131–132, 142
Judaism xv, xviii–xix, xxii–xxiii, 3, 5, 8, 15, 20, 22, 32, 33–34, 37–38, 42, 44, 46–47, 51, 54–57, 59–60, 62–70, 72, 74, 80, 82–88, 90–91, 93–95, 102, 107, 109, 117, 129–130, 133, 152–158, 160–161, 163–168, 177–179, 184, 192–193, 196, 199–201, 213, 217–218, 224, 227, 230–231, 236, 239, 243
as the religion of Jesus and Mary 85, 95–101, 185
Christian study of 16, 159
Dialogue within 11–15
Influence upon Christianity xvi–xvii, 11–12, 110–111
'Late Judaism' (*Spätjudentum*) 239
Rabbinic 12, 46, 56, 80, 83, 87, 160, 169–170, 176–177, 179, 195, 225
Reform 12, 86

## INDEX OF NAMES AND SUBJECTS

Relation with Islam 198, 241
Survival of xix, 11, 31, 38,
  171–172, 194, 196
Joshua, biblical figure 149
Julian the Apostate 145
Justin Martyr 158

Kasper, Walter 71, 224
Kierkegaard, Søren 129
Kimhi, Joseph 108
King, Martin Luther 10
Klausner, Joseph 86–87, 240
Kraeling, Carl Hermann 144
Kuschel, Karl-Josef 218

Lapide, Pinchas 88–89
Lazarus, biblical figure 133
Leuenberg Church Fellowship 25,
  29, 37, 73, 154
Levine, Amy-Jill 86, 91–92
Levinas, Emmanuel 192
Limor, Ora 103
Luria, Isaac 48
Luther, Martin 22, 151
Lutheran World Federation 22

Marcion 33, 157, 177
Marquardt, Friedrich-Wilhelm 62
Mary Magdalene 104–105
Mary, Mother of Jesus xvii–xviii,
  93–109, 137, 240 *see also*
  Miriam A
'*Memoria futuri*' xxiii, 223–225
Melchizedek, biblical figure
  118–119, 140
Melito 122–124, 135–136,
  141–142
Messiah xix–xx, 46, 48–49, 65,
  81–84, 89–90, 96, 107, 166–
  167, 170, 176, 178. 228, 231
  Jesus as 53, 69, 79, 81–83, 102,
  168, 238
Metz, Johann-Baptist xvi, 62, 177

Middle East Conflict *see* Arab–
  Israeli Conflict
Middle East Council of Churches
  22
Midrash xxii, 14, 61, 97, 99, 114,
  124, 206, 211
Miriam (Hebrew name of Mary)
  99, 104–105
Miriam, Sister of Moses 99–100
Mishnah 142, 183
Montefiore, Claude 9, 32, 40,
  86–88, 152, 195, 216
Moses, biblical figure 93, 99–100,
  118–120, 140, 143, 149, 158,
  173, 204
Muhammad, Prophet of Islam
  44–45, 217, 219–220, 244
Murray, Charles 133

National Conference of Christian
  and Jews (NCCJ) 9
Nazism 9, 27, 29, 34, 70, 168,
  175, 217
Neher, Andre 184
Netanyahu, Benjamin 5
Netzer, Ehud 149
Neuhaus, David 56
Neusner, Jacob 81, 180
New Atheists 244
New Testament xvi, xviii, 10–11,
  13, 16, 28, 31, 60–61, 64–65,
  67, 69, 79, 81, 84–86, 88–91,
  93, 95–96, 101, 108–111,
  135, 154, 157, 159, 161–162,
  164–165, 167–170, 179, 204,
  219, 238–240 *see also*
  New Covenant
Noahide Laws 63, 72
Noah, biblical figure 133,
  139–140
*Nostra Aetate* 4, 6, 23, 31, 50, 56,
  59, 70, 153, 155, 162, 164, 166,
  216, 230

*Notes on the Correct Way to Present Jews and Judaism in Preaching and Catechesis in the Roman Catholic Church* 31–32, 34, 50, 66, 68–69, 155, 162, 164, 166

O'Boyle, Patrick 72
Old Testament 10, 54, 60, 81, 157, 159, 161–166, 168–169, 238–240 *see also* Old Covenant, Tanach
Origen 112, 114, 118–119, 121, 123, 136
Ottoman Empire 51
Owen, Wilfred 130

Palestine Liberation Organization (PLO) 22, 233
Palestinian Authority 50
Palestinian Theology of Liberation 54, 57
Parkes, James 9, 26, 63, 152
Passion Narratives 80, 169
Passover 16, 141, 220–221
Paul, the Apostle xvi, 11, 14, 63, 67–69, 80, 82, 87, 91, 101, 111, 139, 164–165, 221, 237
Pawlikowski, John x, 64, 70, 98, 178
Perelmuter, Hayim 66
Pharisees 16, 31, 79–81, 85–86, 90, 95–96, 169, 185, 195
Philo 118
*Pikuah nefesh* 183
Pius X 50, 230
Pius XII 51, 94, 236, 244
Pliny the Younger 131
Pontifical Biblical Commission xix, 65, 95, 117, 157, 160, 163, 168, 178

Pontifical Commission for Religious Relations with the Jews xix, 154, 224
Pontifical Council for Promoting Christian Unity 95
Pontius Pilate 79–80, 169
Presbyterian Church (USA) 52
Proclus 102
Pesudo-Ephrem Graecus 210
Pseudo-Philo 100

Qumran 83, 160
Qur'an xxii, 44, 85, 100, 171, 201, 204, 206–207, 209–210, 217, 219, 242

Rabin, Yitzhak 42, 58, 233
Ratzinger, Joseph 71, 152, 154, 168 *see also* Benedict XVI
Rebecca, biblical matriarch 145
Replacement theology xvi, 47, 52, 54, 62, 156, 163, 217 *see also* Supersessionism
*Report on the Christian Approach to the Jews* 20
Ruether, Rosemary Radford 4
Roman Catholic Church vii, xix–xx, 8–9, 15, 23, 25–28, 30–31, 34, 38, 49–50, 55–58, 64, 70–72, 89, 94–95, 111, 117, 153–160, 162–163, 166, 168, 178, 192, 230, 236, 240, 244
Roman Empire 12, 79–81, 84, 103, 177
Romanos 210–211
Rosen, David 6
Rosenzweig, Franz 63, 89, 193, 195
Rubenstein, Richard 179
Rubin, Miri 103, 107
Rufeisen, Brother Daniel 55
Rushdie, Salman 223

# INDEX OF NAMES AND SUBJECTS

Sabbah, Michel 56
Sabbath 16, 44, 80, 105, 176
Sacks, Jonathan viii, 4, 60, 191
Sadat, Anwar 233
Sadducees 79–80, 95–96, 225
Samuel the Prophet 140–143
Sanhedrin 48, 80, 148
Santayana, George xi, 224
Sarah, biblical matriarch 95, 136–137, 139–140, 145, 208–211
Satan 82, 209–211
Second Temple 80, 96–97, 108–109, 128, 144, 150, 163
  Destruction xix, 46, 79–80, 90, 97, 101, 144, 155
  Period 67, 165, 239
Second Vatican Council 23, 71–72, 167, 236
Second World War xiii, 3, 168, 185, 239
Seelisberg Meeting 31, 110, 153
Seleucus I 142
Sepphoris 148–150
Septuagint 60, 146
*Shekhinah* (divine presence) 97–99
*Shema Yisrael* (Jewish prayer) 96
Shoah xiii, xx, 3–7, 9, 15, 22–23, 34, 49, 51, 55, 94, 129, 152, 155, 168, 172, 177–181, 183–184, 194, 215, 222, 224, 231, 236, 238, 244
  Influence on study of the Bible 62, 180
  Reflection by Christian Churches 27
    Catholic Church 27–28
    Methodist Church 28–29
    Reformation Churches 29
    World Council of Churches 33, 70
Simeon the Just 108
Simon the Zealot 79
Smith, Adam 7

Smith, Wilfred Cantwell vii–ix
Solomon, Norman 5
Soloviev, Vladimir Sergeyevich 9
Southern Baptist Convention 37, 74
Stein, Edith 156
Stendahl, Krister 67
Stransky, Thomas 34
Sukkot 53, 144
Supersessionism 46, 60, 62, 164, 198, 217, 236, 242–243 *see also* Replacement Theology

Tacitus, Publius/Gaius Cornelius 80, 131
Tanach 85
*Tafsir* xxii, 206–207, 211–212, 242
Talmud 104, 214
Teresa of Calcutta xi
Tertullian 132, 136
*Tikkun olam* 170
*The Jewish People and their Sacred Scriptures in the Christian Bible (JPSSCB)* xix, 95, 117, 152, 178
'The Other' 45, 191–193, 199
Thoma, Clemens 89
Torah 32, 46, 61, 63, 71–72, 80, 84, 93, 95–96, 101, 128, 143–144, 146, 150, 161, 173, 175–176, 217, 219–220, 222
  Oral 80
*Transitus Mariae* 103
Tridentine Rite 71

Van Buren, Paul 65
Van Woerden, Isabel Speyart 137
Vermes, Geza 86, 89–90, 92, 99, 240
Vulgate 60, 161

Waite, Terry 25
Waldheim, Kurt 27

Waskow, Arthur 172
*We Remember: Reflections on the Shoah* 27–28, 155
Weiss, Zeev 149
Western Wall 55
  Papal visit at 94, 230
Wiesel, Elie 179
Woolf, Harry x
Woolf Institute vii, ix, 195, 198, 213, 235, 241, 243–244
World Jewish Congress (WJC) 24
World Council of Churches (WCC) 3, 20–23, 33, 37–38, 52, 70, 153, 216, 236
  Faith and Order Commission 216
Wyschogrod, Michael 98, 180

Yad Vashem 51, 55, 94, 244

Zealots 79, 90, 95
Zechariah the Prophet 158
Zionism 49, 172, 198, 213, 215, 228–229
  Christian attitudes to 49–58, 230
  Christian anti-Zionism 51, 238
  'Christian Zionism' 5, 51–53
  First Zionist Congress 49
  Religious
    in the Middle Ages 48
  'Zionist entity' 42
  Zionist interpretation of the Bible 54
Zvi, Shabbetai 228

www.ingramcontent.com/pod-product-compliance
Lightning Source LLC
Chambersburg PA
CBHW051352290426
44108CB00015B/1975